MAYFLOWER FULLERS IN NUNDA, NEW YORK

JOSHUA FULLER AND HIS DESCENDANTS, 1833 - 1932

MAYFLOWER FULLERS IN NUNDA, NEW YORK

Joshua Fuller and His Descendants, 1833 - 1932

William A. Paquette, Ph.D.
History Professor

New Dominion Press ● Norfolk ● Virginia

Mayflower Fullers in Nunda, New York:
Joshua Fullers and His Descendants, 1833 – 1932

Published by:

New Dominion Press
New Dominion Media/New Dominion Press
www.NewDominionPress.com

First Printing: October 2024

No part of this book may be reproduced, stored in any information storage or retrieval system, electronic or mechanical, including photocopying, recording or transmission in any form whatsoever, except in the case of short quotations printed in articles or reviews, with attribution and without the written consent of the author, except as provided by the copyright law of the United States of America.

Cover Design, Graphic Design, and Typography by New Dominion Press

Copyright © 2024 by William A. Paquette
All Rights Reserved.

Publisher's Cataloging-in-Publication Data
provided by Five Rainbows Cataloging Services

Name: Paquette, William A., 1947- author.
Title: Mayflower Fullers in Nunda, New York: Joshua Fullers and His Descendants, 1833–1932 / William A. Paquette.
Description: First edition | Norfolk, VA : New Dominion Press, 2024. | Includes bibliographical references.
Identifiers: LCCN 2024918245 (print) | ISBN 978-1-7357483-5-1 (paperback)
Subjects: LCSH: Fuller, Edward, 1575-1621--Family. | Fuller family. | Pilgrims (New Plymouth Colony)--Genealogy. | Mayflower (Ship) | Pilgrims (New Plymouth Colony)--Genealogy. | Nunda (N.Y.)--History. | BISAC: BIOGRAPHY & AUTOBIOGRAPHY / Historical. | HISTORY / United States / State & Local / Middle Atlantic (DC, DE, MD, NJ, NY, PA) | HISTORY / United States / State & Local / New England (CT, MA, ME, NH, RI, VT)
Classification: LCC CS71.F968 2024 (print) | DDC 929/.20973--dc23.

First Edition

Dedication

In Memory of Belle Fuller Root
1881-1914
My Great-Grandmother

Framed photograph of Belle Fuller Root, about 1900.

Table of Contents

Dedication ix

Preface 1

The Genealogy: 5
    Four Generations of Mayflower Descendants
    in Nunda, New York (1833 - 1932)

Appendix I 143
    The Adams Family of Nunda, New York

Appendix II: 181
    The Carter Family of Nunda, New York

Appendix III: 219
    Lists of Photographs 219
    The Photographs 225

Author Biography 275
    Dr. William A. Paquette

Preface

The Township and Village of Nunda, New York are located in southeastern Livingston County in western New York. Nunda is a Seneca name referring to *where a valley meets the hills*. Nunda Township was created in 1808 when the area was opened to settlement as part of the Morris Reserve. The Township originally was a twelve square mile tract when part of Allegany County. Nunda was reduced to six miles by six miles when the region along the Genesee River was separated and later designated a (Letchworth) State Park. The rest of Nunda became part of Livingston County. Nunda histories record only three families living in the Township in 1808 but the number of residents increased to 1,291 in 1830 and to 2,636 by 1840. Farming was the principal occupation.

New England's increasing population and a high reproductive period in world history witnessed a population boom. This placed a strain on the resources of New England to provide farmland for each newly married family. Therefore, migration became the answer. Many of the early residents of Nunda came from New England; evident in the naming of two of the village streets: Massachusetts and Vermont. Among the families leaving Massachusetts was the Joshua Fuller family. Joshua Fuller purchased land in the Township along what was later named Fuller Road where Joshua, his son William C., and a grandson, Henry, all farmed. In his advancing years Joshua Fuller moved from his farm to Massachusetts Street where he resided until his death.

Nunda village was incorporated in 1839 on the site where four Seneca Indian camps were once located. Village life centered around a former frog pond converted into a village square, a newly created post office (1831), and the construction of two commercial blocks: Merchant's Row and Farmer's Exchange. Nunda's population continued to rise with the completion of the Genesee Valley Canal in 1861, which permitted the shipping of local timber and grains to New York City, Syracuse, and Rochester. Unfortunately, the Canal's value quickly declined with the rapid building of railroad lines across New York State. Nunda was not originally included on a railroad route, but a trunk line was later established by 1882. However, many Nunda families were already leaving the area seeking better economic opportunities in the west, particularly Ohio and Michigan. Nevertheless, Nunda took on the symbols of prosperity with the establishment of newspapers, manufacturing, banks, and a variety of commercial businesses.

Nunda farmer Joshua Fuller was a direct descendant of Edward Fuller who arrived on the *Mayflower* in the Americas in 1620 with his wife, son Samuel and brother Dr. Samuel Fuller.

Joshua Fuller was married twice. His first wife, Polly Brewer, died soon after giving birth to a son, Pliny, in Ludlow, Massachusetts. Joshua Fuller remarried to Mercy Pease and had eight more children. Joshua brought his second wife and their eight children, five daughters and three sons, to Nunda. His son, Pliny Brewer Fuller, came later but did not stay, moving around in quest of suitable farm land until finally settling in Humphrey, New York in nearby Cattaraugus County. By the time Joshua Fuller's eight other children became adults, Nunda could not fulfill their economic expectations. Son James relocated to Michigan while son George Washington Fuller moved to Philadelphia where their respective descendants still live. Joshua Fuller's son William and daughters Polly, Clarissa, and Maria married into local Nunda families (Guy, Carrier, Goldthwaite, and Warren, respectively) and remained for several more generations. Daughters Louisa and Sophia married into local Nunda families (Tabor and Chittenden), but relocated to Michigan and Wisconsin, respectively.

I always knew my maternal great-grandmother, Belle Fuller, was born in Nunda, New York. While in high school living in Wellsville, New York I found a copy of the Centennial History of Nunda where I located the section on the Fullers and learned they were descended from *Mayflower* passengers. This line of descent I documented and used to obtain membership in the General Society of Mayflower Descendants, later serving as Governor of the Virginia Society and Education Chairman of the General Society. For the next several decades I gradually searched for as much information as I could find on the Fullers of Nunda. This book is the result.

In searching for Fullers, I learned that my great-grandmother, Belle, was the daughter of Albert James Fuller (William Fuller's son), and his first wife, Edith Carter. Edith was the daughter of Nunda farmer, Daniel Carter, and his wife, Mary Elizabeth Adams. Mary Elizabeth was the daughter of Nicholas Adams, another Nunda farmer. Therefore, I included two appendices that document the genealogical information on Adams and Carter relatives for the same period as the Fuller family.

I realize and accept that no genealogical history is ever complete. I understand that new documents and information may be uncovered and hope that any future information will be added to my story on my three Nunda lines of descent. For now, my purpose is to preserve and publish what I know so this knowledge can be shared. My genealogy ends in 1932 with the death of Frederick Fuller, the last Fuller and the last of William's sons to reside in Nunda. Frederick Fuller is believed to be buried in an unmarked grave in Oakwood Cemetery.

A special thank you to Mike C. Beaty for his help in scanning and cleaning up photographs for this book. I thank Teddi Kella for the photographs of Albert Fuller's descendants from his second marriage. I am indebted to the following individuals: Linda Hoffman, Neptune, New Jersey, Secretary for the Fuller Society who provided the genealogy for George Washington Fuller, son of Joshua Fuller, to the late Joan Ball of Scio, New York for her updates on the Goldwaithe line of descent, and Robert Palmer, Ferndale, Washington, for his genealogical updates on the descendants of James and Alta Carter Palmer. A final thank you to Tom Cook, Nunda, New York Historian, for his assistance.

William A. Paquette, Ph. D.
Professor of History

East side of State Street, Looking South, Nunda, New York

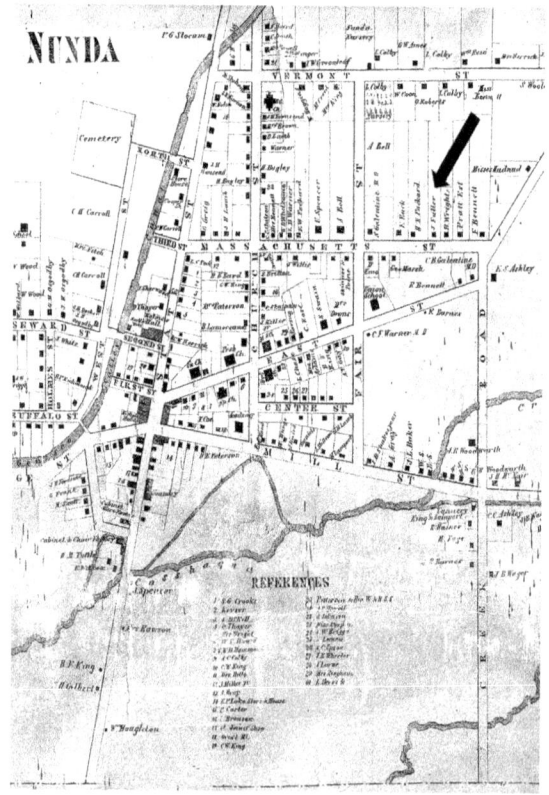

Map of Nunda, New York, 1858 (The arrow points to J. Fuller's Home.)

The Genealogy:

Four Generations of Mayflower Descendants in Nunda, New York (1833 - 1932)

Generation One

1.

Joshua Fuller, b. Ludlow, Massachusetts April 4, 1778, d. Nunda, New York March 28, 1871; m. (1) Massachusetts 1799 Polly Brewer, b. Ludlow, Massachusetts March 4, 1778, d. probably Ludlow, Massachusetts June 3, 1801; m. (2) Ludlow, Massachusetts October 17, 1802, Mercy Pease, b. Ludlow, Massachusetts December 20, 1782, d. Nunda, New York 1869/70, age 88 years. Joshua Fuller was a direct descendant of Mayflower passenger Edward Fuller. The documented line of descent is Edward Fuller, Samuel Fuller, Samuel Fuller, Matthew Fuller, Young Fuller, Joshua Fuller, Elisha Fuller, and Joshua Fuller of Nunda, New York. Joshua Fuller was the third of fourteen children of Revolutionary War soldier Elisha Fuller (1754-1850). His mother was Rebecca Waterman (1754-1796). Polly Brewer was the daughter of Isaac Brewer (1742-1788) and Sybil Miller Brewer (1747-1834). Mercy Pease was the daughter of Job Pease (1745-1814) and Deborah Haskell Pease (1749-1828). The US Census for 1800, 1810, and 1820 record Joshua Fuller's residence in Ludlow, Massachusetts. In 1830, he resided in Granby, Massachusetts. Three years later, Joshua Fuller moved his family to Nunda in Western New York State, where he engaged in farming. Joshua Fuller was one of the Founders of the Universalist Church in Nunda in 1840 and served as one of the Church's first Trustees. He remained a Universalist until his death. He later moved from his farm on what was named Fuller Road to a house on Massachusetts Street in Nunda. His 1871 newspaper obituary noted that Joshua Fuller was esteemed by all who knew him for his intelligence, sincerity, integrity, kindness of heart, charity, and goodwill for all men. Mr. Fuller was a devoted husband, a kind father, a good citizen, and an exemplary Christian. Joshua Fuller was predeceased by both wives. Joshua and Mercy Pease Fuller were buried in Oakwood Cemetery in Nunda, New York with a marker in evidence. The marker has the wrong birth year for Joshua Fuller giving it as 1779, which contradicts the Ludlow Birth Record. His wife's name was listed as Macy instead of Mercy. It is not known where Polly Brewer Fuller was buried. Joshua Fuller had one son by his first wife and five daughters and three sons by his second. (Undocumented sources gave Polly Brewer Fullers death date as June 3, 1801 and Mercy Pease Fuller's birth date as December 20, 1781 and her death date as March 24, 1868).

Children (by first marriage):

2.   I.   **Pliny Brewer Fuller**, f.

Children (by second marriage):

3.   I.   **Polly Fuller**, b. Ludlow, Massachusetts July 30, 1802, d. place and date not known. Undocumented sources identify her husband as either Jesse Carrier or a son or brother of Erastus Carrier of Nunda, New York, where they resided near County Line Road. Mary Carrier, a granddaughter of Joshua Fuller, resided with him in 1855 and was 18 years of age. In the 1860 New York State Census a Mary B. Carrier resided with her cousin, James W. Fuller in Allegany, New York. There is no further information on Mary Carrier, Polly Fuller Carrier, or Polly's husband. Polly Fuller Carrier was not mentioned in her father's 1871 obituary.

4.   II.   **Clarissa Caroline Fuller**, f.

5.   III.   **Louisa Fuller**, f.

6.   IV.   **Sophie Fuller**, f.

7.   V.   **James S. Fuller**, f.

8.   VI.   **William C. Fuller**, f.

9.   VII.   **Maria Fuller**, f.

10.   VIII.   **George Washington Fuller**, f.

References: US Census: 1800, 1810, 1820, 1830, 1840, 1850, 1860, 1870; New York State Census: 1855, 1865; Oakwood Cemetery Records, Nunda, New York; Massachusetts Birth Records 1620-1968 for Joshua Fuller, Polly Brewer Fuller, Mercy Pease Fuller, and Polly Fuller; Massachusetts Marriage Records 1620-1988 for Joshua Fuller's second marriage; The Nunda News April 1, 1871 obituary for Joshua Fuller; William H. Fuller, The Genealogy of Some Descendants of Edward Fuller of the Mayflower, Palma, MA: C. B. Fiske & Co, 1908; W. Wells Hand, The Centennial History of the Town of Nunda 1808-1908, Rochester, New York: Rochester Herald Press, 1908; James H. Smith, The History of Livingston County, NY 1687-1881, Syracuse, New York: D. Mason and Co., 1881.

Generation Two

2.

Pliny Brewer Fuller, son of Joshua (1), b. Ludlow, Massachusetts a. 1800/1801, d. Humphrey, New York December 1863; m. place and date not known, Rebecca Cowing, b. Oneida County, New York August 4, 1805, d. Humphrey, New York, April 4, 1871. Pliny Fuller's occupation was farming. Over his lifetime, he traveled to different parts of New York State and Pennsylvania to establish a profitable farm. In 1830, he and his wife resided in Hounsfield in Jefferson County, New York. The 1840 US Census found him and his growing family living in Italy, New York. Keating, McKean County, Pennsylvania, was where the Fullers resided based on the 1850 US Census. The Fullers cannot be found on the 1855 New York State Census; therefore, the last move to Humphrey, New York, occurred sometime in the 1850s. Based on the New York State Census for 1860, Pliny Fuller's farm consisted of seventy acres, with thirty acres farmed and forty acres unimproved. The cash value of the farm was $2,100, and the equipment value at $70. He had two horses, two milch cows, eight other cattle, eighteen sheep, and one swine. The value of the livestock was $450. His farm produced ten bushels of wheat, ten bushels of oats, three hundred pounds of rice, sixty pounds of wool, twenty-five bushels of Irish potatoes, seventy pounds of butter, and two tons of hay. The value of the slaughtered animals was $10. There is no documentation to show that Pliny Fuller and his family ever resided in Nunda, New York. However, their 1840 location was in the neighboring county to the east and in 1860 they resided in Cattaraugus County to the southwest. Rebecca Fuller was the daughter of James Cowing (1768-1840) and Rebecca Putnam Cowing (1775-1858). She continued to work the farm with the help of their daughter, Mary, and youngest son, Oren, after Pliny's death. Pliny and Rebecca Fuller were buried in Chapellsburg Burying Ground, Humphrey, New York. Markers are in evidence under a grove of trees. Pliny and Rebecca had five children.

Children:

11. I.   *James W. Fuller*, f.

12. II. *George Pliny Fuller*, f.

13. III. *Mary Fuller*, b. Pennsylvania 1836/37, d. place and date not known. She resided with her parents based on the US Census records for 1850, 1860, and 1870 and the New York State Census for 1865. The New York State Census for 1875 found Mary Fuller employed with the Mathias Mosman family in Humphrey, New York. There are no further records for Mary Fuller after this date. It is not known if she married. No burial record can be found.

14. IV. *Oscar Fuller*, b. Pennsylvania August 29, 1844, d. Allegany, New York February 1, 1861. Oscar Fuller resided with his parents. It is not known why he relocated to Allegany, New York or what he died from at age sixteen years, five months, and three days. He was buried in Allegany Cemetery, Allegany, New York. A marker is in evidence.

15. V.   *Oren Fuller*, f.

References: US Census: 1830, 1840, 1850, 1860, 1870; New York State Census: 1865, 1875; US Census Non-Population Schedules, New York 1850-1880 for Pliny Brewer Fuller; Chapellsburg Burying Ground Records, Humphrey, New York; Allegany Cemetery Records, Allegany, New York.

4.

Clarissa Caroline Fuller, daughter of Joshua (1), b. Ludlow, Massachusetts

November 25, 1803, d. Nunda, New York February 11, 1888; m. Granby, Massachusetts October 18, 1832, Alfred Goldthwaite, b. Massachusetts April 21, 1803, d. Nunda, New York November 11, 1875 aged 72 years, six months, and 21 days. Various histories on Nunda, New York and the Fuller family stated incorrectly that Alfred Goldthwaite was married twice to two sisters, Clarissa Fuller and Caroline Fuller. Alfred Goldthwaite was married only once and his wife's full name was Clarissa Caroline Fuller. For unknown reasons Clarissa Fuller's name was changed to Caroline on later US Census records. Alfred Goldthwaite was the son of Elijah Goldthwaite (1766-1846) and Rachel Snow who died in 1827. Mr. Goldthwaite was a farmer. He probably moved to Nunda, New York in the same year as his father-in-law, Joshua Fuller. In 1860 his farm consisted of twenty acres of farmed land and five acres unimproved. The value of his farm was $750 with additional $50 in value for the farm equipment. He had two milch cows and one other cattle, three sheep, and two swine. The livestock value was $85. His farm produced 85 bushels of wheat, twenty bushels of Indian Corn, twenty bushels of oats, twelve pounds of wool, twenty tons of hay, 200 pounds of butter, ten bushels of peas and beans, thirty bushels of Irish potatoes, thirty bushes of barley, and thirty bushels of buckwheat. The Goldthwaite family cannot be found on the 1870 US Census. After her husband's death Clarissa (Caroline) moved in with her daughter Harriet and son-in-law, George Breen, who resided in Nunda Station (Dalton). Alfred and Clarissa Goldthwaite were buried in Oakwood Cemetery, Nunda, New York. There is a marker for Alfred Goldthwaite but not for Clarissa.

Children:

16.	I.	*Gilbert Nelson Goldthwaite*, f.	
17.	II.	*Helen Maria Goldthwaite*, f.	
18.	III.	*Norton Smith Goldthwaite*, f.	
19.	IV.	*Milo Starkey Goldthwaite*, f.	
20.	V.	*Harriet Ermina Goldthwaite*, f.	

References: US Census: 1840, 1850, 1860, 1880; New York State Census:

1855, 1865, 1870; Massachusetts Vital Records 1620-1988 for Clarissa Fuller's birth; Massachusetts Vital Records for marriage of Clarissa Fuller and Alfred Goldthwaite; Oakwood Cemetery Records, Nunda, New York; US Federal Census Non-Population Schedules 1850-1880, 1860 for Alfred Goldthwaite; Descendants of Thomas Goldthwaite of Salem, Massachusetts by Charlotte Goldthwaite, Hartford Press, 1899.

5.

Louisa M. Fuller, daughter of Joshua (1), b. Ludlow, Massachusetts June 13, 1808, d. Hastings County, Michigan November 1, 1880 from heart disease; m. place and date not known, Mr. Tabor/Taber. The full identify of Louisa Fuller's husband is not currently known. At the time of the 1840 US Census she resided in Hastings, Michigan where she was raising three children. No occupation was given for Louisa on US Census records. The death certificate for Louisa's son, Henry Tabor, records his father's name as James Tabor, but his mother's name is not listed. It is believed that Louisa's daughter, Eliza, was deceased by the time of the 1860 US Census because she can no longer be found on any records. In 1860 Louisa resided with her son Alfred. Joshua Fuller's 1871 obituary names Louisa as Mrs. Louisa Tabor residing in Hastings, Michigan. Beginning in 1870 and until her death Louisa resided with her son Henry. It is not known where Louisa Fuller Tabor was buried.

Children:

21. I.   **Henry Tabor**, f.

22. II. **Eliza Tabor**, b. Michigan a. 1838. She only appears on the 1850 US Census.

23. III. **Alfred Tabor**, b. Michigan a. 1843, d. place and date not known but in 1864. In the 1850 and 1860 US Census records, he resided with his mother. On May 13, 1861 Alfred enlisted with Company E, Michigan Third Infantry Regiment. Civil War records indicate he was wounded May 6, 1864 in Wilderness, Virginia and died from his wounds. He was a corporal at the time of his death. His burial location is not known.

References: US Census: 1850, 1860, 1870, 1880; Massachusetts Vital Records 1620-1988 for Louisa Fuller's birth; Michigan Death Records 1867-1995; US Civil War Soldier Records and Profiles 1861-1865 for Alfred Tabor; Civil War Records 1861-1865.

6.

Sophie Barton Fuller, daughter of Joshua (1), b. Ludlow, Massachusetts July 12, 1810, d. Madison, Wisconsin December 27, 1891; m. Nunda, New York April 6, 1834 Dr. Nelson Harvey Chittenden, b. Shelburne, Vermont November 11, 1806, d. Madison, Wisconsin February 12, 1873. Nelson Harvey Chittenden was the son of Bela Chittenden (1767-1842) and Phebe Hard Chittenden (1778-1830). The Chittenden family resided on East Street in Nunda. He was a highly respected dentist and a teacher of vocal music. His dental office was next to the parsonage for Nunda's Methodist Church. In 1852 Dr. Chittenden had an attack of pneumonia followed by an abscess of the left lung which discharged externally for over two and one-half years. He went to Wisconsin in 1854 for his health and fully recovered, which led to his decision to relocate his dental practice and family to Madison in June of 1855. Dr. Nelson Chittenden was a practicing dentist until his death from heart disease. He was the Past Master of Masonic Lodge # 50 in Madison, Wisconsin. Sophia Fuller Chittenden remained in the family residence until her death, with one or more of her children residing with her. Sophia and Nelson Chittenden were buried in Forest Hill Cemetery, Madison, Wisconsin.

Children:

24. I. ***Ella A. Chittenden***, b. Nunda, New York January 15, 1835, d. Madison, Wisconsin, November 26, 1893. Ella never married and resided at the family home at 402 W. Main Street in Madison with her parents and some of her siblings. Her twin sister was Flora. The 1870 US Census recorded her occupation as a music teacher, but after that date, no occupation was given. Ella was buried in Forest Hill Cemetery, Madison, Wisconsin.

25. II. ***Flora E. Chittenden***, f.

26.   III.   *Roselle Lillie Chittenden*, f.

27.   IV.   Eliza Jane Chittenden, b. Nunda, New York January 1, 1840, d. Nunda, New York, January 6, 1840. It is assumed she was buried in Nunda, but no record can currently be found. She was a twin with Charlotte.

28.   V.   *Charlotte S. Chittenden*, f.

29.   VI.   *Charles Curtis Chittenden*, f.

30.   VII.   *Mary Sophia Chittenden*, f.,

31.   VIII.   *Kate Adelle Chittenden.* b. Nunda, New York January 28, 1850, d. Madison, Wisconsin, July 18, 1934. Kate never married and resided most of her life at the Chittenden family residence. Her brother and six sisters predeceased her. At the time of her death, she was living with a great-niece, Kathryn Pierce. Kate was buried in the family plot at Forest Hill Cemetery, Madison, Wisconsin.

References: US Census: 1840, 1850, 1860, 1870, 1880, 1900, 1910, 1920; New York State Census: 1855; William Chittenden of Guilford, Connecticut and his Descendants, by Alvan Talcott, no publisher, 1882; Forest Hill Cemetery Records, Madison, Wisconsin; Vermont Vital Records 1720-1908 for Nelson Chittenden's birth; The Capital Times July 19, 1934 obituary for Kate Chittenden.

7.

James S. Fuller, son of Joshua (1), b. Ludlow, Massachusetts 1812, d. Schoolcraft, Michigan September 30, 1877 from fever; m. Granby, Massachusetts April 14, 1833 Sarah Reed Nutting, b. Brimfield, Massachusetts July 26, 1812, d. Vicksburg, Michigan December 5, 1883. James Fuller was a farmer who moved from Massachusetts to Nunda, New York about the same time as his father, Joshua Fuller, and soon after his 1833 marriage. His wife, Sarah, was the daughter of Asa and Olive Nutting of Brimfield, Massachusetts. In the 1840 US Census, James Fuller and his wife had two sons and resided in Nunda, New York. Sometime after the birth of his son, Samuel who was born in Nunda, New York in 1843, and the birth of his son Oscar who was born in 1847 in Michigan James Fuller moved his growing family to a farm in Brady, Michigan. He now had five sons: Myron, Edward, James, Samuel, and Oscar. In 1860 James Fuller's two eldest sons had moved out of the residence leaving at home James, Oscar, and a daughter, Adelia. In 1870, James and Sarah had moved to Schoolcraft, Michigan with Adelia. James died from fever in 1877. The 1880 US Census lists a daughter Martha residing with the widowed Sarah R. Fuller. However, this is incorrect because if Martha was James and Sarah's daughter, she would have been listed in the 1870 US Census. I suggest that the Martha Fuller who was living with Sarah Fuller was her granddaughter, Martha Agatha Fuller, a daughter of Sarah's son, Myron Fuller. The birth years match up. James and Sarah were buried in Clement Cemetery, Vicksburg, Michigan with two of their sons.

Children:

32.   I.   *Myron A. Fuller*, f.

33.   II. *Edward R. Fuller*, f.

34.   III. *James E. Fuller*, f.

35.   IV. *Samuel A. Fuller*, b. probably Nunda, New York May 1, 1843, d. Michigan February 1, 1852, at age eight years and nine months. Samuel was buried in Clement Cemetery, Vicksburg, Michigan, with a marker as evidence.

36.   V.   *Oscar E. Fuller*, b. Michigan January 4, 1847, d. in a hospital in Chattanooga, Tennessee, June 6, 1865, at age eighteen years, five months, and two days. Oscar enlisted in Company E of the 11th Michigan Infantry. He died from wounds and chronic diarrhea. He may have been buried in a military cemetery in Tennessee, but he also has two grave markers in Clement Cemetery, Vicksburg, Michigan.

37.   VI. *Adelina Adelaide Fuller*, Michigan 1852; m. Brady, Michigan February 10/14, 1873 Charles W. Pursel or Pursails. There is no further information on her.

References: US Census: 1840, 1850, 1860, 1870, 1880; Michigan Death Index 1867-1995 for James S. and Sarah Fuller; Massachusetts Vital Records 1620-1988 for the wedding of James Fuller and Sarah Nutting; Massachusetts Vital Records 1620-1988 for birth of Sarah Reed Nutting; Clement Cemetery Records, Vicksburg, Michigan for Sarah, Samuel, and Oscar Fuller; Civil War Soldier Records and Profiles 1861-1865 for Oscar E. Fuller; Michigan Marriage Records.

8.

William C. Fuller, son of Joshua (1), b. Ludlow, Massachusetts February 7, 1819, d. Nunda, New York July 4, 1904 from old age after a thirty-day illness; m. (1) Nunda, New York January 1, 1842 Louisa C. Guy, b. Cayuga County, New York July 22, 1825, d. Nunda, New York May 28, 1895; m. (2) Nunda, New York, a. 1895, Mrs. Jane L. Brewer, b. New York State July 1832, d. New York State after the 1910 US Census. William C. Fuller moved to Nunda, New York with his father, Joshua Fuller, in 1833. He was a farmer and purchased a fifty-four-acre farm in 1868 on what became known as Fuller Road. The US Non-Population Census for 1850-1880 described his farm as consisting of sixty-five acres of farmed land and nine acres of unimproved land. The farm value was $2,320 with farm equipment value of $90. Mr. Fuller had two horses, three milch cows, forty sheep, and two swine with a value of $300. His farm produced ten bushels of wheat, one-hundred bushels of Indian Corn, 175 bushels of oats, eighty pounds of wool, 120 bushels of Irish potatoes, and two hundred pounds of butter. The value of slaughtered animals was $22. His first wife, Louisa, was the daughter of Alexander and Aurelia Guy of Mt. Morris, New York. William Fuller led a distinguished career in local service. He was appointed Postmaster of Nunda on June 15, 1869, reappointed December 15, 1871, and reappointed again January 15, 1875 holding the position until 1881. In addition, William Fuller served as deputy sheriff from 1861-1870, tax collector, appointed in 1868 and 1879, and town constable. Unlike his father, William Fuller attended the Nunda Baptist Church. He remarried after Louisa's death to Jane L. Brewer. Jane was married to Joel C. Brewer (1822-1877). The 1900 US Census noted that she had had three children with only one living, a son named Albert. Jane Fuller was last documented on the 1910 US Census residing in Rochester, New York with her son.

Albert Brewer never married and on November 14, 1911 was committed to the Alms House for the Poor with kidney trouble. He was last recorded there on the 1930 US Census in Geneseo, New York. William and Louisa Fuller were buried in Oakwood Cemetery, Nunda, New York. It is not known where Jane Brewer Fuller was buried.

Children (by first marriage):

38.   I.   *Henry Franklin Fuller*, f.

39.   II.   *Mary S./L. Fuller*, f.

40.   III.   *Martha E. Fuller*, f.

41.   IV.   *Arthur William Fuller*, f.

42.   V.   *George C. Fuller*, f.

43.   VI.   *Charles O. Fuller*, f.

44.   VII. *Frederick A. Fuller*, f.

45.   VIII. *Albert James Fuller*, f.

References: US Census: 1840, 1850, 1860, 1870, 1880, 1900, 1910; New York State Census: 1855, 1865, 1875, 1892; US Census Non-Population Schedules 1850-1860; New York State Death Index 1852-1956 for William and Louisa Fuller; US Appointments of US Postmasters 1832-1971 for 1869, 1871, and 1875; Oakwood Cemetery Records, Nunda, New York; Nunda Historian's Notes; W. Wells Hand, Centennial History of Nunda, New York 1808-1908, 1908; William H. Fuller, Descendants of Edward Fuller of the Mayflower, 1908; New York State Census of the Inmates of Almshouses and Poorhouses 1830-1920 for Albert Brewer.

9.

Maria/Mariah/Maria Ann Fuller, daughter of Joshua (1), b. probably Ludlow, Massachusetts a. 1824, d. Nunda, New York June 14, 1856 from complications from childbirth; m. probably Nunda, New York, date not known, Porter Warren, b. Middlefield, Otsego County, New York December 11, 1818, d. Dalton, New York May 12, 1910 from partial lung congestion and convulsions. Maria Fuller died after the birth of her youngest daughter, Cora. It is not known where she was buried. Porter Warren was a farmer who worked in both Nunda, New York and Grove, New York. He was the son of Noah Warren (1793-1881) and Ursula Cole Warren (1791-1871). Porter Warren remarried twice after the death of Maria. His second wife was Caroline Remington Scoville whose first husband, Norton Scoville was deceased. Caroline had two children by her first marriage, Cora, born in 1854 and Norton, born in 1855. It is not known when she married Porter Warren nor is it known when she died, but it was after the 1865 New York State Census and before the 1870 US Census. I suggest she was buried with her first husband, but there is no documentation to support this. By 1870 Porter Warren had remarried to Ruth Parker, born about 1830 and died in Dalton, New York December 13, 1900 where she was living with Porter and her step-daughter, Julia Warren Parker and Julia's husband and family. It is not known where Ruth Warren was buried. The 1850 US Non-population Census described Porter Warren's farm in Nunda, New York when he was married to Maria Fuller as consisting of forty-six acres with an additional unimproved six acres with a total value of $2,250. The farm equipment added another $80 in value. Porter Warren had one horse, two milch cows, two other cattle, and seventeen swine with a value of $97. His farm produced 200 bushels of wheat, 100 bushels of Indian Corn, 500 bushels of oats, thirty-five pounds of wool, forty bushels of Irish potatoes, sixty bushels of buckwheat, 300 pounds of butter, and fifteen tons of hay. The farm sold $13 in homemade items and made $21 from slaughtered animals. Porter Warren's obituary noted that he came to Nunda when six months old (1819), that all three of his wives had predeceased him, and he was survived by four of his five children from his first marriage. Mr. Warren attended the McSweeney log school in Nunda when Nunda consisted of only two buildings. Porter Warren did not have any children by his second or third wives. At the time of his death Porter Warren was Nunda's oldest living resident and was buried in Dalton Union Cemetery, Dalton, New York. There is no marker.

Children:

46.   I.   **Emiline or Emma Warren**, b. Nunda, New York, a. 1846 and believed deceased after the 1860 US Census. There are no further

records on Miss Warren, and it is not known where she was buried.

47. II.   *Edward D. Warren*, f.

48. III. *Julia Warren*, f.

49. IV.   *Laura Warren*, f.

50. V.   *Cora Warren*, f.

References: US Census: 1850, 1860, 1870, 1880, 1900, 1910; New York State Census: 1855, 1865, 1875, 1892; New York State Death Index 1852-1956 for Porter Warren and Ruth Parker Warren; The Nunda News May 7, 1910 for Porter Warren's Obituary; US Census Non-Population Schedules, New York 1850-1889, 1850; Dalton Union Cemetery Records, Dalton, New York; Nunda, New York death records for Maria Fuller Warren and Porter Warren.

10.

George Washington Fuller, son of Joshua (1), b. Ludlow, Massachusetts September 20, 1827, d. Philadelphia, Pennsylvania January 4, 1897; m. Philadelphia, Pennsylvania at St. Michael's and Zion Church October 15, 1857 Martha Rote, b. Germany December 7, 1836, d. Philadelphia, Pennsylvania December 19, 1923. In 1860 George Fuller resided in Nunda, New York with his wife and two eldest daughters. He was a farm laborer. By the 1870 US Census he had moved his family to Philadelphia, Pennsylvania. No occupation was given. In addition to his wife George Fuller's family consisted of daughters Mary, Jennie, Martha and sons George Washington, Jr., William, and Matthew. The 1880 US Census recorded Mr. Fuller's occupation as a cooper still residing in Philadelphia with two more sons, Edward and Walter. After George Fuller's death, his widow continued to reside in Philadelphia with her children Jennie, George, William and Walter and a granddaughter Esther. Martha Fuller cannot be found on the 1910 US Census but in 1920 she was living with her granddaughter, Esther Fuller Peacock and Esther's family in Philadelphia. Death Certificates indicate that George and Martha Fuller were buried in Fernwood Cemetery, Philadelphia.

Children:

51. I.   *Mary Ellen Fuller*, f.

52. II.   *Jennie D. Fuller*, f.

53. III. *George Washington Fuller*, f.

54. IV.   *Martha A. Fuller*, b. probably Nunda, New York October 1, 1864, d. Philadelphia, Pennsylvania October 20, 1881 from typhoid and buried in Bethel Vault, Arlington Cemetery, Drexel Hill, Pennsylvania.

55. V.   *William Fuller*, f.

56. VI.   *Matthew Fuller*, f.

57. VII. *Frank Fuller*, b. Philadelphia, Pennsylvania September 8, 1872, d. Philadelphia, Pennsylvania, December 28, 1873. The burial location is unknown.

58. VIII. *Edward Gregory Fuller*, f.

59. IX.   *Walter Fuller*, f.

60. X.   *Lillie Fuller* (a twin), b. Philadelphia, Pennsylvania April 24, 1881, d. Philadelphia, Pennsylvania, July 4, 1881, from marasmus caused by malnutrition and lack of food. She was buried in Bethel Vault, Arlington Cemetery, Drexel Hill, Pennsylvania.

61. XI.   *Flora Fuller* (a twin), b. Philadelphia, Pennsylvania April 24, 1881, d. Philadelphia, Pennsylvania, July 4, 1881, from marasmus caused by malnutrition and lack of food. She was buried in Bethel Vault, Arlington Cemetery, Drexel Hill, Pennsylvania.

62. XII. *Anna Fuller*, b. Philadelphia, Pennsylvania December 10, 1885, d. Philadelphia, Pennsylvania May 9, 1896. The burial location is unknown.

References: US Census: 1860, 1870, 1880, 1900, 1920; Pennsylvania Death Certificate 1803-1915 for George Washington Fuller, Martha A. Fuller, Lillie Fuller, and Florence Fuller; Pennsylvania Death Certificates 1906-

1967 for Martha Rote Fuller; Pennsylvania Church and Town Records 1708-1985 for the marriage of George Fuller and Martha Rote.

Generation Three

11.

James W. Fuller, son of Pliny (2), grandson of Joshua (1), b. New York State 1833, d. place and date not known; m. New York State by 1859 Mary Jane Harris, b. New York State a. 1835; d. place and date not known. James W. Fuller resided with his parents based on the 1850 US Census and the 1855 New York State Census. In 1860 James and his wife, Mary Jane, resided in Allegany, New York where he was employed as a wagon maker. In 1865 they moved to nearby Olean, New York where James continued to be employed as a wagon maker. By 1875 James Fuller moved his family to Andover, New York where he built wagons. In 1880 the Fuller family relocated to Canton, Illinois where James built carriages. There were many James W. Fullers and Mary Jane Fullers in New York, Illinois, and Michigan and documentation to trace both Fullers after 1880 cannot be currently be found. James and Mary Jane adopted a daughter named Ida who was born in 1859. Ida's parentage is not known. James and Mary Jane Fuller had two children of their own, Hattie and Clarence. It is not known where James W. and Mary Jane Fuller were buried.

Children:

63. I. ***Ida Fuller***, b. New York State January 25, 1859, d. Scio, New York March 15, 1874, age fifteen years, one month, and 18 days. Her grave maker indicates she was the adopted daughter of James and Mary Jane Fuller. Her cause of death is not known. Ida Fuller was buried in Fairlawn Cemetery, Scio, New York.

64. II. ***Hattie L. Fuller***, f.

65. III. ***Clarence Henry Fuller***, f.

References: US Census: 1850, 1860, 1870, 1880; New York State Census: 1855, 1865, 1875; Fairlawn Cemetery Records, Scio, New York for Ida Fuller.

12.

George Pliny Fuller, son of Pliny (2), grandson of Joshua (1), b. Italy, New York November 21, 1834, d. Kalamazoo, Michigan April 10, 1901 from kidney disease and exhaustion; m. Limestone, New York February 10, 1856 Nancy Jane Webb, b. Limestone, New York July 18, 1832, d. Kalamazoo, Michigan May 27, 1905 from heart disease. The 1860 US Census records George Fuller's occupation as a Methodist Clergyman residing in Allegany, New York with his wife and son, Charles. In 1870 George Fuller moved his family to Humphrey, New York where he resided on a farm next to his mother's. He was employed as a patent right's agent and had two more sons: Frank and Fred. After his mother's death George Fuller moved his family to New Richmond, Wisconsin where his family resided with his mother-in-law and he was employed as a book agent. George P. Fuller organized the Fuller Brothers Manufacturing Company which made the Northern Queen Washboard, which he invented. He served as the Company's President and moved the business to Kalamazoo in 1896. Mr. Fuller was also interested in coal mining in eastern Kansas. George Pliny Fuller was a poet writing The Charm of the Ages, At Fifty, and The Great Problem. The 1900 US Census recorded George and Nancy Fuller in Kalamazoo, Michigan where he was employed as a laborer. George Pliny Fuller and Nany Jane Webb Fuller were buried in Riverside Cemetery, Kalamazoo, Michigan.

Children:

66. I. *Charles Dwight Fuller*, f.

67. II. *Frank DeWitt Fuller*, f.

68. III. *Fred Adelbert Fuller*, f.

References: US Census: 1850, 1860, 1870, 1880, 1900; Michigan Death Records 1867-1952 for George and Nancy Fuller; Riverside Cemetery Records, Kalamazoo, Michigan; Kalamazoo Daily Telegraph for George Pliny Fuller April 11, 1901.

15.

Oren/Orren/Orrin Fuller, son of Pliny (2), grandson of Joshua (1), b. Pennsylvania 1847, d. Minneapolis, Minnesota April 11, 1888; m. New York State a. 1872 Orpha Bullard, b. Humphrey, New York, 1852, d. Andover, New York March 5, 1932. Oren Fuller resided in Humphrey, New York where he worked the family farm based on US Census records for 1860 and 1870 and New York State Census records for 1865. After the death of his father in 1863, he worked the farm where his mother and sister resided. After the death of his mother in 1873 Oren Fuller moved to Great Valley, New York where he was employed as a wagon maker. His wife, Orpha, lived with him. By 1880 Oren moved to Olean, New York where he continued to be employed as a wagon maker. His family included two daughters and three sons. A third daughter was born after 1880. After the 1880 census Oren Fuller relocated to Minneapolis where he continued to be employed as a wagon maker until his sudden death in 1888 from a spinal compression. His remains were returned to Kalamazoo, Michigan where he was buried in Riverside Cemetery. Orpha Fuller remarried July 15, 1899 to Thomas M. Comstock of Andover, New York. She moved to Andover with her two youngest daughters who married and resided in either Andover or Whitesville, New York. Orpha Bullock Fuller Comstock was buried in Riverside Cemetery, Kalamazoo, Michigan. Thomas Comstock was buried with his first wife in Hillside Cemetery, Andover, New York.

Children:

69. I. ***Minnie A. Fuller***, b. Great Valley, New York 1871, d. Kalamazoo, Michigan March 11, 1897 from peritonitis; m. Kalamazoo, Michigan June 19, 1895, Simon Sliter, b. 1870, d. Clarksville, Michigan, September 1951. Minnie Sliter was buried in Riverside Cemetery, Kalamazoo. There is no marker for Minnie.

70. II. ***Elmer L. Fuller***, f.

71. III. ***Frank Fuller***, f.

72. IV. ***George W. Fuller***, f.

73. V. *Hattie M. Fuller*, f.

74. VI. *Grace Edith Fuller*, f.

References: US Census: 1850, 1860, 1870, 1880, 1900, 1910, 1920, 1930; New York State Census: 1855, 1865, 1875; Riverside Cemetery Records, Kalamazoo, Michigan; Kalamazoo Daily Telegraph April 14, 1888 obituary for Oren Fuller and August 14, 1899 for Orpha Fuller's remarriage; Michigan Death Records 1867-1995 for Oren Fuller and Minnie Fuller Sliter; Michigan Marriage Records 1867-1952 for Minnie Fuller; Hillside Cemetery Records; Andover, New York.

16.

Gilbert Nelson Goldthwaite, son of Clarissa (4), grandson of Joshua (1), b. Nunda, New York March 27, 1834, d. Northeast, Pennsylvania February 5, 1908 from cardiac disease; m. place and date not known, Mary Hunt, b. place not known, 1838, d. place not known, 1914. Gilbert Goldthwaite resided with his parents until his marriage in Nunda. The 1865 New York State Census recorded him working in Caneadea, New York as a laborer with his wife and four children: Minnie, Jennie, Libbie, and Freddie. He continued to work a farm in Caneadea in 1870 but moved to Carroll, New York by 1880 where he continued to farm until the end of the century. In 1905 Gilbert Goldthwaite farmed in Mina, New York and in 1907 in Erie, Pennsylvania where he died. Gilbert and Mary Goldthwaite were buried in Pine Hill Cemetery, Falconer, New York. Gilbert Goldthwaite's grave stone gave his birth year as 1835 but this is conflict with his sister Helen's birth year of 1835.

Children:

75. I. *Minnie E. Goldthwaite*, f.

76. II. *Jennie Goldthwaite*, f.

77. III. *Elizabeth "Libbie" Goldthwaite*, f.

78. IV. *Fred Alfred Goldthwaite*, f.

References: US Census: 1850, 1870, 1880, 1900; New York State Census:

1855, 1865, 1892, 1905; Pine Hill Cemetery Records, Falconer, New York; Pennsylvania Death Certificate 1906-1967 for Gilbert Goldthwaite.

17.

Helen Maria Goldthwaite, daughter of Clarissa (4), granddaughter of Joshua (1), b. August 1835, d. Oxford, New York May 25, 1912; m. (1) Springwater, New York August 31, 1856 George W. Fuller (no relation), b. Springwater, New York 1824, d. Petersburg, Virginia August 25, 1864 from battle wounds; m. (2) New York March 23, 1870 George Breen, b. New York 1812, d. New York December 20, 1880; m. (3) place and date not known, William Close, b. Nunda, New York September 29, 1833, d. Nunda, New York January 20, 1900. George W. Fuller was employed as a carpenter and his family resided on East Hill in Nunda, New York. He joined the Union Army during the Civil War on August 6, 1862 and served with the 126th New York Volunteers. Mr. Fuller was 6' tall with blue eyes and brown hair. He was killed in action at Reams Station, Virginia. His grave location is not known. Helen's second and third husbands were both farmers. Helen and George Breen resided in Conesus, New York. William Close, Helen's third husband, also served in the Civil War with Company I, 136th New York Volunteers. He was wounded in action in 1863 and served under General Sherman in Georgia. Mr. Close was 6' 7" tall with blue eyes and light hair. He was wounded at the Battle of Kennesaw Mountain June 20, 1864. William Close was previously married to Catherine Boyd (1836-1892) by whom he had three children: Harriet, David, and Katie. Helen was buried with her son, William Alfred Fuller in Oakwood Cemetery, Nunda, New York. William Close was buried with his first wife in Oakwood Cemetery. It is not known where George Breen was buried.

Children (by first marriage):

79. I. *Frank Beecher Fuller*, b. March 25, 1857. He is listed on the 1860 and 1870 US Census records only. He was not mentioned in his mother's 1912 obituary and in the 1900 Census, his mother was listed as having only five children, which would not include him.

80. II. *William Alfred Fuller*, f.

81. III. **Cara S. Fuller**, b. Nunda, New York a. 1861. She was listed in the 1870 US Census and the 1865 and 1875 New York Census records. She married Mr. Comstock and moved to California but was deceased by 1912 when her mother died and was listed as deceased in her mother's obituary.

Children (by second marriage):

82. I. **Lewis Henry Breen**, f.

83. II. **William James Breen**, f.

84. III. **John C. Breen**, f.

References: US Census: 1850, 1860, 1870, 1880, 1900, 1910; New York State Census: 1865, 1875; Oakwood Cemetery Records, Nunda, New York; The Nunda News obituary for Helen Close; New York Clerk's Register Civil War Soldiers 1861-1865; Civil War Muster Roll Abstracts 1861-1900; Civil War Records and Profiles 1861-1865.

18.

Norton S. Goldthwaite, son of Clarissa (4), grandson of Joshua (1), b. Nunda, New York October 14, 1837, d. Nunda, New York August 5, 1886 age 48 years, nine months, and 22 days; m. Nunda, New York a. 1866 Hannah Jane Seager, b. Grove, New York September 2, 1846, d. Nunda, New York December 31, 1922 from apoplexy at her home on Mill Street, Nunda. Norton Goldthwaite enlisted with the First New York Dragoons on August 14, 1862 Company I. He was mustered out on April 3, 1865 because of disabilities caused by military combat. Norton Goldthwaite suffered from inflammation of the lungs the rest of his life. Mr. Goldthwaite was a farmer. Norton and Jane Goldthwaite were buried in Oakwood Cemetery, Nunda, New York. There is a marker for Norton Goldthwaite but not for Jane.

Children:

85. I. **Jerome Goldthwaite**, f.

86. II. **Adelbert Goldthwaite**, b. Nunda, New York June 1869, d.

Nunda, New York March 10, 1907, from consumption. He never married and was buried in Oakwood Cemetery, Nunda with a marker in evidence.

87. III. *Clara Goldthwaite*, f.

88. IV. *Isabelle "Belle" Goldthwaite*, b. Nunda, New York February 12, 1886, d. Geneseo, New York November 16, 1968. Isabelle never married. She resided with her mother or by herself. Sometimes, she was employed as a servant in private homes. Isabelle was buried in Oakwood Cemetery, Nunda, New York.

References: US Census: 1850, 1860, 1870, 1880, 1900, 1910, 1920, 1930, 1940; New York State Census: 1855, 1865, 1875; Oakwood Cemetery Records, Nunda, New York; The Nunda News November 21, 1968 obituary for Isabelle Goldthwaite; New York State Death Index 1852-1956; New York Clerk's Register of Civil War Soldiers 1861-1865; Civil War Muster Roll Abstract's 1861-1900; Civil War Records and Profiles 1861-1865; The Dalton Enterprise May 22, 1896 obituary; Nunda News obituary January 1922; Nunda News March 16, 1907 obituary for Adelbert Goldthwaite.

19.

Milo Starkey Goldthwaite, son of Clarissa (4), grandson of Joshua (1), b. October 26, 1841, d. Warsaw, New York February 28, 1922; m. place and date not known Elizabeth J. Mills, b. New York January 1850, d. Scottsville, New York May 12, 1942. Milo Goldthwaite enlisted on August 13, 1862 with Company I, First New York Dragoons. He was promoted to commissary January 3, 1865 and when mustered out held the rank of corporal. Milo Goldthwaite was Nunda, New York's Town Clerk from 1870-1871. He resided at 199 Walnut Street and was a dry goods salesman, a career which began in 1870 and continued until his retirement in 1910. For a time, he was in partnership with Alfred C. Dodge. Milo Garthwaite's obituary described him as courteous and kind to all, a good citizen, friend, and neighbor and had a pleasing appearance. He and his wife were buried in Oakwood Cemetery, Nunda, New York. There is a marker for Milo Goldthwaite.

Children:

89. I. **Howard M. Goldthwaite**, f.

90. II. **Dora K. Goldthwaite**, b. Jamestown, New York February 6, 1879, d. January 21, 1881. Her burial location is not known.

91. III. **Elizabeth Goldthwaite**, b. Olean, New York July 2, 1881, d. Nunda, New York May 1977. Popularly known as Bessie, she never married, resided with her parents, and was trained as a nurse. She worked for Columbia University in New York City and later was the superintendent for Hahnemann Hospital in Rochester, New York. She was buried next to her parents in Oakwood Cemetery, Nunda.

92. IV. **Unnamed Goldthwaite**, b. Olean, New York 1894, d. Jamestown, New York 1895. The burial location is unknown.

References: US Census: 1850, 1860, 1870, 1880, 1900, 1910, 1920, 1930, 1940; New York State Census: 1855, 1865; Social Security Death Index 1935-2014 for Elizabeth Goldthwaite; New York State Birth Index 1881-1942 for Elizabeth Goldthwaite; Oakwood Cemetery Records, Nunda, New York; New York State Death Index 1852-1856 for Milo and Elizabeth Mills; New York Town Clerks Registers for Men who served in the Civil War 1861-1865; The Nunda News March 3, 1922 obituary for Milo S. Goldthwaite.

20.

Harriet E. Goldthwaite, daughter of Clarissa (4), granddaughter of Joshua (1), b. Nunda, New York October 20, 1846, d. Canaseraga, New York December 30, 1932; m. probably Nunda, New York, a. 1875, Robert Craig, b. Sparta, New York March 2, 1845, d. Canaseraga, New York November 29, 1920. Robert Craig was a farmer and moved from Nunda, New York to Canaseraga, New York where he worked one of the largest farms in the area. A few years before his death Mr. Craig suffered an accident that crushed one of his legs, which was later amputated. After her husband's death Harriet resided with her son James until her death. Harriet and Robert Craig were buried in Canaseraga Cemetery, Canaseraga, New York in the Hulbert Section.

Children:

93. I. **Grace Badger Craig**, f.

94. II. **James Goldthwaite Craig**, f.

95. III. **Elizabeth "Bessie" Craig**, b. Nunda, New York July 11, 1881, d. Buffalo, New York February 24, 1965; m. Burns, New York March 22, 1914 William Gustav Quade, b. September 1, 1878, d. East Aurora, New York October 11, 1954. William Quade was a barber by profession. They did not have any children and were buried in Canaseraga Cemetery, Canaseraga, New York in the Hulbert Section.

References: US Census:1850, 1860, 1870, 1880, 1900, 1910, 1920, 1930; New York State Census: 1855, 1865, 1915, 1925; Canaseraga Cemetery Records, Canaseraga, New York; New York State Death Index 1881-1942 for Harriet and Robert Craig; New York State Marriage Index 1881-1942 for Elizabeth Craig; Dansville Express December 2, 1920 obituary for Robert Craig; Buffalo Evening News October 13, 1954 obituary for William Quade; The Nunda News March 4, 1965 obituary for Elizabeth Craig Quade.

21.

Henry D. Tabor, son of Louisa (5), grandson of Joshua (1), b. Nunda, New York August 14, 1833, d. Fife Lake, Michigan February 17, 1900; m. Oxford, Ontario, Canada November 12, 1867 Mary Leadbetter, b. Galashiels, Scotland August 13, 1847, d. Petoskey, Michigan September 1, 1898. Henry Tabor resided with his mother until his marriage. The 1870 US Census noted that he was employed as a carriage maker residing in Hastings, Michigan with his wife and children: Jennie and James and his mother, Louisa. In 1880 he was managing a hotel in Fife Lake, Michigan and a second son, Freddy had been born in 1879. It is not known where Henry Tabor was buried but his wife, Mary, was buried in Greenwood Cemetery, Petoskey, Michigan.

Children:

96. I. **Jennie Tabor**. b. Michigan a. 1869. She was listed on

the 1870 and 1880 US Census records only. Further information is not currently available.

97. II. **James Albert Tabor**, b. Hastings, Michigan June 8, 1870, d. Harvey, Michigan, March 8, 1903, when killed by a train; m. Wise, Michigan June 6, 1900, Minnie Lattimore. In the 1900 US Census, James resided with his younger brother in Grand Traverse, Michigan, where he was employed as a restaurant proprietor. In 1903, he lived in Harvey, Michigan, and worked for the GR and I Railroad as a brakeman. He was buried at Haring Charter Township Cemetery, Michigan.

98. III. **Alfred Dewitt Tabor**, f.

References: US Census: 1850, 1860, 1870, 1880, 1900; Ontario Marriage Records 1801-1920; Greenwood Cemetery Records, Petoskey, Michigan for Mary Tabor; Michigan Death Records 1867-1952 for Mary Tabor and James Albert Tabor; Haring Charter Township Cemetery Records, Haring, Michigan for James Tabor; Michigan Marriage Records 1822-1940 for marriage of James Tabor; Michigan Birth Records 1869-1911 for James Tabor.

25.

Flora Eglantine Chittenden, daughter of Sophie (6), granddaughter of Joshua (1), b. Nunda, New York January 15, 1835, d. Wisconsin November 10, 1910; m. September 29, 1857 Julius B. Devendorf, b. New York, 1831, d. Walworth County, Wisconsin March 27, 1882. Julius Devendorf resided with his parents in Columbia, New York where he was employed as a clerk in the 1850 US Census. The 1860 US Census noted his residence in Delavan County, Wisconsin, married to Flora and with one daughter, Kate. In the 1870 US Census for Sharon, Wisconsin Julius Devendorf was employed as a hardware dealer. By 1880 the family had moved to Delavan, Wisconsin where Mr. Devendorf was an agent for windmills. The 1900 US Census noted that Flora Devendorf had had eight children, but only three were living. Flora Chittenden Devendorf was buried in Forest Hill Cemetery, Madison, Wisconsin while Julius was buried in Spring Grove Cemetery, Delavan, Wisconsin.

Children:

99. I. **Kate Devendorf**, b. Wisconsin October 1858, d. Milwaukee, Wisconsin, February 25, 1929, from mitral regurgitation. Kate never married. She was employed as a music teacher, a seamstress, and a nurse residing with her mother. Kate Devendorf was buried in Forest Hill Cemetery, Madison, Wisconsin. A marker is in evidence

100. II. **Fred C. Devendorf**, b. Delavan, Wisconsin August 3, 1860, d. Los Angeles, California August 22, 1899. Fred resided with his parents until after the 1880 US Census when he moved to California. The cause of death is not known. He was buried in Angelus Rosedale Cemetery, Los Angeles. A marker is in evidence

101. III. **Charles Devendorf**, b. Wisconsin August 8, 1862, d. Wisconsin November 1863. He was buried in Spring Grove Cemetery, Delavan, Wisconsin with his brother Nelson with his name on the lower portion of the shared tombstone.

102. IV. **George Edward Devendorf**, b. Wisconsin January 1, 1867, d. Wisconsin January 13, 1880. He was buried in Spring Grove Cemetery, Delavan, Wisconsin. The cause of death is not known. A marker is in evidence.

103. V. **Nelson Devendorf**, b. and d. Wisconsin 1870. He was buried in Spring Grove Cemetery, Delavan, Wisconsin, with his brother Charles. His name is on the upper half of the tombstone.

104. VI. **Ralph Reeves Devendorf**, b. Wisconsin October 11, 1870, d. Madison, Wisconsin August 30, 1927. Ralph continued the family tradition and became a dentist. He never married and was buried in Forest Hill Cemetery, Madison, Wisconsin. A marker is in evidence.

105. VII. **Marlon Devendorf**, b. Wisconsin December 12, 1873, d. Wisconsin April 16, 1876/7, and was buried in Forest Hill Cemetery, Madison, Wisconsin. The cause of death is not known. There are no dates on the marker.

106. VIII. **Mabel Devendorf**, f.

References: US Census: 1850, 1860, 1870, 1880, 1900, 1910, 1920; Forest Hills Cemetery Records, Madison, Wisconsin; Spring Grove Cemetery Records, Delavan, Wisconsin; Wisconsin Death Records for Marlon Devendorf; Madison, Wisconsin City Directories for Dr. Ralph Devendorf; Los Angelus Rosedale Cemetery Records, Los Angeles, California; William Chittenden of Guilford, Connecticut and his Descendants by Alvan Talcott, 1882.

26.

Roselle L. Chittenden, daughter of Sophie (6), granddaughter of Joshua (1), b. Nunda, New York April 13, 1836, d. Madison, Wisconsin July 22, 1917; m. Wisconsin a. 1861 Lyall C. Stewart, b. Scotland a. 1832, d. Madison, Wisconsin November 20, 1910. Roselle married a dentist, which continued the profession within the family. Dr. Stewart resided with his parents in 1850 in Chester, Wisconsin and in Westfield, Wisconsin in 1860. Thereafter they resided in Waupun, Wisconsin. The 1900 US Census noted that they were married for thirty-nine years, but never had any children. Roselle and Dr. Lyall Stewart were buried in the Chittenden family lot at Forest Hill Cemetery, Madison, Wisconsin.

References: US Census: 1850, 1860, 1870, 1880, 1900, 1910; Wisconsin State Census: 1895, 1905; Forest Hill Cemetery Records, Madison, Wisconsin; William Chittenden of Guilford, Connecticut and his Descendants by Alvan Talcott, 1882.

28.

Charlotte S. Chittenden, daughter of Sophie (6), granddaughter of Joshua (1), b. Nunda, New York January 1, 1840, d. Wisconsin September 11, 1869; m. Wisconsin February 1, 1860 Christopher C. Pierce/Peirce, b. New York a. 1829, d. Chicago, Illinois November 20, 1882. Christopher was a master carpenter. Charlotte died at the home of her father. The cause is not known. She was buried in the Chittenden family plot at Forest Hill Cemetery, Madison, Wisconsin. Christopher Pierce was buried in Pierceville Cemetery, Sun Prairie, Wisconsin.

Children:

107. I. *Charles Tisdale Pierce*, f.

108. II. *Frances Ella Pierce*, f.

109. III. *Harry Lee Pierce*, b. Wisconsin September 29, 1866, d. Wisconsin, July 9, 1873, after falling through railroad ties on a bridge into a lake. He was living with his grandmother, Sophia Fuller Chittenden, and was buried in the Chittenden family lot at Forest Hill Cemetery, Madison, Wisconsin.

References: US Census: 1850, 1860, 1870, 1880; Wisconsin State Journal September 16, 1869 obituary for Charlotte Pierce; Forest Hill Cemetery Records, Madison, Wisconsin; Pierceville Cemetery Records, Sun Prairie, Wisconsin; William Chittenden of Guilford, Connecticut and his Descendants by Alvan Talcott, 1882.

29.

Charles Curtis Chittenden, son of Sophie (6), grandson of Joshua (1), b. Nunda, New York May 10, 1842; d. Madison, Wisconsin December 15, 1905; m. Wisconsin May 18, 1867 Virginia C. Winter, b. Wisconsin July 4, 1842, d. Madison, Wisconsin March 5, 1868. Charles Chittenden followed his father and entered the dentistry profession, which he practiced until his death. He never remarried after the death of his wife, Virginia. From the time of her death until his own, Charles resided with his mother or several of his sisters. Charles and Virginia Chittenden were buried in the Chittenden family plot, Forest Hill Cemetery, Madison, Wisconsin.

References: US Census: 1850, 1860, 1870, 1880, 1900; New York State Census: 1855; Forest Hill Cemetery Records, Madison, Wisconsin; William Chittenden of Guilford, Connecticut and his Descendants by Alvan Talcott, 1882.

30.

Mary Sophia Chittenden, daughter of Sophie (6), granddaughter of Joshua (1), b. Nunda, New York July 2, 1844, d. Madison, Wisconsin August 23,

1903; m. Dane County, Wisconsin October 15, 1872 Richard Walton Hurd, b. Little Mountain, Ohio 1848, d. Madison, Wisconsin July 24, 1934. Mary Chittenden's husband was dentist like her father, brother, brother-in-law, and nephew. The 1900 US Census indicated she was separated and lived with her son at the home of her brother. After her death Richard Hurd remarried to Julia E. Dalton (1866-1946). Mr. Hurd practiced dentistry until his death. Mary Chittenden Hurd was buried in the family plot in Forest Hills Cemetery, Madison, Wisconsin. Richard Hurd was buried in Resurrection Cemetery with his second wife in Madison.

Children:

110.   I.   ***Charles Frederick Hurd***, f.

References: US Census: 1850, 1860, 1870, 1880, 1900; New York State Census: 1855; Forest Hill Cemetery Records, Madison, Wisconsin; Resurrection Cemetery Records, Madison, Wisconsin; Wisconsin Marriage Index 1820-1907 for Chittenden/Hurd marriage; William Chittenden of Guilford, Connecticut and his Descendants by Alvan Talcott, 1882.

32.

Myron A. Fuller, son of James (7), grandson of Joshua (1), b. Nunda, New York January 11, 1835, d. Pleasant Plains, Arkansas January 3, 1903; m. (1) Michigan, date not known Martha E. Hill, b. place not known February 19, 1839, d. Michigan October 9, 1861, age twenty-two years, seven months, and twenty days; m. (2) Michigan 1862, Mary Jane Merritt, b. Michigan April 27, 1841, d. Brady Township, Michigan January 7, 1918 from apoplexy. Myron Fuller had moved to Brady, Michigan with his parents and siblings based on the 1850 US Census. He was recorded at Mendon, Michigan in the 1860 US Census working a farm. His first wife, Martha Hill, died one month after the birth of their daughter Martha Augusta in 1861. Myron and Martha had at least three children. He remarried to Mary Jane Merritt. In 1870 Myron Fuller and his family resided in Hastings, Michigan and was employed as a grocer. He returned to farming by the 1880 US Census in Grand Traverse, Michigan, which he continued in Independence, Arkansas to the end of the century. The 1900 US Census recorded that Mary Jane Fuller had had seven children with only two living. The identities of three are known. Myron Fuller died in Pleasant Plains, Arkansas and was buried in McMullin Cemetery there. His first wife, Martha, was buried in Mint Cemetery, St. Joseph County, Michigan. Mary Jane Merritt Fuller remarried twice more. In 1904 she married John Hindman and after he died Mary Jane married in 1909 John Fisher (1843-1912). Mary Jane was buried in Dutton Cemetery, St. Joseph County, Michigan.

Children (by first marriage):

111.   I.   *Jessie Fuller*, f.

112.   II. *Lillie J. Fuller*, b. Michigan November 25, 1858, d. Michigan November 16, 1860, age one year, eleven months, and twenty-two days. She was buried in Mint Cemetery, St. Joseph County, Michigan.

113.   III. *Martha Augusta Fuller*, f.

Children (by second marriage):

114.   I.   *Merritt Vorhees Fuller*, f.

115.   II. *Minnie Adelle Fuller*, f.

116.   III. *Mary Mande Fuller*, b. Mendon, Michigan 1869, d. Hastings, Michigan April 26, 1873 from spinal fever. It is not known where she was buried.

References: US Census: 1850, 1860, 1870, 1880, 1900, 1910; Mint Cemetery Records, St. Joseph County Michigan; McMullen Cemetery Records, Pleasant Plains, Arkansas; Dutton Cemetery Records, St. Joseph County Michigan; Michigan Death Records 1867-1952 for Mary Mande Fuller.

33.

Edward Randolph Fuller, son of James (7), grandson of Joshua (1), b. Nunda, New York August 15, 1836, d. Blair, Michigan November 3, 1920 from lobar pneumonia and a total physical collapse; m. (1) place and date not known, Diantha A. Ricket, b. place not known, July 30, 1840, d. Michigan October 16, 1891; m. (2) Traverse City, Michigan August 15,

1894 Susan A. Deen, b. Michigan March 14, 1848, d. Michigan August 23, 1920 form aortic insufficiency. Edward Fuller moved to Michigan with his parents and siblings by the 1850 US Census. He was a farmer his entire life either in Brady or Cleon, Michigan. He had three children by his first marriage but no children with his second wife. Edward Fuller and both his wives were buried in Cleon Township Cemetery, Cleon, Michigan.

Children (by first marriage):

117. I. **Arthur Fuller**, f.

118. II. **Belle/Maybelle Fuller**, b. Michigan 1865. She appeared in the 1870 and 1880 US Census residing with her parents in Brady, Michigan. No further information.

119. III. **Jennie Fuller**, f.

References: US Census: 1850, 1860, 1870, 1880, 1900, 1910, 1920; Cleon Township Cemetery Records, Cleon, Michigan.; Michigan Death Records 1867-1952 for Diantha Ricket Fuller; Michigan Marriage Records 1867-1952 for Edward Fuller's second marriage.

34.

James E. Fuller, son of James (7), grandson of Joshua (1), b. Nunda, New York 1841, d. Bloomington, Michigan February 27, 1894 from consumption; m. (1) place and date not known, Arrie A. Pomeroy, b. Indiana 1838, d. Schoolcraft, Michigan July 12, 1872; m. (2) Allegan, Michigan October 2, 1875 Agatha R. Crumly, b. Germany June 22, 1852, d. Otsego, Michigan July 5, 1917 from heart disease and paralysis. James Fuller resided with his parents in Brady, Michigan until his first marriage. He then resided in Mendon, Michigan with his first wife, Arrie, and her mother in Mendon, Michigan. He was employed as a dentist, a career he continued until his death in 1894. The cause of death for his first wife is not known. James Fuller had three children by his second wife, Agatha. Arrie Pomeroy Fuller was buried in Clement Cemetery, Vicksburg, Michigan. It is not known where James and Agatha Fuller were buried.

Children (by first marriage):

120.   I.   *Arrie Gertrude Fuller*, f.

Children (by second marriage):

121.   I.   *Anna C. Fuller*, f.

122.   II.   *Sara Fuller*, b. Michigan a. 1879. She only appears on the 1880 US Census. The 1900 US Census indicated that her mother had three children with only two living, therefore, Sara must have died. Her burial location is not known.

123.   III.   *Grover Fuller*, f.

References: US Census: 1850, 1860, 1870, 1880, 1900, 1910; Clement Cemetery Records, Vicksburg, Michigan for Arrie Pomeroy Fuller; Michigan Marriage Records 1867-1952; Michigan Death Records 1867-1952 for James and Agatha Fuller.

38.

Henry Franklin Fuller, son of William (8), grandson of Joshua (1), b. Nunda, New York July 6, 1843, d. Nunda, New York March 10, 1875 age 32 years and four months from consumption after a long and painful illness; m. Nunda, New York June 11, 1864 Esther A. Barker, b. Nunda, New York November 16, 1843, d. Oneida, Kansas December 6, 1880 at age 37 years and 19 days from pleura-pneumonia. Henry Fuller enlisted September 11, 1862 joining Company F, 33rd New York Infantry. He was mustered out April 13, 1863 because of battlefield injuries suffered at White Oak Church, Virginia. At the time of his enlistment Henry Fuller's occupation was a farmer in business with his father, William Fuller on Fuller Road. He was 5' 8" tall with brown eyes and fair hair. His wife, Esther Fuller was the daughter of Newton and Jane Bradley Barker of Nunda. In 1875 after her husband's death Esther was employed as a school teacher in Nunda. The 1880 US Census listed Esther and her two sons as residents of Portage, New York. Her second son, Ord Fuller, was born after Henry Fuller's death. Sometime after the 1880 US Census Esther Fuller went to Oneida, Kansas to visit her eldest son, Elmer Fuller, and died there. Her remains were returned to Oakwood Cemetery, Nunda, New York for burial beside her husband. Markers are in evidence for both Henry and Esther Fuller.

Children:

124.   I.   ***Elmer Ellsworth Fuller***, f.

125.   II.   ***Ord/Ore/Ora Fuller***, b. Nunda, New York a. 1876 after the death of his father, d. by June 1897 based on his will filed in Nunda, New York June 1897. It is assumed he was buried in Oakwood Cemetery, but no record can currently be found.

References: US Census: 1850, 1860, 1880; New York State Census: 1855, 1865, 1875; New York Civil War Muster Roll Abstracts 1861-1900; New York State Wills and Probates 1659-1999, Livingston County, 1897 for Ora Fuller. Oakwood Cemetery Records, Nunda, New York; W. Wells Hand, The Centennial History of Nunda, New York 1808-1908, 1908; William H. Fuller, Descendants of Edward Fuller...., 1908.

39.

Mary L./S. Fuller, daughter of William (8), granddaughter of Joshua (1), b. Nunda, New York August 1846, d. Sandy Creek, New York September 6, 1911; m. (1) probably Nunda, New York, date not known, John B. Paine/Payne, b. New York State a. 1838, d. Nunda, New York March 8, 1869; m. (2) probably Nunda, New York, date not known, Edward Slater, b. place and date not known, d. place and date not known; m. (3) Nunda, New York January 1, 1881 Charles Rolison, b. New York State August 1851, d. Nunda, New York April 7, 1921, divorced 1899. I suggest that Mary Fuller's middle initial was L for Louisa, the name of her mother and also a sister of her father's. Her first husband, John Paine, served in the Civil War with Company F, 33rd New York Volunteers. He enlisted on September 11, 1862, and was mustered out with a disability after the battle of White Oak Church, Virginia. Mary and John Paine were married after the 1865 New York State Census because she had been living with her parents until then. John Paine was killed in an explosion in Dalton (previously Nunda Station), New York. He was buried in Oakwood Cemetery, Nunda, in the Joshua Fuller lot. They had a daughter, Jennie. Edward Slater remains a mystery. In the 1870 US Census, Mary and Edward Slater were married, but by the time of the 1875 New York State Census, she had resumed use of the Fuller name and was living with her father. Local and Fuller family histories record that Mary Fuller Slater had two sons by her second marriage. These two brothers could not be found in the documents currently available. Mary had a son, Harry Rolison, by her third husband, Charles Rolison. However, in 1886, a year after her son's birth, Mary was committed to an asylum, and Charles divorced her in 1899. The Rolinson descendants interviewed stated that Harry Rolison never knew who his mother was, and there is no evidence to indicate that mother and son were ever reunited. Local Nunda, New York historians and the 1908 History of the descendants of Edward Fuller claim that Mary Fuller was married a fourth time to Harrison Hagadorn of Mt. Morris. The 1900 US Census recorded Mary was employed at the Hagadorn residence as a servant, but there are currently no records to indicate a marriage between them. Mary Slater could not be found on the 1905 New York State Census or the 1910 US Census. Mary Fuller moved to Sandy Creek, New York, where her daughter Jennie Paine Edgett lived with her husband and children. Mary was buried with her daughter's family in the Edgett lot, Woodlawn Cemetery, Sandy Creek, New York.

Children (by first marriage):

126. I. ***Jennie Paine***, f.

Children (by second marriage):

127. I. ***William Slater***, b. New York a. 1873. He was only mentioned in the 1875 New York State Census. The 1908 History of Edward Fuller's Descendants claims he moved to New York City.

128. II ***Frank Slater***, b. Michigan a. 1874. He was only mentioned in the 1880 US Census. The 1908 History of Edward Fuller's Descendants claims he moved to New York City.

Children (by third marriage):

129. I. ***Harry Rolison***, f.

References: US Census: 1850, 1860, 1870, 1880, 1900; New York State Census: 1855, 1865, 1875; US Civil War Registrations Records 1863-1865 for John B. Payne; US Headstones for Deceased Union Civil War Veterans 1861-1904 for John B. Payne; Oakwood Cemetery Records, Nunda, New York for John Paine; Nunda Historian's Notes for Mary Fuller's marriages; The Nunda News January 1881 for Mary Fuller's third marriage; August 15, 1896, and November 4, 1899; William H. Fuller, Descendants of Edward Fuller of the Mayflower; W. Wells Hand, The Centennial History of Nunda, New York 1808-1908; Woodlawn Cemetery records, Sandy Creek, New York.

40.

Martha E. Fuller, daughter of William (8), granddaughter of Joshua (1), b. Nunda, New York May 20, 1849, d. Kalamazoo, Michigan March 26, 1937 from myocarditis; m. (1) probably Nunda, New York, date not known, Samuel J. Drury, b. Nunda, New York 1850, d. Minneapolis, Minnesota August 24, 1889 from pneumonia; m. (2) Kalamazoo, Michigan May 21, 1891 John C. Cragin, b. New Hampshire, February 13, 1839, d. Kalamazoo, Michigan September 23, 1914 from anemia and general disability; m. (3) place and date not known, John Underwood, b. Ohio, 1849, d. place and date not known. Samuel J. Drury was the son of Samuel (1824-1893) and Margaret Gordon Drury (1816-1895) of Nunda. The date of Martha and Samuel Drury's marriage is not known. The 1880 US Census found them married and living in Holland, Michigan with three sons: George, Willie, and Eddie. George was twelve years old, therefore, he was born a. 1869 even though the 1870 US Census recorded that Martha and Samuel were still single. In the 1900 US Census it is recorded that Martha had had five children with four living. Buried in the Drury cemetery lot are a daughter Maggie, b. a. 1868. A son, George, was born about 1869. Samuel Drury was a carpenter by profession and moved to Michigan and later to Minnesota where he resided starting in 1884 and was employed with the Phelps Well and Windmill Company. His remains were returned to Kalamazoo, Michigan where he was buried. John Cragin was previously married to Mary A, Morse (1838-1890) and by whom he had three children. John was a carriage maker and a wood worker. Sometime before the 1920 US Census Martha remarried to John Underwood. He was deceased by the 1930 US Census because Martha Underwood was listed as a widow and had a grandson, George W. Drury, a granddaughter, Ila Drury, and a nephew, Donald Fuller, residing with her. The address for Martha for the 1900, 1910, 1920, and 1930 US Census was 908 N. Church Street. Martha was buried with her first husband, Samuel Drury in Riverside Cemetery, Kalamazoo, Michigan. John Cragin was buried with his first wife also in Riverside Cemetery. Burial information on John Underwood is not currently available. I suggest that the identities of four of her children are known.

Children (by first marriage):

130. I. *Maggie Drury*, b. place not known. 1868, d. Kalamazoo, Michigan July 18, 1872, three and ½ years of age. She was buried in Riverside Cemetery, Kalamazoo, Michigan.

131. II. *George Drury*, b. place not known, a. 1869, d. Kalamazoo, Michigan, October 17, 1922, age 53 years. He was buried in Riverside Cemetery.

132. III. *William S. Drury*, f.

133. IV. *Edward Franklin Drury*, f.

References: US Census: 1850, 1860, 1870, 1880, 1900, 1910, 1920, 1930; New York State Census: 1855, 1865; Oakwood Cemetery Records, Kalamazoo, Michigan; Michigan Death Records 1867-1995 for Martha Fuller Drury Cragin, Samuel J. Drury, and John C. Cragin; Michigan Marriage Index 1867-1952 for Martha Drury's second marriage.

41.

Arthur William Fuller, son of William (8), grandson of Joshua (1), b. Nunda, New York July 14, 1851, d. Nunda, New York March 12, 1898 from uremia; m. place and date not known, Rose/Rosina Morris, b. place not known, October 1859, d. place and date not known. Arthur Fuller was a barber by profession. Some local historians' notes indicated that he and Rose had a child born in 1878 that died young. No documentation could be found to confirm that claim. Edith Carter was employed as a servant by Arthur Fuller and she married his youngest brother, Albert, in 1880. William C. Fuller was made the executor of Arthur Fuller's estate as noted in Arthur's April 18, 1898 will. The 1900 US Census recorded that Rose had three children with two living. However, the 1910 US Census noted that Rose had three children and all three were alive. There is documentation for three living children in both 1900 and 1910. Arthur Fuller was buried in the Joshua Fuller lot in Oakwood Cemetery, Nunda, New York. In 1900 Rose moved to Sayre, Pennsylvania where she was a housekeeper for an attorney. The 1910 US Census noted she remarried in 1908 to Isaac Newton Evans, also a lawyer, who was considerably older being born in New York October 7, 1826. Mr. Newton died October 6, 1922 in Pittsburgh, Pennsylvania. He was a widower at the time of his death, therefore, it could be suggested that Rose had died between 1920 and 1922, although there is no documentation to confirm this. Isaac Evans was buried in Allegheny Cemetery, Pittsburgh, Pennsylvania. It is not known where Rose Morris Fuller Evans was buried.

Children:

134.   I.   *William Fuller*, f.

135.   II. *Grace Fuller*, f.

136.   III. *Morris Fuller*, f.

References: US Census: 1850, 1860, 1870, 1880, 1900, 1910, 1920; New York State Census: 1855, 1865, 1875; Oakwood Cemetery Records, Nunda, New York for Arthur Fuller; New York State Death Index 1867-1952 for Arthur Fuller; New York, US Wills and Probates 1699-1999.

42.

George Curtis Fuller, son of William (8), grandson of Joshua (1), b. Nunda, New York August 1856, d. Kalamazoo, Michigan November 3, 1915 from a mitral lesion; m. (1) Kalamazoo, Michigan December 25, 1882 Rosie Bell Soles, b. Michigan a. 1862, d. Kalamazoo, Michigan 1885, interred May 1, 1885; m. (2) Kalamazoo, Michigan June 6, 1887 Mary Quick, b. Kalamazoo, Michigan April 11, 1868, d. Kalamazoo, Michigan January 23, 1911 from cirrhosis of the liver, divorced; m. (3) Kalamazoo, Michigan March 9, 1895

Ida M. Sheppard, b. Pennsylvania August 1868, d. Kalamazoo, Michigan January 9, 1919 from apoplexy at the home of Martha Cragin, her sister-in-law. The 1908 History of the Descendants of Edward Fuller recorded that George C. Fuller married a Louise Ludwig. There is no documentation to support that assertion. That same genealogical history also stated that George Fuller moved to the West. Maybe Michigan was considered the West? George Fuller resided in either Nunda, New York or Kalamazoo, Michigan. Some family histories contend that George Fuller's second wife was Ida M. Boekeloo. That is incorrect. George's third wife was Ida M. Sheppard and she had a sister Mrs. O. K. Boekeloo of Kalamazoo. George Curtis Fuller resided in Nunda, New York until after the 1880 US Census when he relocated to Kalamazoo, Michigan where relatives resided. It is not known what Rose Fuller died from but it could have been from childbirth complications given their son was born in September 1884 and she died in late April 1885. The date of divorce for George Fuller and his second wife is not known, but each remarried. Mary Quick Fuller remarried November 21, 1896 to Louis Marker of Kalamazoo. George Fuller had one son by his first marriage and no children by his second or third wives. He was a wood worker employed by Wood Wind Manufacturing, a casket company, in Kalamazoo. George C. Fuller was buried in Riverside Cemetery, Kalamazoo, Michigan lot 006, grave 5. His first wife, Rose, was buried in the same lot, grave 6, and his third wife, Ida, was buried in lot 006, grave 7. Mary Quick Fuller Marker was buried in Mount Home Cemetery, Kalamazoo while her second husband was buried in Riverside Cemetery.

Children (by first marriage):

137. I. **Frank R. Fuller**, b. Kalamazoo, Michigan September 27, 1884. He resided with his father until his departure sometime after 1907. Frank Fuller was regularly listed in the Kalamazoo, Michigan City Directories from 1901 to 1907 living at his father's residence at 421 W. North Street. There is no further information on him. His father's 1915 obituary indicated he had moved out west.

References: US Census: 1860, 1870, 1880, 1900, 1910; New York State Census: 1865, 1875; Riverside Cemetery Records, Kalamazoo, Michigan;

Mount Home Cemetery Records, Kalamazoo, Michigan; Michigan Marriage Records 1867-1952 for George Fuller's second and third marriages; Michigan County Marriages 1822-1940 for George Fuller's first marriage; Michigan Birth Index 1867-1911 for Mary Quick; Michigan Death Records 1867-1952 for George C. Fuller, Mary Quick Fuller Marker, and Ida Sheppard Fuller; Kalamazoo Gazette obituaries for George C. Fuller November 4, 1915 and January 10, 1919; Michigan Birth Index 1867-1911 for Frank R. Fuller; Kalamazoo City Directories 1901, 1902, 1904, 1906, 1907 for Frank R. Fuller; William H. Fuller Descendants of Edward Fuller of the Mayflower, 1908. Markers are in evidence for George and Ida Fuller.

43.

Charles O. Fuller, son of William (8), grandson of Joshua (1), b. Nunda, New York August 30, 1857, d. Nunda, New York August 8, 1922; m. place not known, 1885 Harriet Spoon, b. Swain, New York October 4, 1861, d. Nunda, New York March 24, 1935. Charles Fuller resided with his parents in Nunda, New York until his marriage. He was a farmer working in Nunda or Warsaw, New York. The 1920 US Census recorded his occupation as a painter. Charles and Hattie Fuller had two children. They were buried in Oakwood Cemetery, Nunda, New York. Markers are in evidence for Charles, Hattie, and Minnie Fuller.

Children:

138.   I.   ***Minnie Fuller***, b. Nunda, New York November 5, 1891, d. Nunda, New York December 11, 1891 and buried in Oakwood Cemetery, Nunda.

139.   II.   ***Roy Elwood Fuller***, f.

References: US Census: 1860, 1870, 1880, 1900, 1910, 1920, 1930; New York State Census: 1865, 1875, 1915; Oakwood Cemetery Records, Nunda, New York.

44.

Frederick A. Fuller, son of William (8), grandson of Joshua (1), b. Nunda,

New York July 1860, d. Mt. Morris, New York May 27, 1932; m. Mt. Morris, New York October 8, 1906 Margaret Coleman Spencer Stives, b. New York June 1865, d. place and date not known. Fred Fuller resided with his parents until their respective deaths. The 1908 History of the Descendants of Edward Fuller recorded he married a Mrs. Strong, but there is no documentation to support this. After Fred's marriage he resided in Geneseo, New York employed as a farm laborer. His wife, Margaret, had eight children with five living from a previous marriage. Margaret's living children included an Arthur Spencer, a Mary Stives who was sometimes listed incorrectly as Mary Fuller, and another son named Arthur Durock. The 1915 New York State Census found Fred and Margaret Fuller living in Mount Morris, New York where he continued to find farm work. Fred Fuller remained a farm laborer in Mt. Morris until his death. He was buried in Oakwood Cemetery, Nunda, New York. No marker is in evidence. It is not known what happened to his wife.

References: US Census: 1870, 1880, 1900, 1910, 1920, 1930; New York State Census: 1865, 1875, 1915, 1925; New York State Marriage Index 1881-1967; Oakwood Cemetery records, Nunda, New York: William H. Fuller, Descendants of Edward Fuller of the Mayflower, 1908.

45.

Albert James Fuller, son of William (8), grandson of Joshua (1), b. Nunda, New York July 10, 1864, d. Kalamazoo, Michigan June 8, 1944 from old age; m. (1) Nunda, New York April 19, 1880 Edith Estelle Carter, b. Nunda, New York September 13, 1865, d. Binghamton, New York October 22, 1911 from internal obstruction, divorced, place and date not known; m. (2) m. Kalamazoo, Michigan May 19, 1897 Nancy B. Larrabee, b. Michigan August 1865, d. Comstock, Michigan April 10, 1938 from depression leading to suicide, divorced Kalamazoo, Michigan June 26, 1930; m. (3) Lake, Indiana May 16, 1931 Lulu May Bailey, b. Allegan County, Michigan June 19, 1898, d. Kalamazoo, Michigan June 8, 1953 from acute myocardial failure. Edith Carter was the daughter of Daniel and Mary Elizabeth Adams Carter of Nunda, New York. She was employed as a servant in the home of Albert's brother, Arthur Fuller, in 1880, the same year they married. Edith Carter also appears on the 1880 US Census living with her parents and siblings, also in Nunda. It is not known when Albert and Edith separated. They had three children. Edith Carter moved to Olean, New York by 1900 with her two youngest children and moved in with her eldest daughter and her family. Edith later moved to Binghamton, New York where she remarried April 19, 1902 to Lemuel Stalker (1855-1931). Edith was buried in Floral Park Cemetery, Binghamton, New York. Albert Fuller's application for his second marriage indicated that he had never been married, which was not correct. Albert and Nancy Fuller had two children including one who was born and died the same day. Nancy Fuller's divorce was based on depression and extreme cruelty. She was buried in Cedar Creek Cemetery, Hastings, Michigan. Lulu and Albert Fuller did not have any children. She was previously married to Lloyd Lockwood on January 31, 1917 and divorced June 21, 1919. After the death of Albert Fuller, Lulu remarried July 7, 1949 to Chester V. Hyde (1893-1953). Lulu was buried with Albert Fuller in Riverside Cemetery, Kalamazoo, Michigan with a common stone in evidence. There are no markers for either Edith Carter Fuller Stalker or Nancy Larrabee Fuller. Albert Fuller was employed at various times as a machinist, teamster, real estate salesman, flagman for the New York Central Railroad, and a salesman for the C. H. Palmer Company, Kalamazoo.

Children (by first marriage):

140.   I   *Belle Fuller*, f.

141.   II. *Jesse Nicholas Fuller*, f.

142.   III. *Louise Fuller*, f.

Children (by second marriage):

143.   I.   *Male Fuller*, b. and d. January 28, 1899 and buried First Presbyterian Columbarium, Kalamazoo, Michigan.

144.   II. *Donald R. Fuller*, f.

References: US Census: 1870, 1880, 1900, 1910, 1920, 1930, 1940; New York State Census: 1875, 1905, 1915; Floral Park Cemetery Records, Johnson City, Pennsylvania; Riverside Cemetery Records, Kalamazoo, Michigan; Cedar Creek Cemetery Records, Hastings, Michigan; First

Presbyterian Columbarium, Kalamazoo, Michigan; Michigan Marriage Records 1867-1952 for Albert Fuller's second marriage; Michigan Death Records 1867-1952 for Albert Fuller, Nancy Fuller, and Lulu Fuller Hyde; Michigan Divorce Records 1897-1952 for Albert Fuller's second marriage; Indiana Marriage Records 1810-2001 for Albert Fuller's third marriage; William H. Fuller, Descendants of Edward Fuller of the Mayflower, 1908 for Albert Fuller's first marriage; New York State Death Certificate October 22, 1911 for Edith Stalker; Kalamazoo Gazette obituary June 9, 1944 for Albert Fuller; Kalamazoo City Directories: 1904, 1905, 1906, 1922, 1926, 1927. 1931, 1934.

47.

Edward Dwight Warren, son of Maria (9), grandson of Joshua (1), b. Nunda, New York December 25, 1847, d. Beloit, Wisconsin June 23, 1933; m. (1) Nunda, New York a. 1867 Charlotte "Lottie" Schwartz, b. Grove, New York February 2, 1847, d. Cedar Rapids, Iowa May 12, 1925, divorced by 1888; m. (2) Flint, Michigan March 25, 1889 Emma McColloch, b. place not known December 29, 1847, d. place and date not known, divorced; m. (3) Indiana a. 1897 Rose Ella Shank, b. Indiana June 15, 1867, d. Albany, Indiana April 30, 1919 from influenza; m. (4) Albany, Indiana November 15, 1920 Gertrude "Gertie" Della Murray Barry Barton, b. place not known, August 8, 1874, d. Indiana September 3, 1932 from heart disease and nephritis, separated. Edward Warren resided in Nunda, New York until 1870 where he was employed as a teamster. In the 1875 New York State Census, Mr. Warren had moved his family to nearby Warsaw, New York where he worked as a carpenter. Edward and Lottie Warren had two children: a son William Edward Warren and an unnamed child who was born and died between 1870 and 1880 based on local historian notes. In 1880 the Warren family moved to Portage, New York near Nunda where Edward Warren was employed as a railroad clerk. Some years later the family moved to Indiana where Edward and Lottie divorced. Edward Warren married his second wife in 1889. They were divorced by 1897 because Edward Warren had remarried to Rose Ella Shank by whom he had four children: Archie, Lillian, Richard, and Charlotte before she died from influenza. In 1920 Mr. Warren remarried a fourth time to Gertie Murray Barry Barton who had been twice married before her marriage to Edward.

In the 1930 US Census Edward and Gertie were living in separate states, Edward with his eldest son Archie in Wisconsin and Gertie in Indiana where she was listed as a widow. Edward Warren was last employed as a laborer for a tinware factory. Lottie Schwartz Warren remarried in 1892 in Iowa Falls, Iowa to John Henry Lilly. They did not have any children. She died in Cedar Rapids, Iowa May 12, 1925 at the home of her son William Warren and was buried in Oak Hill Cemetery, Cedar Rapids, Iowa. It is not known what happened to Emma Warren, Edward's second wife. She was last recorded in the 1900 US Census and was employed with the Women's Christian Association for Orphans in Kansas City, Missouri. Ella Warren was buried in Moreland Cemetery, Moreland, Indiana with Edward Warren. Gertie Warren was buried in Strong Cemetery, Albany, Indiana. She had two children by first husband, Emery Barry.

Children (by first marriage):

145.   I.   **William Edward Warren**, f.

Children (by third marriage):

146.   I.   **Archie F. Warren**, f.

147.   II.   **Lillian Warren**, f.

148.   III.   **Richard Warren**, f.

149.   IV.   **Charlotte Warren**, f.

References: US Census: 1850, 1860, 1870, 1880, 1900, 1910, 1920, 1930; New York State Census: 1855, 1865, 1875; Moreland Cemetery Records, Moreland, Indiana; Oak Hill Cemetery Records, Cedar Rapids, Iowa; Strong Cemetery Records, Albany, Indian; Michigan Marriage Index 1836-1934 for Edward Warren's second marriage; Indiana Marriage Records 1810-2002 for Edward Warren's fourth marriage; Indiana Death Certificate 1897-2011 for Ella Warren; Belfast Blaze obituary for Lottie Warren Lilly May 14, 1925 and May 22, 1925; William H. Fuller, Descendants of Edward Fuller of the Mayflower, 1908.

48.

Julia Warren, daughter of Maria (9), granddaughter of Joshua (1), b. Nunda, New York July 1849, d. Nunda, New York April 29, 1912; m. probably Nunda, New York, a. 1870 Frank Parker, b. Nunda, New York March 1848, d. Nunda, New York May 23, 1911. Julia Warren resided with her parents or father and step-mother in Nunda, New York except for a brief sojourn in Granger, New York until her marriage to Franklin Parker. In 1860 Frank lost a leg in a threshing machine accident. He was employed as a drover and later owned a farm on State Road, Nunda. Mr. Parker was a stock buyer and highly regarded in the Nunda community at the time of his death. Julia and Frank Parker had three children with only two who survived to adulthood. Julia's father, Porter Warren, and her step-mother, Ruth, resided with them until their respective deaths. Julia and Frank Parker were buried in Oakwood Cemetery, Nunda, New York.

Children:

150.   I.   ***Grace May Parker***, f.

151.   II. ***Roy Parker***, f.

References: US Census: 1850, 1860, 1870, 1880, 1900, 1910; New York State Census: 1855, 1865, 1875; New York State Death Index 1852-1956 for Julia and Frank Parker; Oakwood Cemetery Records, Nunda, New York; Historian's Notes, Nunda, New York.

49.

Laura L. Warren, daughter of Maria (9), granddaughter of Joshua (1) b. Nunda, New York July 1853, d. Brooks Grove, New York April 25, 1920; m. probably Nunda, New York, a. 1870 Samuel Christopher, b. New York State February 1841, d. Brooks Grove, New York June 13, 1921. Samuel Christopher was a life-long farmer in the Brooks Grove section of Mount Morris, New York. He and his wife had two children. Laura and Samuel Christopher were buried in Oakwood Cemetery, Nunda, New York.

Children:

152. I. *Minnie Maude Christopher*, f.

153. II. *Ernest W. Christopher*, f.

References: US Census: 1860, 1870, 1880, 1900, 1910, 1920; New York State Census: 1855, 1865, 1875, 1915; New York State Death Index 1852-1956 for Laura and Samuel Christopher; Oakwood Cemetery Records, Nunda, New York.

50.

Cora E. Warren, daughter of Maria (9), granddaughter of Joshua (1), b. Nunda, New York September 1855, d. Mt. Morris, New York September 3, 1937; m. Nunda, New York March 20, 1878 Egbert Bartholomew, b. Brooks Grove, New York March 3, 1855, d. Mt. Morris, New York July 2, 1934. Egbert Bartholomew was a life-long resident and farmer in the Brooks Grove section of Mt. Morris, New York. Cora resided with her parents in Nunda, New York or her father and step-mother in either Nunda or Granger, New York until her marriage in 1878. They had two daughters. They were buried in Oakwood Cemetery, Nunda, New York. A joint marker is in evidence.

Children:

154. I. *Irene "Rena" Bartholomew*, f.

155. II. *Genevieve "Neva" Bartholomew*, f.

References: US Census: 1860, 1870, 1880, 1900, 1910, 1920, 1930; New York State Census: 1865, 1875, 1915, 1925; New York State Death Index 1852-1956; Oakwood Cemetery Records, Nunda, New York.

51.

Mary Ellen Fuller, daughter of George (10), grandson of Joshua (1), b. Philadelphia, Pennsylvania June 20, 1858, d. Philadelphia, Pennsylvania December 10, 1938; m. place and date not known, John Buzzard Slack, b. Pennsylvania January 19, 1859, d. Philadelphia, Pennsylvania November

12, 1925. Mary Ellen Fuller resided with her parents until her marriage sometime after the 1880 US Census. She was employed as a coat maker. By 1900 Mary Ellen and John Slack had had two children with only one living. He was a wire worker and they resided in Philadelphia. In 1910 Mr. Slack was employed as a janitor in an apartment house and their surviving son was a silversmith for a drugstore. The 1920 US Census still recorded their residence in Philadelphia where John worked as an iron worker for Wire and Iron Company. Both Mary Ellen and John Slack died from the complications of chronic endocarditis. They were buried in Fernwood Cemetery, Yeadon, Pennsylvania.

Children:

156. I.   *George Slack*, b. Philadelphia, Pennsylvania March 25, 1882, d. Philadelphia, Pennsylvania December 23, 1889 and buried in Fernwood Cemetery.

157. II. *John Buzzard Slack*, Jr., f.

References: US Census: 1860, 1870, 1880, 1900, 1910 1920, 1930; Pennsylvania Church and Town Records 1708-1985 for Mary Ellen Fuller's baptism October 15, 1863; Pennsylvania Death Certificates 1906-1967 and 1803-1915 for George Slack; Fernwood Cemetery Records, Yeadon, Pennsylvania.

52.

Jennie D. Fuller, daughter of George (10), granddaughter of Joshua (1), b. Nunda, New York May 14, 1861, d. Philadelphia, Pennsylvania March 13, 1923; m. Philadelphia, Pennsylvania June 28, 1888 John Cavanaugh, Jr., b. Philadelphia, Pennsylvania January 1865, d. Philadelphia, Pennsylvania November 27, 1896. Jennie resided with her parents until her marriage. After the death of her husband Jennie returned to reside with her mother and siblings. She was employed as a box maker. John Cavanaugh was employed as an electrotyper. They were buried in Fernwood Cemetery, Yeadon, Pennsylvania. They did not have any children.

References: US Census: 1870, 1880, 1900, 1910, 1920; Pennsylvania Marriage Records 1852-1968; Pennsylvania Death Certificates 1803-1915;

Fernwood Cemetery Records, Yeadon, Pennsylvania.

53.

George Washington Fuller, son of George (10), grandson of Joshua (1), b. New York State August 22, 1862, d. Pitman, New Jersey December 9, 1950; m. Philadelphia, Pennsylvania June 11, 1902 Emma Bessie Bradley, b. Philadelphia, Pennsylvania December 24, 1876, d. Pitman, New Jersey May 30, 1960. George Fuller resided with his parents and/or mother until his marriage. In 1880 he was a cooper and in 1900 a hatter. After his marriage Mr. Fuller moved to Pitman, New Jersey where he resided the rest of his life. He was employed as a presser in a hat factory (1910), a laborer at a plow plant (1920), a factory watchman (1930), and a guard (1940). They had two children. George Washington and Emma Bessie Fuller were buried in Hillcrest Memorial Park, Hurffville, New Jersey with their daughter Kathryn Fuller Hoffman. A common marker for all three is in evidence.

Children:

158.   I.   ***John Bradley Fuller***, f.

159.   II. ***Kathryn Elizabeth Fuller***, f.

References: US Census: 1870, 1880, 1900, 1910, 1920, 1930, 1940; New Jersey Death Index 1798-1971; Hillcrest Memorial Park records, Hurffville, New Jersey; Pennsylvania Marriage Index 1885-1951.

55.

William Fuller, son of George (10), grandson of Joshua (1), b. Batavia, New York July 4, 1867, d. Camden, New Jersey June 29, 1951; m. place and date not known, Matilda R., last name not known, b. Pennsylvania 1875, d. New Jersey 1927. William Fuller resided with his parents and/or mother in Philadelphia until his marriage. In 1910 William lived with several of his siblings in Philadelphia where his was employed as a shipper for wholesale groceries. By 1920 he married and moved to Gloucester, New Jersey when he was employed as a guard for Victor Talking Machines. The 1930 US Census found him a widower living in Camden, New Jersey where he was worked as a watchman for a radio factory. Matilda Fuller died in 1927 after an eleven-week long illness based on her newspaper obituary. She was buried in Mt. Moriah Cemetery, Philadelphia with Mary C. Murphy who may have been her sister. William Fuller was buried in New Camden Cemetery, Camden, New Jersey. They did not have any children. A marker is in evidence for William Fuller.

References: US Census: 1870, 1880, 1900, 1910, 1920, 1930; New Camden Cemetery records, Camden, New Jersey; Mt. Moriah Cemetery records, Philadelphia, Pennsylvania; Camden (NJ) Courier Post obituary for Mathilda Fuller November 7, 1927.

56.

Matthew Fuller, son of George (10), grandson of Joshua (1), b. Philadelphia, Pennsylvania August 16, 1869, d. Pitman, New Jersey November 14, 1936; m. Camden, New Jersey April 24, 1889 Mary Virginia Williams, b. Philadelphia, Pennsylvania 1871, d. Pitman, New Jersey October 23, 1935. Matthew resided with his parents and/or his mother until his marriage. The 1900 US Census recorded that Matthew and Mary Virginia had four children with two deceased. They later had a fifth child. The identities of the two children who died are not known. In 1900 they resided in Philadelphia where Matthew was employed at a hat factory. They continued to reside in Philadelphia through 1910. By the time of the 1920 US Census Matthew Fuller had moved his family to Pitman, New Jersey where he was employed as a laborer in a shipyard. Only their youngest son, Bickley, lived with them. In 1930 Matthew and Mary continued to reside in Pitman where Matthew was employed as a church janitor, Mary as a trimmer in a dress factory, and Bickley as a furniture salesman. Matthew and Mary were buried in Hillcrest Memorial Park, Hurffville, New Jersey sharing a common stone with their youngest son.

Children:

160. I.   *Geary Vanartsdalen Fuller*, f.

161. II.   *Raymond Matthew Fuller*, f.

162. III. *Henry Bickley Fuller*, f.

References: US Census: 1870, 1880, 1900, 1910, 1920, 1930; Hillcrest Memorial Park records, Hurffville, New Jersey.

58.

Edward Gregory Fuller, son of George (10), grandson of Joshua (1), b. Philadelphia, Pennsylvania April 2, 1876, d. Philadelphia, Pennsylvania January 18, 1910; m. (1) place and date not known, Annie Furman, b. Philadelphia, Pennsylvania December 10, 1875, d. Philadelphia, Pennsylvania May 4, 1896; m. (2) Philadelphia, Pennsylvania December 11, 1899 Madeline Anna Oppermann, b. place and date not known, d. place and date not known. It is not known what caused the death of Edward's first wife. She was buried in Fernwood Cemetery, Yeadon, Pennsylvania. Edward Fuller died from typhoid fever and myocarditis. He was buried in St. Denis Cemetery, Havertown, Pennsylvania. A marker is in evidence. Edward's second wife was alive at the time of the 1940 US Census in Philadelphia where her two daughters: Edna and Marion, and Marion's son, Francis resided. There is no further documentation on her after 1940.

Children (by first marriage):

163.   I.   *Esther Lillie Fuller*, f.

Children (by second marriage):

164.   I.   *Edna Regina Fuller*, f.

165.   II. *Marion Anna Fuller*, f.

References: US Census: 1880, 1900, 1910, 1920, 1930, 1940; Pennsylvania City and Town Death Records 1708-1985 for Annie Furman and Edward Fuller; Pennsylvania City and Town Marriage Records 1906-1967 for Edward Fuller's second marriage; Fernwood Cemetery records, Yeadon, Pennsylvania; St. Denis Cemetery records, Havertown, Pennsylvania.

59.

Walter Fuller, son of George (10), grandson of Joshua (1), b. Philadelphia, Pennsylvania November 2, 1878, d. Philadelphia, Pennsylvania January 5, 1936; m. place and date not known, Catherine Pfitzenmeir, b. place not known, June 10, 1888, d. place not known, May 1963. Walter Fuller was employed as a hatter residing in Philadelphia with his mother in the 1900 US Census. The 1910 US Census noted that Walter continued to reside in Philadelphia with several of his siblings and was employed as a trolley conductor. His World War I Draft Registration Card described him as being of medium height and build with brown hair and eyes. He continued to be employed as a trolley conductor. He belonged to the Methods Mariners Bethel Methodist Episcopal Church. He died from hypertension and cardiovascular disease. His death certificate indicated his body was donated to an anatomical board. Walter Fuller cannot be found on the 1920 and 1930 US Census records. It is not known where Catherine Fuller was buried.

Children:

166. I. *Walter Matthew Fuller*, f.

167. II. *George Washington Fuller*, b. Pitman, New Jersey March 1924, d. Pitman, New Jersey August 1924.

168. III. *Hannah Minnie Fuller*, f.

References: US Census: 1880, 1900, 1910; Pennsylvania Church and Town Records 1708-1985 for religious affiliation; Pennsylvania Death Certificates 1906-1967; World War I Draft Registration Card 1917-1918.

Generation Four

64.

Hattie Fuller, daughter of James (11), granddaughter of Pliny (2), b. New York State August 31, 1867, d. Canton, Illinois April 21, 1955; m. Kalamazoo, Michigan February 19, 1890 William W. Russell, b. place not known, September 13, 1856, d. Canton, Illinois March 6, 1913. Mr. Russell was employed as a clothier (1900) and later as a carpenter at a grocery store (1910). They had one child. Hattie and William Russell were buried in Greenwood Cemetery, Canton, Illinois.

Children:

169. I. *Dorothy Russell*, b. Michigan April 7, 1896, d. February 20, 1984; m. Edward McPheeters, b. May 8, 1895, d. October 7, 1970.

Children:

i. *Robert McPheeters*, b. March 12, 1918, d. January 4, 2002.

References: US Census: 1870, 1880, 1900, 1910, 1920, 1930, 1940; Greenwood Cemetery records, Canton, Illinois; Michigan Marriage Index 1867-1952.

65.

Clarence Henry Fuller, son of James (11), grandson of Pliny (2), b. Olean, New York May 18, 1870, d. Kalamazoo, Michigan August 16, 1949; m. Will County, Illinois October 18 1893 Flora Belle Brundage Fuller, b. Chicago, Illinois June 16, 1874, d. Kalamazoo, Michigan July 9, 1939. They had four children and based on the 1900 US Census had adopted Jenny Clawson. Clarence and Belle were buried in Riverside Cemetery, Kalamazoo, Michigan.

Children:

169. I. *Howard Russell Fuller*, b. Michigan April 1894, d. Sequim, Washington February 15, 1983. He was buried next to his mother.

170. II. *Frances Fuller*, b. Michigan 1896; no further information.

171. III. *Warren Brundage Fuller*, b. 1899, d. 1970; m. Gladys Elizabeth Vandegiessen, b. Portage, Michigan November 19, 1903, d. Louisville, Kentucky April 9, 2002. They were buried in Riverside Cemetery, Kalamazoo, Michigan.

Children:

i. *Robert Warren Fuller*, b. January 25, 1926, d. October 1, 2003 and buried in Riverside Cemetery, Kalamazoo, Michigan.

ii. **Lois Fuller**, b. 1937, d. 1976; m. a Mr. Angelo. Buried in Riverside Cemetery, Kalamazoo, Michigan.

172. IV. **Claire Wesley Fuller**, b. Kalamazoo, Michigan July 14, 1914, d. Portage, Michigan May 11, 2011; m. Kalamazoo, Michigan June 22, 1938 Guelda Carolyn Teipening.

References: US Census: 1870, 1880, 1900, 1910, 1920, 1930, 1940; Riverside Cemetery records, Kalamazoo, Michigan; Illinois Marriage Index 1860-1920; Michigan Marriage Index 1867-1952.

66.

Charles Dwight Fuller, son of George (12), grandson of Pliny (2), b. Humphrey, New York September 8, 1858, d. Detroit, Michigan October 12, 1921; m. Stark, Illinois May 28, 1879 Lucinda A. Andrews, b. Princeville, Illinois January 5, 1853, d. Detroit, Michigan July 10, 1934. Charles Fuller resided with his parents until their move to Richmond, Wisconsin by the 1880 US Census. In 1880 he was a painter and had recently married. By 1900 Charles had moved his family to Kalamazoo, Michigan where he was involved in the manufacture of iron products. In 1910 he was a broker for Fruit Lands and by 1920 had moved to Detroit, Michigan where he was the President of a medical firm. Charles Fuller died from uremia and prostate problems. Charles and Lucinda Fuller were buried in Riverside Cemetery, Kalamazoo, Michigan. Markers are in evidence.

Children:

173. I. **Florence E. Fuller**, b. Wisconsin December 1883, d. place and date not known. She resided with her parents until her June 12, 1907 Kalamazoo marriage to Harry V. Thomas. The marriage did not last and by 1910 she returned to her parents' home and resumed the use of the Fuller name. She was last recorded on the 1930 US Census living in Detroit. It is not known where she was buried.

179. II. **Harry LeRoy Fuller**, b. Minneapolis, Minnesota February 19, 1887, d. Kalamazoo, Michigan October 1969; m. Kalamazoo, Michigan June 22, 1910 Berenice W. Anderson, b. Kansas October 11, 1885, d. Broward County, Florida September 12, 1974. At the time of his marriage Harry

was employed on a steamboat for a land resort in Kalamazoo. By 1920 he moved to Detroit, Michigan where he was secretary and later President of a Medical Manufacturing company. His niece, Ellen Fuller, resided with them in 1930. They moved backed to Kalamazoo by 1940 where Harry was working as a chemist. His World War I Draft Registration Card described him as being stout with a medium build and had light brown hair and blue eyes. He was the superintendent of the Dionel Company. Harry Fuller's World War II Draft Registration Card described him as being 5' 7" tall, weighed 185 pounds with blue eyes and gray hair. He was the owner and manager of the Q-Vita Company. They did not have any children and were buried in Mountain Home Cemetery, Kalamazoo, Michigan. There are no markers in evidence.

180.   III.   **Maurice Eugene Fuller**, b. Kalamazoo, Michigan June 9, 1890, d. Contra Costa, California October 18, 1950; m. place and date not known, Ruth H. Hanck, b. Columbus Grove, Ohio December 6, 1891, d. Hobe Sound, Florida January 6, 1988. Maurice Fuller's World War I Draft Registration Card described him as being slender and tall with dark brown hair and blue eyes. He was a machinist foreman for the Ford Motor Company. Mr. Fuller was married with one child. His World War II Draft Registration Card noted he was 5' 8" tall, weighed 185 pounds with blue eyes and gray hair. He resided in Martinez, California where he owned Fuller Auto Parts. It is possible that Maurice and his wife separated based on the information on their son's death record. Maurice Fuller was cremated and the whereabouts of his remains are not known. It is not known where Ruth Fuller was buried.

Children:

i.   **Ellen Fuller**, b. Oklahoma a. 1915; no further information.

ii.   **John T. Fuller**, b. August 30, 1917, d. Michigan, November 20, 1937, from a heart condition. He was employed with the body department for Chrysler. It is not known where he was buried.

References: US Census: 1860, 1870, 1880, 1900, 1910, 1920, 1930,

1940; World War I Draft Registration Card 1917-1918; World War II Draft Registration Card 1942; Riverside Cemetery records, Kalamazoo, Michigan; Illinois Marriage Records 1800-1940 for Charles Fuller's marriage; Michigan Death Records 1867-1952 for Charles Fuller; Michigan Marriage Records 1822-1940 for Florence Fuller and Harry Fuller; Mountain Home Cemetery records, Kalamazoo, Michigan; Social Security Death Index 1935-2014 for Harry Fuller; California Death Index 1940-1997 for Maurice Fuller; Michigan Death Records 1867-1952 for John Fuller.

67.

Frank DeWitt Fuller, son of George (12), grandson of Pliny (2), b. Allegany, New York December 13, 1862/3, d. Los Angeles, California September 16, 1958; m. St. Croix, Wisconsin August 24, 1884 Cora Lucretia Webster b. Warren, Wisconsin December 14, 1865, b. Pasadena, California January 25, 1941. Frank resided with his parents in Humphrey, New York and New Richmond, Wisconsin until his 1884 marriage. By 1900 he moved his wife and four children to Chicago, Illinois where he was a general agent. By 1910 he relocated to Kalamazoo, Michigan where he managed an automobile company and by 1920 was the company's President. He later moved to California where he apparently lived off the income from the company's sale. Frank and Cora Fuller were buried in Mt. View Cemetery and Mausoleum, Altadena, California. Markers are in evidence.

Children:

181. I. *Lawrence Cecil Fuller*, b. Richmond, Wisconsin March 16, 1886, d. Fallbrook, California September 8, 1978; m. (1) Kalamazoo, Michigan June 22, 1912 Minnie M. Harmon, b. Kalamazoo, Michigan September 12, 1886, d. Kalamazoo, Michigan, November 24, 1915, from childbirth complications; m. (2) Pontiac, Michigan September 26, 1921 Margaret E. Hanson, b. place not known, 1894, d. California, 1969. Lawrence was employed with a dairy business in 1910 and by 1920 was the Vice President of a family manufacturing company making transmissions. He was not employed in 1930 and, in 1940, moved to California, residing in San Gabriel. Lawrence and Margaret Fuller were buried in Eternal Hills Memorial Park, Oceanside, California. Minnie Harmon Fuller was buried

in Riverside Cemetery, Kalamazoo, with her infant unnamed daughter. There are no markers in evidence.

    Children (by first marriage):

    i.   **Dorothy Irene Fuller**, b October 7, 1913, d. Orange County, California September 27, 1978; m. Donald O. Boudeman May 31, 1935, Kalamazoo, Michigan, b. 1911, d. 1973. They had one child: Don Oernst Boudeman (1940-2019). Dorothy and her husband were buried in Eternal Hills Memorial Park with her parents, and their son was buried in Mt. View Cemetery, Orwell, Vermont. Markers are in evidence.

    ii.   **Baby Girl Fuller**, b. and d. Kalamazoo, Michigan, November 15, 1915, and buried in Riverside Cemetery, Kalamazoo.

182.   II.   **Stella E. Fuller**, b. Minnesota June 10, 1887, d. Laguna Hills, California December 17, 1976; m. Kalamazoo, Michigan March 24, 1917 Carl Oscar Mainburg, b. Red Oak, Iowa May 30, 1882, d. Laguna Hills, California April 7, 1972. Carl's World War I Draft Registration Card described him as slender and tall with brown hair and grey eyes. He was employed by Franklin Manufacturing Company. His World War II Draft Registration Card noted he was 5' 11" tall, weighed 156 pounds, had gray hair and hazel eyes, and had a light and ruddy complexion. In 1942, he was employed by A. J. Lynch in Los Angeles. Mr. Mainburg's career included employment as an asbestos salesman in Chicago (1920), an architect in Kalamazoo (1930), and the supervisor for sales of a chemical industry (1940). Stella and Carl did not have any children. It is not known where they were buried.

183.   III.   **Walter Pliny Fuller**, b. Kalamazoo, Michigan May 4, 1889, d. Pasadena, California November 25, 1972; m. Kalamazoo, Michigan July 12, 1913 Helen May Conarroe, b. Middletown, Ohio May 12, 1881, d. Los Angeles, California February 7, 1948. Walter Fuller was employed with a dairy company (1910), Frear Manufacturing (1920), and after that had his own income while residing in both Kalamazoo and Pasadena, California.

Walter and Helen were buried in Mt. View Cemetery and Mausoleum, Altadena, California. Markers are evident.

      Children:

         i.   *Robert Dale Fuller* (1916-1997).

         ii.   *Donald Everett Fuller* (1918-1989).

         iii.   *Maryon Elizabeth Fuller* (1920-1987).

         iv.   *Virginia Louise Fuller* (1928-2011)

         v.   *Carol Jeanne Fuller* (1930-2003).

184.   IV.   *Edith Mabel Fuller*, b. Kalamazoo, Michigan June 29, 1892, d. Kalamazoo, Michigan, October 23, 1919, from tuberculosis. She was employed as a clerical worker with Northwest National Life Insurance. Edith was buried in Riverside Cemetery, Kalamazoo, Michigan.

References: US Census: 1870, 1880, 1900, 1910, 1920, 1930, 1940; Mt. View Cemetery and Mausoleum records, Altadena, California; Riverside Cemetery records, Kalamazoo, Michigan; Eternal Hills Memorial Park records, Oceanside, California; World War I Draft Registration Card 1917-1918; World War II Draft Registration Card 1942; Michigan Birth Records 1867-1952 for Edith Fuller; Michigan Death Records 1867-1952 for Edith Fuller. Mt. View Cemetery records, Orwell, Vermont.

68.

Fred Adelbert Fuller, son of George (12), grandson of Pliny (2), b. probably Nunda, New York December 1868, d. Denver, Colorado August 13, 1948; m. Winnebago, Wisconsin December 23, 1890 Mary Alberta Stebbins, b. Wisconsin January 1871, d. Denver, Colorado June 12, 1944. Fred Fuller resided in Humphrey, New York (1870) and New Richmond, Wisconsin (1880) with his parents. The 1900 US Census found Fred Fuller with his wife and children residing in Kalamazoo, Michigan, where he was employed as a woodworker, but by 1910 he had moved his family to Denver, where he was engaged in mining. He remained in Denver, where he was an oil well supplies broker based on 1920 and 1930 US Census records. In 1940, Fred was an engineer. Fred and his brothers Charles and Frank created the Fuller Brothers Company, which introduced the Atlantic Queen washboard. The company's successful transition to automobiles and transmissions led to the three men becoming financially independent. Mary Fuller's remains were cremated and given to the family. Fred Fuller was buried in Fairmount Cemetery, Denver, Colorado, in an unmarked grave.

Children:

185.   I.   **Mildred Imogene Fuller**, b. Kalamazoo, Michigan April 7, 1892, d. Denver, Colorado March 1978; m. Manhattan, New York March 21, 1936 Burnham Hoyt, b. Denver, Colorado February 3, 1887, d. Denver, Colorado, April 3, 1960. Mildred Fuller resided with her parents until her move to New York City by 1930. There, she met architect Burnham Hoyt, and they married. Mildred was an accomplished interior designer. Mr. Hoyt's World War II Draft Registration Card described him as 5' 7 ½ "tall, weighing 135 pounds, with gray eyes and black hair. He designed the interior of Riverside Church, Manhattan, for J. D. Rockefeller, the Red Rocks Amphitheater, the Fourth Church of Christ Scientist, and the Denver Public Library, Park Hill Branch in Denver. He died of Parkinson's Disease and was buried in Fairmount Cemetery, Denver. It is assumed that Mildred was also buried there, but there is no confirmation. They did not have any children.

186.   II.   **Ruth Fuller**, b. Kalamazoo, Michigan January 27, 1894, d. Guatemala December 26, 1974; m. place and date not known Rodney Dean Wells, b. Pueblo, Colorado October 17, 1896, d. Guatemala City, Guatemala, November 26, 954, from a gastric ulcer. Rodney Wells was a merchant. They had three children, two of whom died young. Ruth and Rodney Wells were buried in General DeHuitan Cemetery, Quetsahenanyo, Guatemala, along with two of their children.

Children:

i.   **Mildred Barratt Wells**, b. Guatemala February 23, 1923, d. San Bernadino, California September 10, 1993; m. Walter James McKenzie, Jr., b. Portland, Oregon June

6, 1923, d. Washington State November 29, 2014. They were buried in Victor Valley Memorial Park, Victorville, California.

    ii.   ***Claire Ruth Wells***, b. Guatemala June 25, 1927, d. Guatemala, March 23, 1934, from scarlet fever and buried with parents.

    iii.   ***Rodney Deane Wells***, Jr., b. Guatemala June 1931, d. Guatemala June 13, 1931, and buried with parents.

187.   III.   ***Thornton Paul Fuller***, b. Kansas City, Missouri September 10, 1897, d. Denver, Colorado July 17, 1970; m. 1937, Margaret Louise Arndt, b. Colorado June 1, 1907, d. Denver, Colorado, July 31, 1974. They were buried at All Souls Walk at St. John's Cathedral, Denver, Colorado, with her parents. His World War II Draft Registration Card described him as 6' 1" tall, weighing 180 pounds, with brown hair and gray eyes. He was self-employed with Thornton Fuller, Inc., a design firm. They did not have any children.

References: US Census: 1870, 1880, 1900, 1910, 1920, 1930, 1940; Fairmount Cemetery records, Denver Colorado; World War II Draft Registration Card 1942 for Burnham Hoyt; Michigan Birth Index 1867-1911 for Mildred Fuller; New York Marriage Index 1907-2018 for Mildred Fuller and Burnham Hoyt; US Departs of American Citizens Deaths Abroad 1835-1974 for Ruth Fuller, Rodney Wells, Claire Wells, and Rodney Wells, Jr.; Victor Valley Memorial Park records, Victorville, California; All Souls Walk records, St. John's Cathedral, Denver, Colorado; Wisconsin Marriage Index 1820-1907 for Fred Fuller's marriage.

70.

Elmer Leslie Fuller, son of Oren (15), grandson of Pliny (2), b. Andover, New York May 11, 1873, d. Hennepin, Minnesota August 24, 1944; m. Hartford, Michigan January 15, 1902 Theo L. Anderson, b. place not known, October 10, 1878, d. Minnesota March 1, 1966. Elmer Fuller resided with his parents in Andover, Great Valley, and Olean, New York and Kalamazoo, Michigan until his marriage in 1902. After the death of their only child they moved to Minneapolis, Minnesota where both died. Elmer Fuller's World War I Draft Registration Card described him as being tall and stout with gray eyes and brown hair. Mr. Fuller was employed as a bookkeeper (1900), a corn salesman (1910), a wholesale shoes salesman (1920), a radio salesman (1930), and later an agent (1940). Both Elmer and Theo Fuller were cremated and their ashes spread at Lakewood Cemetery, Minneapolis, Minnesota.

Children:

188. I. *Edward Leslie Fuller*, b. Kalamazoo, Michigan May 3, 1903, d. Kalamazoo, Michigan May 5, 1903 from lung issues at birth. He was buried in Riverside Cemetery, Kalamazoo, Michigan. There is a marker.

References: US Census: 1880, 1900, 1910, 1920, 1930, 1940; Michigan Marriage Records 1867-1952; New York State Census: 1875; Minnesota Death Index 1908-2002; World War I Draft Registration Card 1917-18; Michigan Death Record 1867-1952 for Edward Leslie Fuller; Riverside Cemetery records, Kalamazoo, Michigan; Lakewood Cemetery Records, Minneapolis, Minnesota.

71.

Frank Charles Fuller, son of Oren (15), grandson of Pliny (2), b. Olean, New York January 24, 1875, d. Kalamazoo, Michigan March 30, 1940; m. Kalamazoo, Michigan September 6, 1899 Catherine Eleanor Chapman, b. place not known 1876, d. Kalamazoo, Michigan 1966. Frank resided in Chicago with his wife in 1900 and was employed as a cashier. By 1904, they moved to Kalamazoo, Michigan, where they lived the rest of their lives. In 1910, Frank was a salesman for a sled company, in 1920 a bookkeeper for a foundry, and in 1930 a vacuum cleaner salesman. His World War I Draft Registration Card described him as medium height and weight with blue eyes and gray hair. Frank Fuller died from influenza and bronchitis complicated by a heart condition. Frank and Catherine Fuller were buried in Riverside Cemetery, Kalamazoo, Michigan, where they share a monument.

Children:

189. I. **Marion Eleanor Fuller**, b. Kalamazoo, Michigan March 27, 1904, d. Kalamazoo, Michigan, June 9, 1905, from nephritis. She was buried in Riverside Cemetery, Kalamazoo, Michigan. No marker is evident.

References: US Census: 1880, 1900, 1910, 1920, 1930; World War I Draft Registration Card 1917-18; Michigan Death Records 1867-1952; Michigan Marriage Records 1867-1952; Riverside Cemetery Records, Kalamazoo, Michigan.

72.

George Washington Fuller, son of Oren (15), grandson of Pliny (2), b. Humphrey, New York March 29, 1877, d. Kalamazoo, Michigan January 19, 1950; m. Kalamazoo, Michigan November 29, 1900 Edna Rebecca Mead, b. Barry County, Michigan July 5, 1881, d Kalamazoo, Michigan March 1964. In 1880 George Fuller resided in Olean, New York with his parents. By 1900 he moved to Kalamazoo, Michigan and lived with his cousin, Clarence Fuller. George and Edna Fuller resided in Kalamazoo the rest of their lives where he was employed as a clerk (1910), a corsets salesman (1920), a traveling salesman for the Fuller Brush Company (1930), and a trucking salesman (1940). Mr. Fuller's World War I Draft Registration Card described him as being of medium build and height with brown hair and blue eyes. George and Edna Fuller were buried in Riverside Cemetery, Kalamazoo, Michigan with a joint marker.

Children:

190. I. **Dorothy Jane Fuller**, b. Ann Arbor, Michigan June 17, 1913, d. Walker, Michigan December 15, 1991; m. Allegan County, Michigan January 19, 1940 Cyrus Vincent Kean III, b. Otsego, Michigan September 8, 1912, d. Grand Rapids, Michigan June 3, 2006. Dorothy was employed as a stenographer while Cyrus was in advertising for a heating equipment company. They did not have any children. It is not known where they were buried.

References: US Census: 1880, 1900, 1910, 1920, 1930, 1940; World War I Draft Registration Card 1917-1918; Riverside Cemetery records, Kalamazoo, Michigan; Michigan Death Records 1867-1952; Michigan Marriage Records 1867-1952.

73.

Hattie M. Fuller, daughter of Oren (15), granddaughter of Pliny (2), b. Olean, New York January 2, 1880, d. Andover, New York May 20, 1935; m. Alfred, New York January 4, 1905, George H. Baker, b. New York State January 4, 1869, d. Andover, New York, November 19, 1947. Hattie resided in Olean, New York, with her parents in 1880. After her father's death and her mother's remarriage, she moved to Andover, New York, where she resided for the rest of her life. Hattie's mother and stepfather lived with her, her husband, and their three children in 1910. George Baker was a carpenter by profession but later worked for a silk mill in Andover, New York. They briefly resided in Angelica, New York, in 1905, where Mr. Baker farmed. Hattie and George Baker had four children. They were buried at Hillside Cemetery in Andover, New York.

Children:

191. I. ***Doris B. Baker***, b. Andover, New York December 30, 1905, d. Wellsville, New York February 11, 1997; m. place and date not known Edward F. Graves, b. January 1, 1879, d. November 12, 1963. Doris and Edward Graves had no children and were buried in York's Corner Cemetery, York's Corner, New York.

192. II. ***Susan Dorothy Baker***, b. Andover, New York March 15, 1907, d Andover, New York May 6, 2003; m. Andover, New York June 4, 1933, Roger Phillip Baker, b. July 29, 1911, d. Andover, New York February 25, 1977. Roger Baker was employed as a printer for a printing mill. They were buried at Hillside Cemetery in Andover, New York.

Children:

i. ***Jacqueline Baker***, b. Andover, New York, October 15, 1935, no further information.

ii. ***Lorraine Edith Baker***, b. Andover, New York February 23, 1937, d. Andover, New York, June 29, 2005, and buried at Hillside Cemetery.

193. III. ***Howard Fuller Baker***, b. Andover, New York August 16, 1909, d. Andover, New York October 1, 1953. Howard resided with his parents until their respective deaths and was a farmer. He was a Tec4 with the 3814 Om Gas Supply Company during World War II. Howard Baker did not marry and was buried in Hillside Cemetery, Andover, New York.

194. IV. ***Eleanor Baker***, b. Allegany County, New York April 19, 1914, d. Genesee, Pennsylvania September 1976; m. Wellsville, New York June 16, 1945, Roy C. Lunn, b. Oswayo, New York 1903, d. Andover, New York, February 13, 1954. Eleanor and Roy Lunn did not have any children. He was employed with the Steuben Silk Mills, Andover, New York, as a weaver, and Eleanor was employed as a quiller. Roy Lunn was previously married and had two daughters by his first marriage. Eleanor and Roy Lunn were buried in Rathbone Cemetery, Oswayo, Pennsylvania.

References: US Census: 1880, 1900, 1910, 1920, 1930, 1940; Hillside Cemetery records, Andover, New York; Rathbone Cemetery Records, Oswayo, Pennsylvania; New York State Marriage Records 1881-1967; York's Corner Cemetery records, York's Corners, New York.

74.

Grace Edith Fuller, daughter of Oren (15), granddaughter of Pliny (2), b. Olean, New York July 6, 1885, d. Independence, New York April 16, 1933; m. Andover, New York May 12, 1909, Linford Adrian Potter, b. Andover, New York January 26, 1885, d. Independence, New York, July 14, 1977. Mr. Potter was a lifelong farmer in Independence, New York. Grace and Linford Potter were buried in Whitesville Rural Cemetery, Whitesville, New York.

Children:

195. I. ***Edith Dottie Potter***, b. Allegany County, New York October 10, 1919, d. Whitesville, New York June 6, 2006; m. Allegany County, New York Walter Alanson Childs, b. Allegany County, New York June 14, 1901,

d. Andover, New York March 25, 1985. Mr. Childs was previously married to Edna Mae Sisson, who died in 1966. Edith was buried in Whitesville Rural Cemetery, Whitesville, New York, and Walter was buried in West Genesee Cemetery, Obi, New York, with his first wife.

196. I. *Joseph Orren Potter*, b. Allegany County, New York December 9, 1922, d. 1999; m. Wellsville, New York October 19, 1949, Mary Catherine Rindgen, b. May 29, 1923, place and date of death not known. Joseph Potter was buried in Whitesville Rural Cemetery, Whitesville, New York.

References: US Census: 1900, 1910, 1920, 1930, 1940; Whitesville Rural Cemetery records, Whitesville, New York; West Genesee Cemetery records, Obi, New York; New York State Birth Index 1881-1942; New York State Marriage Index 1881-1967; New York State Death Index 1852-1956; Wellsville Daily Reporter obituary July 14, 1977 for Linford Potter.

75.

Minnie E. Goldthwaite, daughter of Gilbert (16), granddaughter of Clarissa (4), b. New York State November 13, 1859, d. Jamestown, New York April 3, 1943; m. New York State January 1, 1879 Fred L. Rhodes, b. Carroll, New York August 10, 1857, d. Chautauqua County, New York February 21, 1942. Minnie resided with her parents in Caneadea, New York until her 1880 marriage to Fred Rhodes. They moved to Ellery, New York where Fred was employed as a carpenter. By 1910 they relocated to Jamestown, New York where they resided the rest of their lives and where Fred was consistently employed as a carpenter. Minnie and Fred Rhodes were buried in Sunset Hill Cemetery, Lakewood, New York.

Children:

197. I. *Maude Mae Rhodes*, b. Jamestown, New York 1879, d. Pembroke, Maine 1951; m. Jamestown, New York July 3, 1897, William A. Blackwood, b. Pembroke, Maine April 25, 1868, d. Pembroke, Maine 1952. Maude and William Blackwood were buried in Forest Hill Cemetery, Pembroke, Maine.

Children:

i. **Lester Rodgers Blackwood**, b. Pembroke, Maine April 18, 1900, d. Pembroke, Maine December 1974; m. Calais, Maine September 16, 1920 Letitia May Hilton, b. 1902, d. 1996. They had two daughters: Juanita (1922-2013) and Mary Jane (1937-2019). They were buried in Clarkside Cemetery, Pembroke, Maine.

ii. **Cecil Blackwood**, b. Maine September 23, 1906, d. Brewer, Maine November 1977; m. Cecilia, last name not known, b. Maine January 17, 1909, d. Brewer, Maine January 1980. They were buried in Oak Hill Cemetery, Brewer, Maine.

198. II. **Bertha Rhodes**, b. Jamestown, New York May 29, 1882, d. Jamestown, New York July 10, 1968; m. Jamestown, New York June 15, 1905, Wallace E. Tiffany, Jamestown, New York November 17, 1882, d. place and date not known. It is not known where they were buried.

199. III. **Lester L. Rhodes**, b. Jamestown, New York 1887, d. New York State August 13, 1948; m. Chautauqua County, New York September 25, 1909 Florence E. Thompson, b. place and date not known, d. place and date not known. Mr.Rhodes was employed by the Erie Railroad, the Jamestown and Chautauqua Railroad, and Swanson Machine Corporation. He was a lifelong resident of the Jamestown, New York area. Lester was buried in Sunset Hill Cemetery, Lakewood, New York. They had four children: Cecil, Fred, Doris, and June Marie.

References: US Census: 1860, 1870, 1880, 1900, 1910, 1920, 1930, 1940; Sunset Hill Cemetery records, Lakewood, New York; Oak Hill Cemetery records, Brewer, Maine; Clarkside Cemetery records, Pembroke, Maine; Forest Hill Cemetery records, Pembroke, Maine.

76.

Jennie Goldthwaite, daughter of Gilbert (16), granddaughter of Clarissa (4), b. Portland, New York February 23, 1862, d. Jamestown, New York May 31, 1938; m. place and date not known, Frank Arnold, b. June 1858, d. place and date not known. Frank Arnold was a woodworker by profession in Jamestown, New York. In 1920 he changed careers to work as a drill press operator at an axle factory. After Frank's death, Jennie resided with her daughter Pearl and Pearl's family in Jamestown. Jennie was buried in Pine Hill Cemetery, Falconer, New York. It is not known where Frank was buried. They had four children.

Children:

200. I. **Harry A. Arnold**, b. North Warren, Pennsylvania December 9, 1882, d. Falconer, New York November 7, 1951; m. Bernice L., last name not known, b. 1891, d. 1978. They had two sons: Gordon and Gerald. Harry and Bernice were buried in Pine Hill Cemetery, Falconer, New York.

201. II. **Louis P. Arnold**, b. January 14, 1890, d. October 22, 1950. He served as a private with the 152nd Depot Brigade during WW II. Mr. Arnold was buried in Pine Hill Cemetery, Falconer, New York.

202. III. **Pearl Arnold**, b. New York a. 1892, d. New York State August 1958; m. place and date not known Arthur Pearson, b. 1893, d. 1940. Pearl and Arthur were buried in Pine Hill Cemetery, Falconer, New York.

Children:

i. **George Arthur Pearson**, b. Jamestown, New York August 20, 1917, d. December 23, 2005; m. Beatrice E. Hedman, b. Jamestown, New York August 4, 1921, d. Gerry, New York, June 7, 2017. They were buried in Allen Cemetery, Falconer, New York. George and Beatrice had two sons, Richard and Gregory.

203. IV. **Ernest W. Arnold**, b. Jamestown, New York March 19, 1901,

d. Buffalo, New York November 9, 1947; m. Buffalo, New York November 22, 1923, Emma M. Obermeyer, b. New York State March 5, 1903, d. Buffalo, New York, December 1970. Ernest was employed as an engineer for a gas company and later as a government worker. His World War II Draft Registration Card described him as 5' 7" tall, weighed 170 pounds, with blue eyes and brown hair. Ernest and Emma had two daughters, Jean and Noreen. It is not known where they were buried.

References: US Census: 1870, 1880, 1900, 1910, 1920, 1930, 1940; Pine Hill Cemetery records, Falconer, New York; Allen Cemetery records, Falconer, New York; World War II Draft Registration Card 1942 for Ernest Arnold.

77.

Elizabeth "Libbie" Goldthwaite, daughter of Gilbert (16), granddaughter of Clarissa (4), b. Portland, New York January 3, 1864, d. New York State 1936; m. July 4, 1883 Lucious Marsh, b. place not known, March 1860, d. New York State September 13, 1934. The Marsh family were longtime residents of Carroll, New York where Mr. Marsh was employed as a laborer with a door factory (1910), a lumber company (1920), and a furniture company (1925). They had four children with three living. The identity of the fourth child is not known. Libbie and Lucious Marsh were buried in Maple Grove Cemetery, Frewsburg, New York.

Children:

204. I. *Rowena "Rena" Marsh*, b. New York State May 1884, d. Carroll, New York June 16, 1940; m. Busti, New York April 25, 1903, Fred Boswell, b. New York State April 13, 1873, d. Carroll, New York, September 17, 1950. They were buried in Busti Cemetery, Busti, New York, with a joint marker.

Children:

i. *Florence Eleanor Boswell*, b. Frewsburg, New York May 17, 1908, d. Frewsburg, New York April 1974; m. place and date not known, Charles H. Hildum, b. Randolph, New York December 21, 1904, d. Frewsburg, New York October 1973. They were buried in Randolph Cemetery, Randolph,

New York, with their son, Charles Frederick Hildum, b. January 6, 1931, d. December 18, 1993.

 ii. ***Irene J. Boswell***, b. New York State June 6, 1918, d. New York State February 22, 2003, m. place and date not known, William A. Lowery, b. 1913, d. 1996. They had two children: Richard and Susan. Irene and William Lowery were buried in Maple Grove Cemetery, Frewsburg, New York, with a joint marker.

 iii. ***Howard Frederick Boswell***, b. Carroll, New York July 11, 1921, d. Buffalo, New York November 28, 2007; m. North Collins, New York February 19, 1949, Josephine, last name unknown, b. 1920, d. 2014. Howard served with the US Navy from January 22, 1942 to June 19, 1943. He was described as being 5' 8" tall, weighed 130 pounds, and had blue eyes, brown hair, and a dark complexion. They were buried in Holy Sepulcher Cemetery in Cheektowaga, New York.

205. II. ***Edith M. Marsh***, b. Frewsburg, New York September 6, 1868, d. 1946; m. 1907 Eric William Coe, b. Carroll, New York November 27, 1884, d. Erie County, New York, August 15, 1966. They were buried in Jerusalem Corners Cemetery, Jerusalem Corners, New York.

Children:

 i. ***Dorothy E. Coe***, b. Frewsburg, New York April 20, 1911, d. Jacksonville, North Carolina March 28, 1999; m. James Andrew Oring, b. 1904, d. May 1986. They were buried in Hillcrest Memorial Park, Pickens, South Carolina.

 ii. ***Charles Samuel Coe***, b. Deby, New York July 22, 1920, d. Sun Valley, California January 1, 2011; m. Cecilia M., last name not known, b. July 20, 1921, d. October 24, 2015. Charles served during World War II with the US Marines with the rank of Corporal. They had five children: Kenneth (1909-1996), Ruth (1912-1999), Helen (1916-

1999), Eric (1923-2015), Herbert (1925-2009). They were buried in Assumption Catholic Cemetery, Simi Valley, California.

206. III. *Howard Allen Marsh*, b. New York State April 4/5, 1901, d. New York State May 1983; m. Blasdell, New York September 24m 1924 Leona M. Brown, b. 1903, d. 1934. Howard and Leona Marsh were buried in Niles Cemetery, Ellicottville, New York.

References: US Census: 1870, 1880, 1900, 1910, 1920, 1930, 1940; New York State Census: 1905, 1925; Maple Grove Cemetery records, Frewsburg, New York; Niles Cemetery records, Ellicottville, New York; Assumption Catholic Cemetery records, Simi Valley, California; Hillcrest Memorial Park records, Pickens, South Carolina; World War II Draft Registration Card, 1942 for Howard Boswell; Holy Sepulcher Cemetery, Cheektowaga, New York Randolph Cemetery records, Randolph, New York. Busti Cemetery records, Busti, New York.

78.

Fred Alfred Goldthwaite, son of Gilbert (16), grandson of Clarissa (4), b. New York State 1869, d. Cuba, New York February 27, 1937; m. Gowanda, New York August 19, 1900 Estella "Stella" Ramsdell, b. 1874, d. 1966. Fred Goldthwaite was employed as a cheesemaker. They resided in Gerry, New York (1910), Pomfret, New York (1920), and New Hudson, New York (1930). Fred and Stella were buried in Cuba Cemetery, Cuba, New York.

Children:

207. I. *Margareta Fannie Goldthwaite*, b. Jamestown, New York January 24, 1896, d. Falconer, New York March 1979; m Chautauqua County, New York May 19, 1920 John Arthur Haskins.

Children:

i. *Marian Haskins*, (1920).

ii. *Kenneth Haskins*, (1922).

iii. *Dorothy Haskins*, (1925).

iv.   ***Waldo Haskins***, (1927).

v.   ***John Haskins***, (1929).

208.   II.   Hazel Goldthwaite, b. New York State 1897, d. New York State 1971; m. place and date not known, Clark Grimes, b. 1896, d. 1969. They had at least one child. Hazel and Clark were buried in Holland Cemetery, Holland, New York.

Children:

i.   ***Gertrude May Grimes***, b. Gaines, New York May 14, 1918, d. Middleport, New York December 19, 1967 from a heart attack; m. Walter A. Fuller, b. January 2, 1915, d. July 1, 1974. They had six children: Walter, William, Lawrence, Charles, Gerald, and Evelyn. Gertrude and Walter Fuller were buried in Hartland Central Cemetery, Hartland, N.Y.

209.   III.   ***Marion A. Goldthwaite***, b. New York State 1898, d. New York State 1969; m. Joseph F. Hare, Sr., b. 1900, d. 1967. They had at least one child. Marion and Joseph Hare were buried in Evergreen Hill Cemetery, Corfu, New York.

Children:

i.   ***Ruth A. Hare***, b. Kenmore, New York September 4, 1931, d. Batavia, New York May 9, 2020; m. Alton Rudolph Rupp, b. Buffalo, New York September 22, 1930, d. Batavia, New York, January 17, 2015. They were Buried in Evergreen Hill Cemetery, Corfu, New York.

210.   IV.   ***Ernest Merle Goldthwaite***, b. New York State September 1, 1901, d. Cuba, New York July 17, 1977; m. Cuba, New York July 20, 1933 Helen (H.) Jean Campbell, b. Cuba, New York January 21, 1907, d. Friendship, New York July 26, 2005. Ernest's World War II Draft Registration Card described him as being 5' 4" tall, weighed 165 pounds with a ruddy complexion, blue eyes, and brown hair. He was employed by Bell Aircraft Corporation, Niagara Fall, New York. Ernest and Jean Goldthwaite were buried in Cuba Cemetery, Cuba, New York.

211. V. *Madelaine Goldthwaite* (a twin), b. Northeast, Pennsylvania April 4, 1907, d. place and date not known; m. Orchard Park, New York September 20, 1930 William G. Eisensmith. They had two daughters: Merry (1932) and JoAnne (1933).

212. VI. *Evaline Goldthwaite* (a twin), b. Northeast, Pennsylvania April 4, 1907, d. place and date not known; m. Chautauqua County, New York July 6, 1924 Claude Albertman.

References: US Census: 1870, 1880, 1910, 1920, 1930, 1940; New York State Census: 1892; New York State Marriage Index 1881-1967; Cuba Cemetery records, Cuba, New York; Holland Cemetery Records, Holland, New York; Hartland Central Cemetery records, Hartland, New York; Evergreen Hill Cemetery records, Corfu, New York; World War II Draft Registration Card 1942 for Ernest Goldthwaite.

80.

William Alfred Fuller, son of Helen (17), grandson of Clarissa (4), b. Nunda, New York July 10, 1859, d. Dansville, New York February 6, 1924; m. place and date not known, Agnes M., last name not known, b. New York State July 1859, d. Dansville, New York December 27, 1933. William and Agnes Fuller had a daughter based on the 1900 US Census named Inez, b. July 1888. Inez Fuller does not appear on any future census records. William and Agnes Fuller resided in Olean, New York in 1900 where he was employed as a bookkeeper. In 1910 they moved to Manhattan, New York where Mr. Fuller was employed as a railroad clerk. By 1920 the Fullers returned to Livingston County living in Dansville where William Fuller continued his employment as a railroad clerk. In the 1930 US Census Agnes resided with her sister Kate Lyons in Dansville. William and Agnes Fuller were buried in Oakwood Cemetery, Nunda, New York next to William Fuller's mother. There are no dates on Agnes Fuller's gravestone.

References: US Census: 1860, 1870, 1880, 1900, 1910, 1920, 1930; New York State Census: 1875, 1905, 1915; Oakwood Cemetery records, Nunda, New York; New York State Death Index 1852-1956 for William and Agnes Fuller.

82.

Louis/Lewis Henry Breen, son of Helen (17), grandson of Clarissa (4), b. Bath, New York September 14, 1872, d. Corning, New York September 2, 1919; m. (1) Hornellsville, New York April 9, 1899 Nellie A. Peckham, b. New York State 1874, d. Olean, New York November 13, 1912; m. (2) Corning, New York October 28, 1914 Cora Belle Rhoda Humphrey, b. Hornby, New York 1872, d. Hornby, New York 1947. Lewis Breen's marriage record to Cora Humphrey noted that he had two previous marriages. One wife had died and the second was a divorce. Documentation for only two wives could be found. Cora was previously married twice and both husbands were deceased. Documentation could be found for only Cora's marriage to John Humphrey, Sr. In 1875 Lewis Breen resided with his parents in Conesus, New York and in 1880 in Nunda Station (Dalton), New York. The 1900 US Census found Mr. Breen employed as a laborer in a brick yard in Hornell. Lewis Breen lived in Portville, New York in 1905 where he farmed. The 1910 US Census found Mr. Breen living in Olean, New York where he was employed in a glass works. His World War I Draft Registration Card described him as being of medium height and weight with blue eyes and brown hair. He was employed at Corning Glass Works in Corning, New York as a tracer. Census records indicated that Lewis and Nellie did not have any children. It is not known where Lewis and Nellie Breen were buried. Cora Breen was buried in Central Valley Cemetery, Hornby, New York with members of the Humphrey family.

References: US Census: 1880, 1900, 1910, 1920, 1930, 1940; New York State Census: 1875, 1905; World War I Draft Registration Card 1917-18; Central Valley Cemetery records, Hornby, New York; New York State Death Index 1852-1956 for Lewis Breen.

83.

Walter James Breen, son of Helen (17), grandson of Clarissa (4), b. Conesus, New York May 6, 1873, d. Romulus, New York February 2, 1944; m. Canandaigua, New York January 25, 1899 Grace M. Woolverton, b New York State July 1874, d. Scranton, Pennsylvania May 10, 1929 from nephritis and hypertension at a hospital. Walter Breen resided with his parents in Nunda Station (Dalton), New York until his marriage. In 1900 he lived in Gainesville, New York with his wife where he was employed as a railroad clerk and Grace was a milliner. The 1910 US Census Walter was employed as an inspector for a button company in Rochester, New York. They continued to reside in Rochester in 1915 where Mr. Breen worked for a paper mill. Walter Breen changed careers by 1920 when he was recorded working as a railroad station agent, a career he continued until his death. Walter Breen's World War I Draft Registration Card described him as being of medium height and weight with blue eyes and brown hair. After the death of his wife Grace, Walter lived with his son and his son's family in Painted Post. Walter and Grace Breen were buried in Erwin Fairview Cemetery, Painted Post. There is a marker for Grace but not for Walter.

Children:

213. I. *Walter Kenneth Breen*, b. 1900, d. 1947; m. January 20, 1929, Mabel Marie Layton, b. 1906, d. 2000. They had two daughters: Ruth and Doris and one son, John. Walter and Mabel were buried in Erwin Fairview Cemetery.

214. II. *Marjorie Helen Breen*, b. a. 1909, d. place and date not known; m. Erwin, New York Grant Austin Lewis, Jr. They had two sons and two daughters.

References: US Census: 1880, 1900, 1910, 1920, 1930, 1940; New York State Census: 1875, 1915, 1925; New York State Marriage Index 1852-1956; Erwin Fairview Cemetery records, Painted Post; World War I Draft Registration Card 1917-18; Pennsylvania Death Certificates 1906-1967.

84.

John C. Breen, son of Helen (17), grandson of Clarissa (4), b. Nunda, New York November 4, 1875, d. Buffalo, New York January 18, 1953; m. 1900 Mary D. Brien, b. 1877, d. 1955. John Breen resided with his parents until his marriage in Nunda Station (Dalton), New York. He was employed doing odd jobs in Burns, New York in 1910, as a signal laborer in Caneadea, New York in 1920, a laborer in a milk plant in Bolivar, New York in 1930 and in 1940 as a county road construction worker in Canaseraga, New York. John and Mary Breen had two daughters: Helen (1896) and Mary

(1899). John and Mary Breen were buried in Canaseraga Cemetery in the Hulbert Lot, Canaseraga, New York.

References: US Census: 1880, 1900, 1910, 1920, 1930, 1940; New York State Census: 1905; New York State Death Index 1852-1956; Canaseraga Cemetery records, Canaseraga, New York.

85.

Jerome Goldthwaite, son of Norton (18), grandson of Clarissa (4), b. Nunda, New York, b. Nunda, New York September 2, 1867, d. Barkertown, New York May 28, 1959; m. Nunda, New York December 25, 1888 Katherine "Katie" R. Close, b. Nunda, New York August 29, 1872, d. Nunda, New York December 10, 1953. Jerome Goldthwaite was a life-long resident of Nunda, New York where he farmed. They had six children with only one dying in infancy. Mr. Goldthwaite was elected a highway commissioner for Livingston County in 1906. Jerome and Katie Goldthwaite were buried in Oakwood Cemetery, Nunda, New York.

Children:

215. I. **William Goldthwaite**, b. Nunda, New York July 9, 1890, d. Warsaw, New York, in a hospital June 17, 1960; m. LeRoy, New York June 9, 1920 Elsie LaRose Couchman, b. Geneseo, New York July 16, 1897, d. Wellsville, New York, January 9, 1986. Mr. Goldthwaite was employed as a carpenter and for a time was employed by Foote Manufacturing Company, while Mrs. Goldthwaite, a graduate of Geneseo Normal School, was a teacher. Mrs. Goldthwaite moved to Wellsville, New York, in 1964, where she resided until her death. William and Elsie were buried in Oakwood Cemetery, Nunda, New York.

Children:

i. **Dorothy Goldthwaite**; m. Howard Herke and had two children.

216. II. **Harry Jerome Goldthwaite**, b. Nunda, New York July 11, 1892, d. Nunda, New York February 1957; m. Nunda, New York October 6, 1915 Anna Belle Hinderland, b. Canaseraga, New York June 7, 1895, d.

Castille, New York November 28, 1966 in a nursing home. Harry was a thirty-year employee of Foster Wheeler Corporation in Dansville, New York. Driving to work, he had a medical emergency and crashed his car, causing his death. Harry Goldthwaite was buried with his parents. His wife was also buried in Oakwood Cemetery, but there is no grave marker for her. It is not known why they were buried apart.

Children:

    i.   **Leon H. Goldthwaite**, b. Nunda, New York July 20, 1916, d. Nunda, New York, December 22, 1992. He was employed for thirty-three years at the Craig Developmental Center. He served as a trustee for the Village of Nunda and from 1959-1976 was Nunda's Mayor. In addition, Mr. Goldthwaite was the Chief of Nunda's Fire Department and President of Nunda's Rotary Club. He never married and was buried in Oakwood Cemetery, Nunda, New York.

    ii.   *Thelma Goldthwaite*, b. Nunda, New York November 18, 1918, d. Perry, New York January 7, 1999; m. Perry, New York November 12, 1939, James Eugene Ferrell, b. Perry, New York July 19, 1915, d. Perry, New York, July 19, 1971. They had two children: William and JoAnne.

217.   III.   **Ethel Goldthwaite**, b. Nunda, New York January 1894, d. Nunda, New York May 13, 1959; m. Nunda, New York 1919 William Merritt Paine b. Nunda, New York April 6, 1895, d. Dansville, New York, June 25, 1974. William Paine was a farmer his entire life. Ethel and William Paine had no children and were buried in Oakwood Cemetery, Nunda, New York.

218.   IV.   **Unnamed Goldthwaite**, b. and d. 1895 and was buried in Oakwood Cemetery in lot G-51.

219.   V.   **Milo S. Goldthwaite**, b. Nunda, New York March 9, 1896, d. Rochester, New York June 28, 1963; m. place not known, February 1, 1924, Mariam Bruno, b. 1903, d. Zephyrhills, Florida, October 23, 1986. Milo was employed as a salesman and Distributor for Socony Vacuum

Company. After Milo's death, Mariam remarried to Dale Campbell. Milo and Mariam had two children, David and Jean, and three grandchildren. Milo and Mariam were buried in Hunts Hollow Cemetery, Portage, New York.

220. VI. **Alfred Leon Goldthwaite**, b. Nunda, New York March 26, 1904, d. Warsaw, New York hospital June 1, 1949; m. place and date not known Marguerite Luella Kemp, b. West Sparta, New York 1902, d. Dansville, New York, August 22, 1980. Alfred was a member of Nunda's Chamber of Commerce, the Livingston County Farm Bureau, and Master of Hunt Grange. Marguerite was employed by Geneseo State University. They had one daughter: Lois and one grandson. Alfred and Marguerite were buried in Oakwood Cemetery, Nunda, New York.

References: US Census: 1870, 1880, 1900, 1910, 1920, 1930, 1940; New York State Census: 1875, 1905, 1915, 1925; Oakwood Cemetery Records, Nunda, New York; New York State Marriage Index 1881-1967; New York State Death Index 1881-1967; Nunda News obituary December 17, 1953 for Katherine Goldthwaite; Genesee Country Express obituary January 23, 1986 for William Goldthwaite; Nunda News obituary February 21, 1957 for Harry Goldthwaite and December 1, 1996 obituary for Anna Goldthwaite; Glenwood Cemetery records, Perry, New York; Nunda News May 14, 1959 obituary for Ethel Paine; Nunda News July 4, 1963 for Milo Goldthwaite; Livingston County Leader June 9, 1949 for Alfred Goldthwaite; Genesee Country Express August 28, 1980 obituary for Marguerite Goldthwaite; New York State Birth Index 1881-1967.

87.

Clara Goldthwaite, daughter of Norton (18), granddaughter of Clarissa (4), b. Nunda, New York 1872, d. Nunda, New York, May 13, 1896, from consumption. Clara never married, but she did have a son with Edward Walker. Clara Goldthwaite was buried in Oakwood Cemetery, Nunda, New York. No marker is evident.

Children:

221. I. ***James Goldthwaite***, b. Nunda, New York January 13, 1893, d. Sayre, Pennsylvania, November 4, 1948, from kidney cancer; m. (1) Nunda, New York January 25, 1915, Lillie A. Austin, b. Nunda, New York August 15, 1894, d. New York March 1977, divorced 1933; m. (2) Pearl Carnes. His maternal grandparents raised James Goldthwaite from the time of his mother's death. He resided in Bath, New York, for most of his adult life, where he was employed as an inspector for the Ingersoll Rand Company. He was also a talented auto mechanic. James Goldthwaite was buried in Oakwood Cemetery, Nunda, New York. There is a marker for Lillie Goldthwaite but not for James.

Children:

i. ***Robert C. Goldthwaite***, b. Nunda, New York September 7, 1915, d. d. Nunda, New York May 1, 2007; m. place and date not known, Theresa M. Dunlap, b. Black Creek, New York April 14, 1915, d. Nunda, New York, April 23, 1996. They had one daughter, Sandra S. Goldthwaite, who was born and died October 16, 1951. Robert, Theresa, and Sandra were all buried in Cuba Cemetery, Cuba, New York, with markers.

References: US Census: 1880, 1900, 1910, 1920, 1930, 1940; New York State Marriage Index 1881-1967; Oakwood Cemetery records, Nunda, New York; Cuba Cemetery records, Cuba, New York; Pennsylvania Death Certificate 1906-1967 for James Goldthwaite; Nunda News November 12, 1948 for James Goldthwaite.

89.

Howard Mills Goldthwaite, son of Milo (19), grandson of Clarissa (4), b. Jamestown, New York February 1871, d. place and date not known; m. Jamestown, New York June 22, 1901, Mary Adelaide O'Dell, b. Pennsylvania 1874, d. The place and date are not known, but by 1930. Mr. Goldthwaite was a draftsman by trade and, in 1910, had moved to Hamilton, Ohio, where he was the manager for Safe Works. He later became a salesman for office furnishings and moved to Denver, Colorado. He was a widower by the 1930 US Census. The 1910 US Census indicated they had three children with only one living. The identities of the two are known. It is not known where they were buried.

Children:

222. I. **Eleanor Elizabeth Goldthwaite**, b. Manhattan, New York February 27, 1904, d. Manhattan, New York, February 29, 1904. The burial location is not known.

223. II. **Mary Helen Goldthwaite**, b. Brooklyn, New York July 10, 1905, d. New York State May 11, 1994, and buried in Evergreen Cemetery, Brooklyn, New York.

References: US Census: 1880, 1900, 1910, 1920, 1930, 1940; New York State Birth Index 1862-1948 for Eleanor and Mary Goldthwaite; New York State Death Index 1866-1909 for Eleanor Goldthwaite; Social Security Death Index 1935-2014 for Mary Helen Goldthwaite.

93.

Grace Badger Craig, daughter of Harriet (20), granddaughter of Clarissa (4), b. Nunda, New York April 21, 1876, d. Wellsville, New York March 24, 1970; m. Canaseraga, New York September 27, 1899 Samuel Bonner Scott, b. Ossian, New York September 10, 1872, d. Canaseraga, New York February 10, 1941. Grace and Samuel were both invested in Craig and Scott funeral home, Canaseraga, New York and in the Craig and Scott furniture business. They resided in Burns, New York until 1930 when they briefly moved to Bolivar, New York to run a furniture business there. By 1940 they had returned to Canaseraga. Grace and Samuel Scott were buried in Canaseraga Cemetery, Canaseraga, New York. Samuel Scott had a daughter, Ruth Alice Scott (1895-1917) from an earlier marriage who was buried in Wood Cemetery, Ossian, New York.

Children:

224, I. **Phyllis Jeannette Scott**, b. Ossian, New York October 25, 1901, d. Cornwall, New York February 9, 1990; m. Mr. Conroy had four daughters.

225. II. **Elizabeth "Betty" Louise Scott**, b. 1905, d. Wellsville, New York Hospital 1985; m. 1899 Glenn A. Mapes, b. 1904, d. 1987. They ran the Caneadea, New York Country Store, and Mapes Woodworking. From 1972 until their respective deaths, Mr. and Mrs. Mapes resided in Alfred Station. They did not have any children. Betty and Glenn were buried in Canaseraga Cemetery, Canaseraga, New York.

References: US Census: 1880, 1900, 1910, 1920, 1930, 1940; New York State Census: 1915, 1925; Canaseraga Cemetery records, Canaseraga, New York; Sabbath Recorder, May 1985 obituary for Betty Mapes; Wood Cemetery records, Ossian, New York; New York State Marriage Index 1881-1967.

94.

James G. Craig, son of Harriet (20), grandson of Clarissa (4), b. Nunda, New York December 15, 1877, d. Canaseraga, New York April 11, 1956; m. Hornell, New York June 5, 1920 Mae H. Walbridge, b. October 27, 1889, d. October 1984. James Craig's World War I Draft Registration Card described him as being 5' 10" tall, weighed 190 pounds with blue eyes and brown hair. He owned and operated the Craig and Scott furniture business and funeral home in Canaseraga. In addition, James Craig was Director of the Canaseraga Bank. They had one son: Robert James Craig (1921-1977) who married and had two children: Robert and Michele. Robert James Craig was an officer in the US Marines. James and Mae Craig were buried in Canaseraga Cemetery, Canaseraga, New York.

References: US Census: 1880, 1900, 1910, 1920, 1930, 1940; New York State Census: 1915, 1925; New York State Marriage Index 1881-1967; Canaseraga Cemetery records, Canaseraga, New York; California Death Index for Robert J. Craig.

98.

Alfred DeWitt Taber, son of Henry (21), grandson of Louisa (5), b. Walton, Wisconsin January 17, 1879, d. Ann Arbor, Michigan September 22, 1931 from repeated heart attacks; m. (1) Ada, Michigan November 28, 1900

Bessie B. Watson, divorced Ada, Michigan July 3, 1905, b. Grand Rapids, Michigan November 24, 1887, d. Port Huron, Michigan September 27, 1952; m. (2) Milwaukee, Wisconsin March 24, 1907 Ethel Callier Bradfield, divorced Michigan April 29, 1911; m. (3) Detroit, Michigan October 9, 1912 Blanche Hazel Draney Snelling, b. Montana a. 1891, d. place and date not known. Alfred Taber was an electrician by trade and worked for a number of companies in the greater Detroit area. He had five children by his third wife. It is not known where Alfred and Blanche Taber were buried. Bessie, his first wife, remarried two more times after their divorce and was buried in Ada Cemetery, Ada, Michigan. What happened to Ethel, his second wife, is not known.

Children (by third marriage):

226. I. **Alfred D. Taber**, b. January 7, 1914, d. Clinton, Michigan August 3, 1988; m. St. Clair Shores May 11, 1938. He was a painter, and they had at least one child, a son named Ernest, born in 1940.

227. II. **Charles Henry Taber**, b. December 25, 1915, d. St. Clair Shores July 17, 1931, from an accidental drowning.

228. III. **Delores B. Taber**, b. Michigan 1920, d. Michigan 1970; m. Williams, Ohio November 12, 1940 Marvin E. Eichler, b. Michigan September 29, 1914, d. Hillsdale January 20, 1999. Delores and Marvin were buried in Mt. Hope Cemetery, Litchfield, Michigan.

229. IV. **Alice Marie Taber**, b. St. Clair Shores 1929, d. place and date not known; m. (1) Hillsdale, Michigan June 5, 1948, James Arthur Polkow, divorced; m. (2) endocino, California June 10, 1974 William O'Hale. Alice had two children by her first marriage: Margaret and David. It is not known where Alice and James Polkow were buried.

230. V. **Ellen Louise Taber**, b. Michigan 1930, d. place and date not known; m. Mt. Clemens, Michigan August 2, 1947, Lloyd Aolson. Further information is not available.

References: US Census: 1880, 1900, 1910, 1920, 1930; Ada Cemetery records, Ada, Michigan; Michigan Marriage Records 1867-1952; Michigan Divorce Records 1897-1952; Wisconsin Marriage Records 1838-1911;

Michigan Death Records 1867-1952 for Alfred DeWitt Taber and Charles Henry Taber; Mt. Hope Cemetery records, Litchfield, Michigan.

106.

Mabel Devendorf, daughter of Flora (25), granddaughter of Sophie (6), b. Delavan, Wisconsin September 28, 1875, d. Birchwood, Wisconsin 1950; m. Green Lake, Wisconsin January 7, 1901 John Warrington Stowe, b. Dane County, Wisconsin July 1, 1880, d. Wisconsin 1961. John Stowe was a farmer in Wisconsin, residing in Birchwood, Wisconsin, for most of his life. He was briefly a salesman for a retail grocery store in Easton, Wisconsin, in 1920. After Mabel's death, Mr. Stowe remarried in 1956 to Dolores Zimbeck (1903-1961). John and his second wife died in a house fire. Mabel and John Stowe were buried in Woodlawn Cemetery, Birchwood, Wisconsin.

Children:

231. I. *Harold R. Stowe*, b. Plainville, Wisconsin August 18, 1902, d. Birchwood, Wisconsin November 4, 1977; m. Viola B. Strohmeyer, b. 1909, d. 2008. They were buried in Woodlawn Cemetery, Birchwood, Wisconsin.

232. II. *Donald H. Stowe*, b. Adams County, Wisconsin June 16, 1908, d. Birchwood, Wisconsin November 4, 1971. He never married and was buried in Woodlawn Cemetery, Birchwood, Wisconsin.

233. III. *Marion/Maryann Stowe*, b. Adams County, Wisconsin September 10, 1911, d. Birchwood, Wisconsin February 5, 1989; m. Washburn County, Wisconsin April 24, 1976, Kenneth Keith Rhinehart, b. Wisconsin July 26, 1912, d. Easton, Wisconsin, March 14, 1983. Kenneth Rhinehart remarried after Marion's death, but he was buried with Marion at Woodlawn Cemetery, Birchwood, Wisconsin.

234. IV. *Flora Elizabeth Stowe*, b. Wisconsin March 10, 1913, d. Lyndon Station, Wisconsin January 24, 2015; m. 1940 Raymond F. Bowers, b. 1913, d. 1986. They were buried in Woodlawn Memorial Park, Joliet, Wisconsin.

235. V. **Wesley J. Stowe**, b. Wisconsin November 11, 1914, d. Wisconsin June 29, 1995; m. 1940 Phyllis Irene McCauley, b. 1916, d. Monument, Colorado, August 23, 2018. They were buried in Woodlawn Cemetery, Birchwood, Wisconsin. They had six children: Richard, Judy, Joanne, Carol, Teri, and Ronnie. Ronnie, b. May 4, 1941, d. September 26, 1974, in Powell City, Montana, by suicide and was buried in Woodlawn Cemetery.

References: US Census: 1880, 1900, 1910, 1920, 1930, 1940; Woodlawn Cemetery records, Birchwood, Wisconsin; Woodlawn Memorial Park records, Joliet, Wisconsin; Montana Death Records 1907-2016 for Ronnie Stowe.

107.

Charles Tisdale Peirce, son of Charlotte (28), grandson of Sophie (6), b. Wisconsin 1861, d. Chicago, Illinois, February 7, 1922, following surgery on his throat; m. place and date not known, Agnes H. Robinson, b. Wisconsin 1864, d. Madison, Wisconsin, October 19, 1925. Mr. Peirce followed the family tradition and became a dentist. He resided in Janesville, Wisconsin, for almost thirty-five years. They had four children. Charles and Agnes Peirce were buried in Oak Hill Cemetery, Janesville, Michigan.

Children:

236. I. **George Robinson Peirce**, b. Wisconsin April 17, 1886, d. Wisconsin, August 24, 1886, and buried in Oak Hill Cemetery.

237. II. **Griffin C. Peirce**, b. Janesville, Wisconsin June 27, 1893, d. Janesville, Wisconsin, March 27, 1932. He never married and was buried in Oak Hill Cemetery.

238. III. **Kathryn Frances Peirce**, b. Rock, Wisconsin August 12, 1901, d. Madison, Wisconsin December 17, 1961; m. Matthew R. Groth. Mr. Groth was a clerk at Gisholt Machine Company, Madison. He died on June 25, 1944. Mr. and Mrs. Groth had no children, and they were buried in Oak Hill Cemetery.

239. IV. **Henry O. Peirce**, b. Wisconsin 1903, d. Wisconsin 1938.

He never married and was buried in Oak Hill Cemetery.

References: US Census: 1880, 1900, 1910, 1920; Oak Hill Cemetery records, Janesville, Michigan.

108.

Frances Ella Peirce, daughter of Charlotte (28), granddaughter of Sophie (6), b. Wisconsin July 1864, d. Dekalb County, Georgia October 1, 1948; m. Dane County, Wisconsin September 21, 1885 Theodore Carl Zahn, b. District of Columbia 1865, d. Sioux City, Iowa June 10, 1906 from diabetes. Mr. Zahn worked for Olson and Veerhausen of Madison and Sioux City. Theodore Zahn's newspaper obituary said he had a daughter, Louise, but there is no further mention of her. Frances Zahn had a job that took her around the US. When she became unemployed during the depression Frances remained in Atlanta, Georgia where friends gave her a trolley, which Frances placed on squatter's land and made a home for herself dividing the trolley into five parts. Her only survivor was a niece, Mrs. Matthew Groth. Frances was buried in Forest Hill Cemetery, Madison, Wisconsin with her husband.

References: US Census: 1870, 1880, 1900, 1910, 1920, 1930, 1940; Forest Hill Cemetery records, Madison, Wisconsin; District of Columbia Evening Star obituary January 14, 1906 for Theodore Zahn; The Atlanta Constitution April 25, 1937 for article about Frances Zahn's trolley home; Wisconsin Marriage Records 1820-1907; Wisconsin State Journal obituaries October 4 and 5, 1948 for Frances Zahn.

110.

Charles Frederick Hurd, son of Mary (30), grandson of Sophie (6), b. Little Mountain, Ohio April 17, 1876, d. Lodi, Wisconsin November 23, 1944; m. Cottage Grove, Wisconsin November 29, 1904, Mary Maude McComb, b. place not known, 1878, d. Wisconsin 1935. Mr. Hurd followed in the family tradition and became a dentist practicing in Lodi, Wisconsin, for most of his life. After his wife's death, Charles Hurd resided with his daughter and son-in-law. Charles and Mary Hurd were buried in Mt. Pleasant Cemetery, Lodi, Wisconsin.

Children:

240. I. **Gladys Hurd**, b. Lodi, Wisconsin November 14, 1906, d. Wisconsin 1940; m. Rockford, Illinois October 24, 1927, Wallace Falkenstein, b. Wisconsin August 16, 1902, d. Lodi, Wisconsin June 21, 1972. Mr. Falkenstein was a farmer. After the death of Gladys, he remarried in 1945 to Mildred Guethlein. Gladys and Wallace were buried in Mt. Pleasant Cemetery, Lodi, Wisconsin. There is no information about children.

References: US Census: 1880, 1900, 1910, 1920, 1930, 1940; Mt. Pleasant Cemetery records, Lodi, Wisconsin; Wisconsin Marriage Records 1800-1907; Illinois Marriage Records 1800-1940; Social Security Death Index 1935-2014.

111.

Jessie Fuller, daughter of Myron (32), granddaughter of James (7), b. Michigan October 12, 1856, d. Kalamazoo, Michigan August 4, 1926 from apoplexy; m. Vicksburg, Michigan November 13, 1878 Edward Briggs, b. Schoolcraft, Michigan October 31, 1845, d. Vicksburg, Michigan December 12, 1919 from cockroach powder mistakenly put into the food prepared for inmates of a farm labor camp, divorced Kalamazoo, Michigan October 31, 1899 for extreme cruelty. After Jessie's divorce she was employed in a paper mill and she lived alone. Jessie and Edward Briggs had four children two of whom died young and two adult children who died from convulsions. Jessie Briggs was buried in Gourdneck Prairie Cemetery, Vicksburg, Michigan as was Edward Briggs, but not together.

Children:

241. I. **Asa Briggs**, b. Vicksburg, Michigan October 9, 1879, d. Michigan, date not known, and buried in an unmarked grave in Gourdneck Prairie Cemetery.

242. II. **Martha E. Briggs**, b. Vicksburg, Michigan 1882, d. Vicksburg, Michigan, May 10, 1898, from convulsions. She was buried in Gourdneck Prairie Cemetery.

243.   III.   *Daisey Briggs*, b. Vicksburg, Michigan a. 1883, d. Vicksburg, Michigan, date unknown, and buried in an unmarked grave in Gourdneck Prairie Cemetery.

244.   IV.   ***Charles E. Briggs***, b. Vicksburg, Michigan September 11, 1888, d. Michigan, July 23, 1933, from an epileptic seizure. Mr. Briggs's World War I Draft Draft Registration Card described him as being tall with a medium build and having blue eyes and light brown hair. He suffered from convulsions his entire life and, in 1930, was a patient at the Michigan Farm Colony for Epileptics. Charles Briggs was buried in Gourdneck Prairie Cemetery. There is no marker.

References: US Census: 1860, 1870, 1880, 1900, 1910, 1920, 1930; Gourdneck Prairie Cemetery records, Vicksburg, Michigan; Michigan Death Record 1867-1952 for Edward Briggs, Jessie Fuller Briggs, and Charles Briggs; Michigan Marriage Records 1867-1952; Michigan Divorce Records 1897-1952; World War I Draft Registration Card 1917-1918 for Charles E. Briggs.

113.

Martha Augusta Fuller, daughter of Myron (32), granddaughter of James (7), b. St. Joseph County, Michigan September 1861, d. Liberty, Michigan, April 11, 1941, from cerebral apoplexy; m. (1) Fife Lake, Michigan September 5, 1880, Richard Bridson, b. Newburg, Ohio October 22, 1856, d. Grand Traverse, Michigan February 11, 1923 from a heart attack while he slept; (2) Traverse City, Michigan December 3, 1936 William Ferguson, b. place and date not known, d. place and date not known. Richard Bridson was a farmer in Fife Lake, Michigan his entire life. Martha continued to reside on the family farm in 1930 with her daughter Wealtha and a grandson and in 1940 when she had remarried to William Ferguson. Martha was buried in Walton Cemetery, Grand Traverse, Michigan with her first husband. They had ten children. It is not known where her second husband was buried.

Children (by first marriage):

245. I. **Jennie J. Bridson**, b. Michigan June 23, 1881, d. Traverse City, Michigan September 2, 1939; m. Abram Avery; no further information.

246. II. **Martha Elizabeth Bridson**, Fife Lake, Michigan September 28, 1884; no further information.

247. III. **Edward D. Bridson**, b. Walton Junction April 13, 1887, d Bellevue, Washington January 12, 1966; m. Detroit, Michigan, September 17, 1919, divorced. They had one child, Marion, b. 1918. Edward was buried in Mount Pleasant Cemetery in Seattle.

248. IV. **Elmer Richard Bridson**, b. Michigan March 30, 1889, d. Michigan November 1, 1961; m. (1) Traverse City, Michigan October 9, 1915, Wava Bensinger, b. Ottawa City, Michigan May 19, 1899, d. Lake Odessa, Michigan October 30, 1965, divorced; m. (2) place and date not known Marie Bordon; m. (3) Menton, Michigan April 22, 1934, Thelma Young, b. Akron, Indiana April 28, 1902, d. Grand Traverse, Michigan August 6, 1988. Wava remarried twice more times and was buried with her third husband in Lakeside Cemetery, Lake Odessa, Michigan. Elmer and Thelma were buried in Walton Cemetery, Grand Traverse, Michigan.

Children (by first marriage):

i. **Leonard Leroy Bridson**, b. Muskegon, Michigan December 28, 1916, d. Ionia, Michigan August 27, 1967; m. Detroit, Michigan December 23, 1945 Marion E. Haynes (1925-2004). They were buried in Walton Cemetery.

Children (by third marriage):

i. **James Bridson**, b. and d. January 19, 1935, and buried in Walton Cemetery.

ii. **Richard Allen Bridson**, b. Fife Lake, Michigan October 24, 1935, d. Fife Lake, Michigan January 17, 2013; m. Kathleen Johnson b. Detroit, Michigan July 2, 1936, d. Caldwell, Michigan, May 24, 2017. They were buried in Walton Cemetery.

iii. **Kay W. Bridson**, b. Michigan May 10, 1941, d. Flint, Michigan June 5, 1977; m. 1961 John Wesley Powell, Jr. b. Macomb, Michigan May 21, 1941, d. Marion, Michigan November 16, 1999. He remarried to Norma Taylor Mishler (1951-2015) in 1983.

iv. **Keith Bridson**, b. Bloomfield, Michigan May 10, 1941, d. May 11, 2017; m. Linda Huff. They had three children: an infant daughter who died and Craig and Ali.

249. V. **Robert Curtis Bridson**, b. Fife Lake October 5, 1891, d. Tacoma, Washington, April 11, 1954, and buried in Alder Cemetery, New Reliance, Washington.

250. VI. **Albert Myron Bridson**, b. Fife Lake, Michigan January 30, 1894, d. Wexford, Michigan November 29, 1963; m. Roxanne Jenkins (1905-1985). They had one on Stuart Douglas Bridson. Fife Lake December 7, 1928, d. Tucson, Arizona January 2, 1995; m. 1950 Ardith Birgy (1932-2004). They were buried in Walton Cemetery.

251. VII. **Maud S. Bridson**, b. Michigan July 1896. She was listed on the 1900 and 1910 US Census records. No further information.

252. VIII. **Otis Custer Bridson**, b. Fife Lake, Michigan November 7, 1899, d. 1958; m. Arkansas February 20, 1927, Nola Churchill (1909-1959). They had a daughter, Matabell Joy Bridson (1931-2000), who married Austin Spalding (1932-2014), and they, in turn, had a son, Mark Austin Spalding (1957-1977). They were buried in Walton Cemetery.

253. IX. **Wealtha M. Bridson**, b. Grand Traverse, Michigan March 22, 1901, d. Michigan July 24, 1969; m. (1) Lake City, Michigan May 21, 1923 Samuel McKeown, b. Ganges, Michigan May 18, 1894, d. Grand Rapids, Michigan March 16, 1944, divorced; m. (2) Traverse City, Michigan May 12, 1930 Henry J. Fisher, b. Wexford, Michigan April 27, 1894, d. Michigan April 9. 1975. Samuel McKeown raised bees and lost an eye and an arm in a massive bee attack. He was buried in Moorestown Cemetery, Moorestown, Michigan.

Children (by first marriage):

i. **Van Basel McKeown**, b. May 17, 1924, d. Spokane, Washington, December 3, 1973. He was a Master Sergeant in the US Air Force and was buried in Fairmount Memorial Park, Spokane, Washington.

254. X. **Violet Bridson**, b. Fife Lake, Michigan April 10, 1902, d. South Bend, Indiana July 6, 1970; m. 1919 Jay Eugene Hills, b. March 7, 1902. d. May 1980. They were buried in St. Joseph Valley Memorial Park, Granger, Indiana.

References: US Census: 1880, 1900, 1910, 1920, 1930, 1940; St. Joseph Valley Memorial Park records, Granger, Indiana; Fairmount Memorial Park records, Spokane, Washington; Moorestown Cemetery records, Moorestown, Michigan; Walton Cemetery records, Grand Traverse, Michigan; Mount Pleasant Cemetery records, Seattle, Washington; Michigan Death Records 1867-1952; Michigan Marriage Records 1867-1952; Michigan Divorce Records 1897-1952; Michigan Birth Records 1867-1911.

114.

Merritt Vorhees Fuller, son of Myron (32), grandson of James (7), b. Hastings, Michigan September 1864; d. Pleasant Plains, Arkansas November 22, 1906; m. (1) Traverse City, Michigan October 24, 1891 Nellie E. Storrs, b. Ontario, New York October 3, 1875, d. Grand Traverse, Michigan October 4, 1913, divorced; m. (2) Michigan September 6, 1894 Lydia Mae Fuller, b. Cairo, Illinois May 1, 1878, d. Pleasant Plains, Arkansas July 1, 1934. Nellie Storrs Fuller remarried to Osmer B. Leland (1868-1947) in 1897. Merritt and Lydia Fuller were buried in McMullin Cemetery, Pleasant Plains, Arkansas.

Children (by second marriage):

255. I. **Infant Fuller**, b. Arkansas August 21, 1895, d. Arkansas, August 23, 1895, and buried in Pleasant Plains, Arkansas.

256. II. **Zema Adell Fuller**, b. Pleasant Plains, Arkansas April 14,

1897, d. Searcy, Arkansas January 6, 1952; m. White, Arkansas November 25, 1917, William Christopher Huff, b. April 3, 1892, d. February 6, 1963. They had one daughter, Lorene (1924-1992). Zema and William Huff were buried in McMullin Cemetery, Pleasant Plains, Arkansas.

257. III. **Myron Edward Fuller**, b. Pleasant Plains, Arkansas January 18, 1899, d. Arkansas 1964; m. Ruth A., last name not known (1903-1966). They were buried in Crestlawn Cemetery, Conway, Arkansas.

> Children:
>
> i. **Myron Houston Fuller**, b. Huff, Arkansas December 31, 1928, d, Conway, Arkansas December 28, 1993; m. Faulkner, Arkansas April 9, 1967 Billie Jean Dereuisseaux, b. England September 13, 1928, d. Conway, Arkansas, August 5, 1979.

258. IV. **Margaret Alice Fuller**, b. Arkansas January 21, 1901, d. Pleasant Plains, Arkansas 1956; m. Independence City, Arkansas September 25, 1921, Marcus Edward Hays, b. Arkansas January 10, 1902, d. Pleasant Plains, Arkansas February 1971.

> Children:
>
> i. **Oma Mae Hays**, b. Pleasant Plains, Arkansas September 29, 1922, d. Searcy, Arkansas June 2, 2013; m. place and date not known, Royal Hardy Burress, b. Arkansas July 12, 1922, d. Searcy, Arkansas, December 17, 1991. They had a son, Kenneth Wade Burress (1947-2013), who married Priscilla, last name not known, and had two children: Keven and Kristi. They had a second son, Royal D. Burress.
>
> ii. **Marcus Dean Hayes**, b. Pleasant Plains, Arkansas November 9, 1925, d. Pleasant Plains, Arkansas January 11, 1997; m. Lila Mae Griffis (1930-2012). They had two sons and one daughter.

259.   V.   ***John M. Fuller***, b. Arkansas January 15, 1903, d. Arkansas, February 18, 1903, and buried in McMullin Cemetery, Pleasant Plains, Arkansas.

260.   VI.   ***Arie Vida Fuller***, b. Arkansas 1904, d. Pleasant Plains, Arkansas 1975; m. Phuel Roy Catterlin (1905-1968). They had two children: Geneva E. (1924-1999) and Leroy (1927-1996).

261.   VII.   ***Aery Fuller***, b. Arkansas 1906; no further information.

References: US Census: 1870, 1880, 1900. 1910, 1920, 1930; McMullin Cemetery records, Pleasant Plains, Arkansas; Crestlawn Cemetery records, Conway, Arkansas.

115.

Minnie Adelle Fuller, daughter of Myron (32), granddaughter of James (7), b. Michigan September 1867, d. Clinton, Washington July 20, 1921; m. (1) Paradise, Michigan March 9, 1887 David Kingsley, b. New York November 16, 1853, d. Clinton, Washington August 13, 1909; m. (2) Everett, Washington November 12, 1912 Andrew P. McCreight, b. Ireland September 17, 1858, d. Washington State March 21, 1930. Mr. Kingsley was an Arkansas farmer in 1900. They had four children. Sometime after the 1900 US Census the Kingsley family moved to Clinton, Washington where Mr. Kingsley died in 1909. Andrew McCreight was also a farmer. Minnie was buried with her second husband in St. Peter Lutheran Cemetery, Clinton, Washington. David Kingsley was also buried in St. Peter Lutheran Cemetery.

Children (by first marriage):

262.   I.   ***Frank L. Kingsley***, b. Michigan 1888, d. Seattle, Washington March 22, 1931; m. Washington State December 20, 1911, Grace Adeline Fiske, b. Vineland, New Jersey, d. Wenatchee, Washington, August 12, 1953. They were buried in St. Peter Lutheran Cemetery.

Children:

i.   ***Ferne Margaret Kingsley***, b. Clinton, Washington

March 3, 1914, d. Omak, Washington March 23, 1976; m. Roy Knighton, b. Kansas August 5, 1903, d. Omak, Washington September 15, 1969. They were buried in Omak Memorial Cemetery, Okanogan, Washington. Ferne and Roy had one son, James Leroy Knighton (1934-1997). James was buried in Willamette National Cemetery, Portland, Oregon.

  ii. ***Francis Fiske Kingsley***, b. Washington State September 24, 1916, d. Washington State June 9, 1977; m. Spokane, Washington December 29, 1944 June Meyers, b. Butte, Montana July 2, 1921, d. Spokane, Washington, February 5, 2017. Francis Kingsley served in the US Army during WW II as a PFC from April 3, 1941 to September 30, 1945. They had two children: Linda and Paul. They were buried in Fairmount Memorial Park, Spokane, Washington

  iii. ***Doris May Kingsley***, b. Snohomish County, Washington February 13, 1923, d. Spokane, Washington October 6, 1990; m. Arlington, Virginia, February 25, 1950. Mark Landau divorced Los Angeles, California, January 1976. She was buried in Fairmount Memorial Park, Spokane, Washington.

  iv. ***Elon Gates Kingsley***, b. Washington State May 29, 1925, d. Washington State January 1975; m. (1) Kootenai, Idaho June 23, 1950, Lorraine Witte, divorced Marion, Oregon January 29, 1969; m. (2) Virginia, last name not known. Elon served with the US Navy from August 25, 1941, to January 11, 1945. He and Lorraine had five children: Donald, Janice, Julene, Laureen, and Patricia. It is not known where Elon Kingsley was buried.

263. II. *Ferne Marguerite Kingsley*, b. Michigan December 2, 1891, d. Washington State September 28, 1964; m. Clinton, Washington June 5, 1912, John A. Erikson, b. Sweden 1885, d. Clinton Washington 1930. Mr. Erikson was a salesman for General Motors. Ferne and John Erikson were buried in St. Peter Lutheran Cemetery, Clinton, Washington.

Children:

    i.   **Randolph David Erickson**, b. Washington State May 16, 1913, d. Washington State March 27, 1981; m. Sequin, Washington May 28, 1934, Esther M., last name unknown, b. Port Williams, Washington January 25, 1915, d. Washington State October 3, 2013. They had four children: John, Pat, Sharon, and Gus.

    ii.   **Katharine Ann Erikson**, b. Washington State October 11, 1915, d. Milton, Washington March 2, 2006; m. Frank Gerald Fell, b. Iowa April 16, 1911, d. Big Harbor, Washington April 13, 2009. They had two daughters.

    iii.   **Marjorie E. Erikson**, b. Washington State April 6, 1924, d. Washington State August 10, 1962; m. Richard Wayne Robbins, b. Snohomish, Washington March 1919, d. Washington State April 10, 1962. They were buried in Mt. View Memorial Park, Lakewood, Washington.

264.   III.   **Florence Kingsley**, b. December 29, 1893, d. Wenatchee, Washington July 11, 1926; m. Walter Waldon, b. Dorset, England January 25, 1886, d. Mt. Vernon, Washington October 1, 1974. Florence was buried in Wenatchee City Cemetery, Wenatchee, Washington. Walter remarried Florence's sister, Cora, and he and Cora were buried in Hawthorne Memorial Park, Mt. Vernon, Washington.

265.   IV.   **Cora Ann Kingsley**, b. Grand Traverse, Michigan March 12, 1896, d. Mt. Vernon, Washington September 8, 1979; m. Walter Walden, her brother-in-law. They were buried in Hawthorne Memorial Park, Mt. Vernon, Washington.

References: US Census: 1870, 1880, 1900, 1910, 1920, 1930, 1940; Hawthorne Memorial Park records, Mt. Vernon, Washington; Wenatchee City Cemetery records, Wenatchee, Washington; Fairmount Memorial Park records, Spokane, Washington; St. Peter Lutheran Cemetery records, Clinton, Washington; Mt. View Memorial Park records, Lakewood, Washington; Washington Marriage Records 1854-2013; Willamette

National Cemetery records, Portland, Oregon; Omak Memorial Cemetery records, Okanogan, Washington; Social Security Death Index 1935-2014.

117.

Arthur Fuller, son of Edward (33), grandson of James (7), b. Michigan December 1859, d. Superior, Wisconsin 1924; m. Vicksburg, Michigan January 1, 1880, Mary Margaret "Maggie" Spangler, b. Clarion, Pennsylvania June 1860, d. Superior, Wisconsin 1943. Arthur and Maggie did not have any children. For a time, she ran a confectionary store while Arthur was a railroad engineer for his professional career from 1900 until his death. Arthur and Maggie Fuller were buried in Greenwood Cemetery, Superior, Wisconsin.

References: US Census: 1860, 1870, 1880, 1900, 1910, 1920, 1930, 1940; Greenwood Cemetery records, Superior, Wisconsin.

119.

Jennie Fuller, daughter of Edward (33), granddaughter of James (7), b. Kalamazoo, Michigan January 15, 1867, d. Whitewater, Michigan March 20, 1947; m. place and date not known, John Calvin Spangler, b. place not known, March 27, 1863, d. Michigan November 4, 1936, from influenza and pneumonia. John was a lifelong farmer. He and Jennie were buried in Oakwood Cemetery, Traverse City, Michigan.

Children:

266. I. *Lara Belle Spangler*, b. Michigan November 8, 1893, d. Grand Traverse, Michigan June 24, 1913, from typhoid fever; m. Michigan 1911 Oliver S. Moyer, b. 1887, d. Grand Traverse, Michigan, November 11, 1946. Lara was buried in Monroe Center Cemetery, Grand Traverse, Michigan. Mr. Moyer remarried in 1916 to Helen Thomas (1898-1985), with whom he had a daughter, Velma (1923-2018). Lara and Oliver had one child.

Children:

i. *Lorin Moyer*, b. Michigan June 1, 1913, d. Michigan

December 11, 1988; m. 1938 Ruth Knight (1916-2015). They had a son, Frederick (1943-2002).

267.   II.   **Edward A. Spangler**, b. Michigan 1900, d. Grand Traverse, Michigan August 30, 1944; m. 1921 Rose Bartz (1900-1983). They were buried in Monroe Center Cemetery, Grand Traverse, Michigan. They had two sons: Calvin Junior Spangler (192-2015) and Clyde A. Spangler (1940-2013),

References: US Census: 1870, 1880, 1900, 1910, 1920, 1930, 1940; Oakwood Cemetery records, Traverse City, Michigan; Monroe Center, Grand Traverse, Michigan; Michigan Marriage Records 1867-1952; Michigan Death Records 1867-1952.

120.

Arrie Gertrude Fuller, daughter of James (34), granddaughter of James (7), b. Mendon, Michigan August 28, 1870, d. Lansing, Michigan July 19, 1918; m. (1) Allegan, Michigan September 23, 1891, George W. Beadle, b. Michigan 1870, d. Allegan County, Michigan 1893; m. (2) Mendon, Michigan November 29, 1896 Alpheus Williams, b. LaGrange, Indiana February 14, 1859, d. Berwyn, Illinois, March 20, 1930. George Beadle was buried in Hillside Cemetery, Plainwell, Michigan. Arrie Williams was buried in Mt. Hope Cemetery, Lansing, Michigan. Alpheus Williams was buried in Mt. Auburn Memorial Park, Stickney, Illinois.

Children (by second marriage):

268.   I.   **Treasure Williams**, b. Michigan August 29, 1898, d. Illinois October 1975; m. Lansing, Michigan December 30, 1917, Gerald Hinterman, b. Michigan October 11, 1888, d. Illinois June 1972. Gerald was a mechanic with the Telephone Company in Berwyn, Illinois, in 1930 and an inspector in Berwyn in 1940. They had three children: Margaret Ruth (1919-2015), Mary Elizabeth (1921-2015), and Evelyne (1923-2015)). According to the 1920 and 1930 US Census Records, Gerald Williams resided with his sister. It is not known where Treasure and Gerald Hinterman were buried.

269.   II.   **Gerald A. Williams**, b. Wexford, Michigan April 8, 1908,

d. Berwyn, Illinois July 27, 1988; m. Chicago May 22, 1935, Eleanore Katherine Hohit, b. 1911, d. Berwyn, Illinois, July 19, 1988. Gerald and Eleanore had two daughters. Gerald and his wife were buried in Arlington Cemetery, Elmhurst, Illinois.

References: US Census: 1880, 1900, 1910, 1920, 1930, 1940; Michigan Marriage Index 1867-1952; Hillside Cemetery records, Plainwell, Michigan; Mt. Hope Cemetery records, Lansing, Michigan; Mt. Auburn Memorial Park records, Stickney, Illinois; Arlington Cemetery records, Elmhurst, Illinois; Cook County Marriage Index 1930-1960; Cook County Death Index 1908-1988.

121.

Anna C. Fuller, daughter of James (34), granddaughter of James (7), b. Allegan, Michigan August 30, 1876, d. Otsego, Michigan, October 22, 1933, from pneumonia and melancholia; m. (1) Michigan September 4, 1906, William H. Noble, b. New York October 15, 1862, d. Kalamazoo, Michigan January 6, 1922, divorced by Mr. Noble on the grounds of extreme cruelty April 29, 1909; m. (2) South Haven, Michigan August 22, 1912, William H. Noble, her first husband; m. (3) Allegan, Michigan December 31, 1928 Freeman Elijah Schoolcraft, b. Allegan County, Michigan December 31, 1877, d. Kalamazoo, Michigan, May 11, 1957. William Noble was married to Ida Seeley (1887-1904), with whom he had three daughters and two sons. Between Mr. Noble's two marriages to Anna Fuller, he was married to Harriet Dailey, whom he divorced in 1912. Anna was buried in Mountain Home Cemetery, Otsego, Illinois with her son, Clermond. William Noble was buried in St. Margaret Cemetery, Kalamazoo, Michigan with his first wife. Freeman Schoolcraft was buried in Hillside Cemetery, Plainwell, Michigan, with his second wife.

Children (by second marriage):

270. I. *Clermond M. Noble*, b. Michigan April 28, 1913, d. Michigan April 30, 1928 from an accidental drowning while sailing a boat. He was buried in Mountain Home Cemetery with his mother.

271. II. *Virginia Tee Noble*, b. Michigan April 12, 1917, d. Michigan

November 2, 1996; m. Kalamazoo, Michigan December 13, 1939, Gulle Kenneth Lamphere, b. 1918, d. 1996. They were buried in Riverside Cemetery, Kalamazoo, Michigan.

References: US Census: 1880, 1900, 1920, 1930, 1940; Riverside Cemetery records, Kalamazoo, Michigan; Mountain Home Cemetery records, Otsego, Michigan; Hillside Cemetery records, Plainwell, Michigan; St. Margaret Cemetery records, Kalamazoo, Michigan; Michigan Marriage Index 1867-1952; Michigan Divorce Records 1897-1952; Michigan Death Records 1867-1952.

123.

Grover Cleveland Fuller, son of James (34), grandson of James (7), b. Allegan, Michigan July 6, 1885/1886, d. place and date not known; m. Hennepin, Minnesota July 5, 1910 Mary/Marie Schultz. Mr. Fuller was described in 1942 as being 5' 2" tall, weighed 120 pounds with blonde hair and blue eyes. He was employed by Liggett Drug Store in Chicago. Grover Fuller resided in Saugatuck, Michigan (1900), Haskell, Oklahoma (1910), Linton, North Dakota (1920), and in 1930 in Minneapolis, Minnesota. There was no further documentation for Grove Fuller after his World War II Draft Registration Card, 1942. Mr. and Mrs. Fuller did not have any children. It is not known where they were buried.

References: US Census: 1900, 1910, 1920, 1930; World War II Draft Registration Card, 1942; Minnesota Marriage Index 1849-1950.

124.

Elmer Ellsworth Fuller, son of Henry (38), grandson of William (8), b. Nunda, New York March 20, 1868, d. Kansas April 1, 1900; m. Nemaha, Kansas September 11, 1894 Catherine Viola Rockefeller, b. Nebraska May 13, 1877, d. Wilkinsburg, Pennsylvania July 18, 1931 from tuberculosis. In 1898 Mr. Fuller was employed with a newspaper and resided with his family in Iowa. Elmer Fuller was buried in Fairview Cemetery, Smith Center, Kansas. Catherine Fuller remarried Nunda, New York November 9, 1902 Harry McKeown. The marriage did not last and they were probably divorced sometime between the 1910 US Census and the 1915 New York

State Census. In future census records, Catherine listed herself as a widow. Harry McKeown, b. Nunda, New York April 30, 1877, d. Dalton, New York January 24, 1968 remarried and had two sons. Catherine Fuller ran a boarding house in 1910 and 1915 in Perry, New York. By 1930 she moved to Wilkinsburg, Pennsylvania where her son resided and ran a boarding house there. Catherine Fuller was buried in Glenwood Cemetery, Perry, New York.

Children:

272.   I.   *Esther Rose Fuller*, b. Nemaha, Kansas April 11, 1896, d. Greensburg, Pennsylvania September 21, 1987; m. Perry, New York June 24, 1914 Earl William Courtney, b. 1893, d. March 30, 1971. They were buried in Glenwood Cemetery, Perry, New York.

Children:

i.   *Glen Earvin Courtney*, b. Perry, New York November 28, 1915, d. Dade County, Florida July 18, 1992; m. Florida November 26, 1939 Marie Mutz. His World War II Draft Registration Card described him as 5'9" tall, weighing 145 pounds, with red hair and green eyes. He was employed in Wilkinsburg, Pennsylvania, with Kee Lox Manufacturing in 1942. It is not known where he was buried.

273.   II.   *Glenn Ore Fuller*, b. Belmond, Iowa September 13, 1898, d. Pinellas, Florida May 15, 1990; m. Perry, New York June 9, 1926, Marion Luella Barrett, b. December 27, 1899, d. September 8, 1983. Mr. Fuller was employed as a drafting engineer and resided in Wilkinsburg, Pennsylvania. His World War II Draft Registration Card described him as 5'11" tall, weighing 160 pounds, with brown hair and blue eyes. In 1942, he was employed by Westinghouse. Glenn and Marion Fuller were buried in Glenwood Cemetery, Perry, New York.

Children:

i.   *Infant Fuller*, b. Wilkinsburg, Pennsylvania October 11, 1927, d. Wilkinsburg, Pennsylvania, October

13, 1927, from a cerebral Hemorrhage. It is not known where the child was buried.

ii. **Sally Fuller**, b. New York 1933; no further information.

References: US Census: 1870, 1880, 1900, 1910, 1920, 1930, 1940; New York State Census: 1875; Fairview Cemetery records, Smith Center, Kansas; Glenwood Cemetery records, Perry, New York; Kansas Marriage Records 1811-1911; Pennsylvania Death Certificates 1906-1966 for Katherine Fuller and Infant Fuller; New York State Marriage Records 1907-1936; Iowa Birth Records 1856-1944 for Glenn Fuller; New York State Marriage Records 1881-1967; New York State Birth Index 1881-1942; World War II Draft Registration Card 1942; Florida Marriage Index 1927-2001.

126.

Jennie Paine, daughter of Mary (39), granddaughter of William (8), b. Nunda, New York February 1, 1868, d. Camden, New York April 8, 1952; m. 1889 Fred Wellington Edgett, b. New York February 15, 1864, d. Split Rock, New York July 2, 1918. Fred and his son Harold were tragically killed July 2, 1918 at the munitions plant where they worked in Split Rock, New York along with forty-eight other workers. A fire started when a bearing overheated. The Semet-Solvay Company was closed by the end of the 1918 and never reopened. Jennie Edgett moved to Syracuse, New York where she resided with her son, Roy, and daughter, Frances. Jennie and Fred Edgett were buried in Woodlawn Cemetery, Sandy Creek, New York.

Children:

274. I. **Frances M. Edgett**, b. New York State 1891, d. Syracuse, New York, September 11, 1971, and buried in Woodlawn Cemetery. She never married and resided with her mother and/or brother. She was employed as an elevator operator in a dry goods store and later as a nurse.

275. II. **Maude Louise Edgett**, b. New York State 1892, d. Sandy Creek, New York, August 11, 1918, from grief over the death of her father and brother who died at Split Rock, New York. She was buried in Woodlawn Cemetery.

276. III. ***Roy Wellington Edgett***, b. Erie, Pennsylvania April 22, 1896, d. Syracuse, New York, August 24, 1983. His World War II Draft Registration Card, 1942, recorded he was employed by New Process Gear Company, Camden, New York, and was 5'10 ½ "tall, weighed 230 pounds with a ruddy complexion, brown hair, and eyes. It is not known where he was buried.

277. IV. ***Harold Nathan Edgett***, b. New York State 1897, d. Split Rock, New York, in a munitions explosion on July 2, 1918; m. Sandy Creek, New York April 28, 1917 Edna Mary Roberts, b. 1894, d. New York State October 14, 1967. Edna Edgett was a school teacher at Sandy Creek Central School for 43 years, retiring in 1963. Their daughter was born posthumously. Harold and Edna were buried in Woodlawn Cemetery, Sandy Creek, New York.

>Children:
>
>i. ***Betty Norine Edgett***, b. New York State 1919, d. November 26, 1999; m. 1942 James Ward Carey, b. Lacona, New York July 17, 1915, d. Watertown, New York, May 20, 1994. Mr. Carey was a meat cutter and later a custodian for Sandy Creek Schools. They had two children: Patricia and Patrick. Betty and James Carey were buried in Woodlawn Cemetery, Sandy Creek, New York.

278. V. ***Ralph C. Edgett***, b. Sandy Creek, New York March 28, 1907, d. New York State June 6, 1952; m. Weedsport, New York September 13, 1936, Dorothy G. Callen, b. 1913, d. 2004. Mr. Edgett was a mechanic. They had one child, James, b. 1937. Ralph Edgett's World War II Draft Registration Card noted that he was employed at John J. Costello Buick in Syracuse, New York. He resided in Oswego, New York, was 6' 3" tall, weighed 180 pounds, and had brown hair, eyes, and a crooked nose. Ralph and Dorothy Edgett were buried in South Onondaga Cemetery, South Onondaga, New York.

References: US Census: 1870, 1880, 1900, 1910, 1920, 1930, 1940; New York State Census: 1905, 1915, 1925; New York State Birth Index 1881-1942; New York State Marriage Index 1881-1952; South Onondaga

Cemetery records, South Onondaga, New York; World War II Draft Registration Cards 1942; Woodlawn Cemetery records, Sandy Creek, New York; Syracuse Post Standard August 13, 1918 obituary for Maude Edgett;

129.

Harry Rolison, son of Mary (39), grandson of William (8), b. Nunda, New York February 19, 1885/1886, d. Rochester, New York hospital December 9, 1942; m. Mt. Morris, New York July 2, 1906, Edith May Heliker, b. 1886, d. 1959. Interviews with descendants of Harry Rolison indicated that he never knew who his mother was and even claimed he was adopted. Mr. Rolison never talked about his parentage to his children. The 1900 US Census noted he resided with his paternal grandmother and father in Nunda, New York. By 1910 he moved to nearby Mt. Morris, where he began a career as a printer, later becoming the editor and owner of the Mt. Morris newspaper. His World War II Draft Registration Card described him as being 5' 11" tall, weighing 178 pounds with gray eyes, and being bald. It is assumed that Harry and Edith Rolison were buried in Mount Morris Cemetery, Mt. Morris, but there is no confirmation of that from records.

Children:

279. I. **Harry Bruce Rolison**, b. Mt. Morris September 2, 1918, d. Perry, New York August 17, 1994; m. Mt. Morris, New York July 29, 1944 Madeline Louise Jennings, b. Groton, New York June 24, 1919, d. Geneseo, New York December 1, 2006. Mr. Rolison was employed by the Picket Line Post. His World War II Draft Registration Card described him as 5' 11" tall, weighing 170 pounds, with gray eyes and blonde hair. Mrs. Rolison was a teacher at Mr. Morris Schools until her retirement in 1976. Madeline Rolison was buried in Mt. Morris City Cemetery, Mt. Morris, and it is assumed that Harry Rolison was also buried there, but there is no record to confirm this.

Children:

i. **Linda Jean Rolison** b. Mt. Morris, New York August 28, 1947, d. Loris, South Carolina April 14, 2013; m. Mt.

Morris October 1, 1966, David A. Bush. They did not have any children and were buried in Mt. Morris City Cemetery.

    ii.   **Harry Bruce Rolison, Jr.**, b. Mt. Morris February 6, 1955, d. Mt. Morris, New York, September 15, 1976, due to a head-on collision of his car with a truck. It is believed that he was buried in Mt. Morris City Cemetery.

280.   II.   *Carol V. Rolison*, b. New York July 1, 1923, d. Mt. Morris, New York November 17, 2008; m. Harold McCormick. They had two children: a daughter and a son, David H. McCormick, b. September 25, 1955, d. Great Barrington, Massachusetts, May 28, 2012. It is not known where they were buried.

281.   III.   *Jerry Watson Rolison*, b Mt. Morris, New York December 31, 1927, d. Mt. Morris, New York October 13, 2015; m. Mt. Morris, New York, July 9, 1955 Evelyne Chiappone. Mr. Rolison owned and operated the Mt. Morris Shopper starting in 1956 and until he retired 56 ½ years later. They had five children: Jerry, Jeffrey Paul Rolison, Sr., b. Dansville, New York November 18, 1965, d. Mt. Morris, New York November 15, 2020 who married and had two children, Jessica and Jeffrey, James, John, and Janet, b. Dansville, New York October 15, 1957, d. Mt. Morris, New York, July 12, 2011. Jerry, Evelyne, Janet, and Jeffrey Rolison, Sr. were all buried in Assumption Cemetery, Portageville, New York.

References: US Census: 1900, 1910, 1920, 1930, 1940; New York State Census: 1915, 1925; Assumption Cemetery records, Portageville, New York; Mt. Morris City Cemetery records, Mt. Morris, New York; World War II Draft Registration Card, 1942; New York State Marriage Index 1881-1967; New York State Death Index 1880-1956.

132.

William Samuel Drury, son of Martha (40), grandson of William (8), b. Michigan October 13, 1874, d. Kalamazoo, Michigan February 1965; m. (1) Kalamazoo, Michigan January 20, 1894 Louise Marie Pfau, b. Germany 1877, d. Los Angeles, California August 21, 1930, divorced; m. (2) Kalamazoo, Michigan September 1, 1900 Mary Emma Staley, b.

Otsego, Michigan May 29, 1875, d. Kalamazoo, Michigan May 25, 1924. William Drury resided with his parents in Holland, Michigan in 1880. The 1900 US Census found him residing in Kalamazoo, Michigan with his mother and stepfather where he was employed as a wood finisher. The rest of Mr. Drury's career was in Kalamazoo where he worked for the Kalamazoo Paper Company as a truck driver or foreman. After his second wife's death William Drury resided alone with a housekeeper in 1930 and in 1940 with his daughter and youngest sons. His World War I Draft Registration Card described him as being slender and of medium build with blue eyes and light brown hair. William and Mary Drury were buried in Riverside Cemetery, Kalamazoo, Michigan. Louise Pfau Fuller remarried 1899 Frank Elliott Fisher. Her burial location is not known.

Children (by first marriage):

282. I. *Florence Drury*, b. Kalamazoo, Michigan July 7, 1894, d. Osteoma, Michigan March 23, 1972; m. 1917 Charles John Weaver, b. Kalamazoo, Michigan August 16, 1894, d. Waimanalo, Hawaii January 15, 1961. Mr. Weaver was previously married and divorced. Florence Fuller Weaver was buried in Riverside Cemetery, Kalamazoo, Michigan. It is not known where Charles Weaver was buried.

Children (by second marriage):

283. I. *Harry Herbert Drury*, b. Michigan May 28, 1900, d. place not known, 1961; m. Kalamazoo, Michigan May 5, 1923 Mary Vermeulan, b. 1905, d. 1969, divorced Duval, Florida 1946. Harry Drury was employed as a truck driver for the Kalamazoo Paper Company. He and Mary had three children. Although divorced, they were buried together in Mount Ever-Rest Memorial Park South, Kalamazoo, Michigan.

Children:

i. *Dorothy Drury*, b. Michigan December 13, 1923, d. Paw Vermeulen, Michigan November 1980; m. Mr. Coy. No further information.

ii. *Robert William Drury*, b. Michigan July 14, 1925, d. January 6, 1990; m. Kalamazoo, Michigan September

30, 1945, Viola M. Noble, b. Lawrence, Ohio August 24, 1925, d. May 12, 1925. Robert Drury served with the US Navy in WW II from July 7, 1943 to August 20, 1945. He was buried in Arlington National Cemetery, Arlington, Virginia. Viola remarried to Jack Rodarmer, b. 1927, d. 2009. Viola was buried with her second husband in Mount Ever-Rest Memorial Park. It is believed that Robert and Viola had at least one child. A female Drury infant was b. and d. September 11, 1948, and was buried in Riverside Cemetery, Kalamazoo, Michigan.

    iii.   ***Richard Drury***, b. 1927. No further information.

284.   II.   ***William Glenn Drury***, b. Sturgis, Michigan August 6, 1904, d. October 1961; m. (1) Goshen, Indiana December 20, 1928 Eylla Winona Johnson, divorced Kalamazoo, Michigan April 3, 1934; m. (2) Tillie, whose last name is not known. William Drury was a truck driver with the Sutherland Paper Company in Kalamazoo, Michigan. His World War II Draft Registration Card described him as being 5' 11" tall, weighing 170 pounds, with blue eyes, blonde hair, and scars from an operation on the left side of his ribs. He did not have any children with his first wife. William Glenn Drury was buried in South Portage Cemetery, Portage, Michigan. The burial locations of his two wives are not known.

References: US Census: 1880, 1900, 1910, 1920, 1930, 1940; World War I Draft Registration Card, 1918; South Portage Cemetery Records, Portage, Michigan; World War II Draft Registration Card, 1940; Michigan Birth Index 1867-1911; Riverside Cemetery Records, Kalamazoo, Michigan; Michigan Marriage Index 1867-1952; Mount Ever-Rest Memorial Park South, Kalamazoo, Michigan; Arlington National Cemetery Records, Arlington, Virginia; Michigan Divorce Records 1897-1952; US Veterans Death Index 1850-2010 for Robert Drury.

133.

Edward Franklin Drury, son of Martha (40), grandson of William (8), b. Kalamazoo, Michigan April 11, 1878/April 10, 1879, d. Los Angeles, California March 18, 1949; m. (1) Munising, Michigan October 6, 1909

Gertrude S. Gibbard, divorced Michigan December 1, 1919; m. (2) Kalamazoo, Michigan July 24, 1920 Louise Swandrlik, b. May 17, 1897, d. March 12, 1980. Edward Drury worked for as a grocery store manager and later as a superintendent in both Detroit, Michigan and later in Alhambra and San Gabriel, California. They had one child, Donald Drury, b. Detroit, Michigan May 4, 1921. Edward Drury was buried in Forest Lawn Memorial Park, Glendale, California. Louise remarried to a Mr. Swan.

References: US Census: 1880, 1900, 1910, 1920, 1930, 1940; Michigan Birth Index 1867-1911; Riverside Cemetery records, Kalamazoo, Michigan; Michigan Marriage Index 1867-1952; California Death Index 1905-1939 for Louise Pfau Fisher; South Portage Cemetery records, Portage, Michigan; Michigan Divorce Index 1897-1952; World War II Draft Registration Card, 1942; World War I Draft Registration Card 1917-1918; Florida Divorce Index 1927-2001 for Harry Drury; Mount Ever-Rest Memorial Park South records, Kalamazoo, Michigan; Arlington National Cemetery records, Arlington, Virginia; US Veterans Death Index 1850-2010 for Robert Drury; Forest Lawn Memorial Park, Glendale, California.

134.

William Arthur Fuller, son of Arthur (41), grandson of William (9), b. Nunda, New York November 16, 1879, d. Kalamazoo, Michigan May 6, 1951; m. (1) Kalamazoo, Michigan June 23, 1903 Anna Elizabeth Meyers, b. Indiana October 23, 1884, d. Michigan 1965, divorced Kalamazoo, Michigan April 27, 1915 for wife's adultery; m. (2) Kalamazoo, Michigan December 1, 1915 Pearl L. Hooven, b. Chicago, Illinois July 4, 1892, d. Kalamazoo, Michigan May 5, 1926 by suicide, divorced; m. (3) Michigan by 1926 Luella M., last name not known, b. Illinois January 1, 1895, d. Kalamazoo, Michigan February 20, 1967. In the 1900 US Census Mr. Fuller was employed as a farm laborer in Mt. Morris, New York. Soon after he moved to Kalamazoo, Michigan where he married. William Fuller was employed by the Kalamazoo Paper Company rising to the position of foreman. His World War I Draft Registration Card described him as being of medium height and weight with blue eyes and red hair. Anna Meyers Fuller married twice more after their divorce. Her second husband was Ethan Peeke whom she married in 1916 and divorced in 1927. Anna's third husband was Herbert Bell. Anna was buried with her third husband and his first wife in Riverside Cemetery, Union City, Michigan. Pearl Fuller was previously married to John Miller. She committed suicide in front of her home using a shot gun. Pearl Fuller was buried in Riverside Cemetery, Kalamazoo, Michigan. William Fuller had a son by his first marriage. Some census and genealogical records list his first wife's daughter, Doris, as William Fuller's child, but she was not. William and Luella Fuller were buried in Riverside Cemetery, Kalamazoo, Michigan.

Children (by first marriage):

285. I. *Charles Clinton Fuller*, b. Kalamazoo, Michigan April 1, 1910, d. Alexandria, Virginia April 17, 2007; m. Battle Creek, Michigan September 23, 1935, Doris Hazel Wycoff, b. Michigan July 23, 1914, d. Alexandria, Virginia, September 8, 2007. Charles and Doris Fuller were buried in Presbyterian Cemetery in Alexandria, Virginia.

Children:

i. *Julie Ann Fuller*, b. 1939. She was listed in the 1945 Florida Census as residing in Pinellas County, Florida. No further information.

ii. *Charles Thomas Fuller*, b. Michigan April 22, 1942, d. April 13, 2007. His remains were cremated. No further information.

References: US Census: 1880, 1900, 1910, 1920, 1930, 1940; Michigan Marriage Records 1867-1952 for William Fuller's first marriage; Michigan Death Records 1897-1952 for William Fuller's first and second wives; World War I Draft Registration Card 1917-1918; World War II Draft Registration Card 1942; Michigan Death Records 1867-1995 for William Fuller; Riverside Cemetery records, Kalamazoo, Michigan; Kalamazoo City Director 1926; Riverside Cemetery record, Union City, Michigan; Presbyterian Cemetery records, Alexandria, Virginia; Florida Census: 1945.

135.

Grace Fuller, daughter of Arthur (41), granddaughter of William (8), b. Nunda, New York May 1880, d. place and date not known; m. (1) Towanda, Pennsylvania April 27, 1904 Charles C. Yocum, b. Columbia County, Pennsylvania October 1874, d. Shamokin, Pennsylvania April 13, 1924, divorced; m. (2) Mt. Morris, New York June 14, 1928 Joseph Ephraim Wheelock, b. Athens, Pennsylvania October 6, 1853, d. Athens, Pennsylvania April 18, 1930. Grace resided with her parents in Nunda, New York. The 1900 US Census recorded her residence in Windham, New York where she did housework and lived in a boarding house. After her 1904 marriage she and Charles Yocum resided in Sayre, Pennsylvania where he practiced law. They seemed to have divorced sometime after the 1920 US Census based on his death certificate, which noted that Mr. Yocum died from tuberculosis, diabetes, and a pulmonary hemorrhage. Charles Yocum was buried in Glenwood Cemetery, Waverly, New York. The 1923 and 1925 City Directories for Binghamton, New York record Grace and her daughter residing there and Grace was listed as a widow in 1923 even though Charles Yocum died in 1924. Grace's second marriage lasted about two years because Joseph Wheelock died in 1930. Mr. Wheelock was buried in Tioga Point Cemetery, Athens, Pennsylvania. Grace continued to reside in Sayre based on the 1930 and 1940 US Census. No occupation was recorded for her, but her daughter was employed as a proofreader. No records can be found for Grace Fuller Yocum Wheelock after the 1940 US Census. It is not known where she was buried.

Children (by first marriage):

286. I. *Eleanor S. Yocum*, b. Sayre, Pennsylvania 1905, d. Gardner, Massachusetts, date not known; m. Cuyahoga, Ohio October 26, 1926, Edward Harold Farnham, b. Earle, Arkansas July 28, 1904, d. Winchendon, Massachusetts, January 15, 1977.

Children:

i. *Gloria Farnham*, b. Pennsylvania December 13, 1925, d. Medway, Massachusetts March 1977.

References: US Census: 1880, 1900, 1910, 1920, 1930, 1940; New York State Census: 1925; Glenwood Cemetery records, Waverly, New York; Tioga Point Cemetery records, Athens, Pennsylvania; Pennsylvania Marriage Index 1852-1968; Pennsylvania Death Certificates 1906-1967; New York State Marriage Index 1907-1936; Ohio Marriage Records 1774-1993; Binghamton City Directories 1923 and 1925.

136.

Morris Henderson Fuller, son of Arthur (41), grandson of William (8), b. Nunda, New York July 30, 1887, d. Roscoe, Michigan August 29, 1921; m. Chicago, Illinois February 21, 1920 Evelyn Arta Graves, b. Fulton, Illinois September 19, 1889, d. Palm Beach, Florida April 1961. After his father's death, Morris resided with his mother and sister in Sayre, Pennsylvania where his mother later remarried. In 1910 Morris Fuller continued to reside in Sayre with his mother and step-father where he was employed as a tool maker in a machine shop. His World War I Draft Registration Card described him as being tall and slender with brown eyes and light brown hair. In 1918 he was employed in Chicago with the Rockwell Company as a foreman. Morris Fuller was buried in Oakwood Cemetery, Beloit, Wisconsin. It is not known why that cemetery and state. His widow remarried to Emmett J. Covell (1886-1971) and she was buried with her second husband in Hillcrest Cemetery, Albany, Wisconsin.

References: US Census: 1900, 1910, 1920; World War I Draft Registration Card 1917-1918; Cook County Marriage Index 1912-1942; Illinois Death Index 1916-1947; Oakwood Cemetery records, Beloit, Wisconsin; Hillcrest Cemetery records, Albany, Wisconsin.

139.

Roy Elwood Fuller, son of Charles (43), grandson of William (8), b. Nunda, New York October 20, 1893, d. Warsaw, New York January 17, 1934 from pneumonia; m. (1) date and place unknown, Julia, last name unknown, b. a. 1893, d. place and date not known; m. (2) Perry, New York August 12, 1916, Ruth Naomie Bailey, b. place not known August 2, 1897, d. place not known, October 17, 1960. Roy Fuller resided with his parents in Nunda and Perry, New York, based on the 1900 and 1910 US Census records. The

1915 New York State Census recorded that he lived with his parents, his wife Julia, and a son, Niles, b. a. 1914. No record could be found regarding this marriage and birth, and in 1916, Roy married Ruth Bailey. His 1916 marriage record indicated he had never been married before. Julia and Niles Fuller only appear on the 1915 New York State Census. In 1920, Roy resided with his wife, Ruth, and son Melvin, with his parents in Warsaw, New York, where Mr. Fuller was employed as a painter. The 1930 US Census found Roy Fuller and his family living in Castile, New York, where he was employed as a decorator. His World War I Draft Registration Card described Roy Fuller as medium height and weight with dark brown eyes and hair. It said he had three children, but the identities of two of the three are not known. Sometime in 1918, Roy moved his wife and son, Melvin, to DuBois, Pennsylvania, where a stillborn male infant was delivered. When Roy Fuller died, it was at the home of his mother, and there is no mention of a wife or any children in the obituary. Roy Fuller was buried in Oakwood Cemetery with his parents. There is another burial in the Charles Fuller lot for an unnamed Fuller baby who died in 1922 at the age of eleven months and twenty-two days. Ruth remarried to Mr. LacKinsa. It is not known where she was buried. Her remarriage was indicated in the World War II Draft Registration Card for her son Melvin.

Children (by second marriage):

287. I. **Melvin Fuller**, b. Warsaw, New York April 22, 1917, d. place and date not known. His World War II Draft Registration Card indicated he was 5' 8" tall, weighed 150 pounds, had a ruddy complexion and blue eyes, and blonde hair. Mr. Fuller had scars on his right eye and left leg. He was unemployed at the time of his draft registration. There is no further information on him.

288. II. **Male Fuller**, b. and d. DuBois, Pennsylvania, July 28, 1918. The baby was stillborn and buried in DuBois, Pennsylvania.

References: US Census: 1900, 1910, 1920, 1930; New York State Census: 1915; World War II Draft Registration Card 1942; Pennsylvania Death Certificate 1906-1967; New York State Marriage Index 1907-1936; Oakwood Cemetery Records for Roy Fuller and Unnamed Fuller infant; World War I Draft Registration Card 1917-18; New York State Death Index

1906-1967 for Roy Fuller.

140.

Belle Fuller, daughter of Albert (45), granddaughter of William (9), b. Nunda, New York April 16, 1881, d. Binghamton, New York December 14, 1914 from cancer; m. Olean, New York February 19, 1898 Ernest Jerome Root, b. Bolivar, New York July 15, 1873, d. Bolivar, New York July 23, 1904 by suicide. Ernest Root was employed as a blacksmith in Olean, New York and in Smethport, Pennsylvania. Belle and Ernest separated after the birth of their second child and when reconciliation failed, Mr. Root committed suicide. Belle moved to Binghamton, New York where her mother, sister, and brother resided. She operated a dress shop. Ernest Root was buried in Maple Lawn Cemetery, Bolivar, New York. Belle Root was buried in Floral Park Cemetery, Johnson City, New York.

Children:

289.   I.   *Leo C. Root.* See Abel Root, Sr. and His Descendants of Bolivar, New York by William A. Paquette for detailed biographies of Leo Root's eight children and descendants.

290.   II.   *Nordica Thelma Root* is married and has one daughter. (Same as for # 289.)

References: US Census: 1900, 1910; New York State Census: 1905; Floral Park Cemetery records, Johnson City, New York; Maple Lawn Cemetery records, Bolivar, New York.

141.

Jesse Nicholas Fuller, son of Albert (45), grandson of William (8), b. Nunda, New York January 24, 1883, d. Binghamton, New York January 24, 1934 from angina pectoris; m. Binghamton, New York June 6, 1906 Emma Graf, b. Pennsylvania May 30, 1886, d. Clearwater, Florida, January 15, 1978, from natural causes. Jesse was named for his maternal great-grandfather, Jesse Adams, Jr., and for his maternal grandfather, Nicholas Adams. He was employed with the Endicott Johnson Shoe Company, as was his wife, Emma. They did not have any children. Emma Fuller retired to Clearwater, Florida. Her remains were cremated and returned for burial in Floral Park Cemetery, Johnson City, New York, near Jesse Fuller's remains.

References: US Census: 1900, 1910, 1920, 1930, 1940; New York State Census: 1905, 1915, 1925; Floral Park Cemetery records, Johnson City, New York; January 18, 1978 obituary for Emma Fuller.

142.

Louise Fuller, daughter of Albert (45), granddaughter of William (8), b. Nunda, New York February 1884, d. Binghamton, New York March 15, 1904 from pneumonia after a five-day illness; m. Binghamton, New York November 20, 1901 Charles E. Hungerford, b. Broome County, New York August 15, 1880, d. Conklin, New York April 28, 1942. Louise and Charles Hungerford did not have any children. She was buried in the Hungerford lot in Floral Park Cemetery, Johnson City, New York next to her mother. There is no headstone. Charles Hungerford remarried twice more. Charles Hungerford was buried with his third wife in Calvary Cemetery, Johnson City, New York.

References: US Census: 1900, 1910, 1920, 1930, 1940; New York State Census: 1905, 1915, 1925; Floral Park Cemetery records, Johnson City, New York; New York State Marriage Index 1881-1967; New York State Death Index 1852-1956; Calvary Cemetery records, Johnson City, New York.

144.

Donald Robert Fuller, son of Albert (45), grandson of William (8), b. Kalamazoo, Michigan October 15, 1905, d. Punta Garda, Florida May 31, 1976; m. (1) Michigan February 7, 1925 Theodora Blanche Waite, b. Almena, Michigan March 4, 1905, d. Kalamazoo, Michigan October 3, 1957, divorced Michigan June 7, 1930; m. (2) Michigan May 10, 1931 Florence M. Raymond, b. Watseka, Illinois March 22, 1903, d. Kalamazoo, Michigan June 15, 1985, divorced Kalamazoo, Michigan September 17, 1938; m. (3) Indiana October 15, 1938 Sadie, last name not known, divorced March 1, 1941 for cruelty and non-support; m. (4) Ohio November 25, 1941 Garnet

J., Upson, divorced Kalamazoo, Michigan November 17, 1952; m. (5) place and date not known, Arlene Patricia Briney, b. Watervliet, Michigan September 1, 1921, d. Polk, Florida March 4, 1986. Divorce records indicate that Donald Fuller did not have any children by his first wife; one by his second wife; none by his third and fourth wives, and one by his fifth wife. Donald Fuller's World War II Draft Registration Card described Mr. Fuller as being 5' 6" tall, weighed 200 pounds and had blue eyes and red hair. He was employed in 1942 by the Fuller Manufacturing Company of Kalamazoo, Michigan. While married to his fifth wife, Donald Fuller owned and operated with Arlene the Fuller Nursing Home, Eau Claire, Michigan and the Fuller Manufacturing Company, Kalamazoo. Theodora Fuller remarried to Louis Whetham (1906-1982) and was buried with her second husband in Almena Cemetery, Paw Esau, Michigan. Florence Fuller was previously married to William J. Murphy with whom she had two children before divorcing in 1928. Florence was buried in Mt. Ever-Rest Memorial Park South, Kalamazoo, Michigan. Burial information on Mr. Fuller's third and fourth wives is not known. Donald and Arlene Fuller's remains were cremated and given to their son, Albert D. Fuller, Sr.

Children (by second marriage):

291. I. **Donna Fuller**, b. Kalamazoo, Michigan February 14, 1932; m. (1) Indiana January 21, 1950, Donald Dee Shirah, b. Kalamazoo, Michigan November 15, 1928, d. Battle Creek, Michigan December 25, 2014, divorced; m. (2) Michigan September 22, 1973, Stewart Leonard Reger, b. Delton, Michigan August 1, 1925, d. Kalamazoo, Michigan July 24, 2012. Mr. Reger was buried in Hope Cemetery, Texas Corners, Michigan. Donna had three children by her first husband: Ronald (1950-2020), Donald, Jr. (b. and d. May 10, 1952), and Steven. She had a fourth child, Shelby, but it is unclear whether the father was her first or second husband.

Children (by fifth marriage):

292. I. **Albert D. Fuller**, Sr., b. Michigan July 1, 1951/52; m. (1) June Alice Taylor; m. (2) Sharon Emsperger; m. (3) Linda, last name not known. He had a daughter, Patricia, and a son, Albert Jr., by his first marriage.

References: US Census: 1910, 1920, 1930, 1940; Indiana Marriage Records 1810-2001; Michigan Marriage Records 1822-1940; Michigan Divorce Records 1897-1952; Social Security Death Index 1935-2014; World War I Draft Registration Card 1942; Almena Cemetery Paw Asperger, Michigan; Mt. Ever-Rest Memorial Park South, Kalamazoo, Michigan; Florida Death Index 1877-1998; News Palladium, Benton Harbor, Michigan October 24, 1959; Hope Cemetery records, Texas Corners, Michigan; Kalamazoo Gazette, November 26, 1941 for Donald Fuller's fourth marriage.

145.

William Edward Warren, son of Edward (47), grandson of Maria (9), b. Buffalo, New York October 1869, d. Los Angeles, California October 11, 1940 suicide by hanging; m. Shelbina, Missouri December 25, 1893, Abbie Norris, b. Shelbina, Missouri November 21, 1873, d. Cedar Rapids, Iowa, November 12, 1949, from a perforated ulcer on the lower esophagus. William Warren resided in Buffalo, New York, in 1910, where he was employed as a yardmaster. In 1910, Mr. Warren and his family lived in Cranston, Rhode Island, where he continued to be employed as a yardmaster. By 1920, they moved to Iowa Falls, Iowa, where he was a train master. William and Abbie Warren later moved to Cedar Rapids, Iowa, where he was employed by the railroad. For reasons not documented, he was committed to a sanitarium in Rosemead, California, where he committed suicide by hanging. William Warren's remains were cremated and interred in Savannah Memorial Park Cemetery, Rosemead, California. Abbie Warren was buried in Oak Hill Cemetery, Cedar Rapids, Iowa, with other members of the Warren family.

Children:

293. I. *Frank Norris Warren*, b. Buffalo, New York October 10, 1894, d. Iowa City, Iowa January 19, 1962; m. (1) place and date not known, Etta Walton; m. (2) Cedar Rapids, Iowa October 1943 Roselyn Augusta Griffith Cooper. Mr. Warren was buried in Oak Hill Cemetery, Cedar Rapids, Iowa. It is not known if he had any children or where his wives were buried.

294. II. *Twin Warrens*, b. and d. Cedar Rapids, Iowa, August 30,

1908, and buried in Oak Hill Cemetery, Cedar Rapids, Iowa.

References: US Census: 1870, 1880, 1900, 1910, 1920, 1930, 1940; Oak Hill Cemetery records, Cedar Rapids, Iowa; Savannah Memorial Park Cemetery records, Rosemead, California; Missouri Marriage Records 1805-2020; California Death Index 1940-1997; Cedar Rapids Gazette November 12, 1949 obituary for Abbie Warren; Iowa Marriage Records 1880-1951 for Frank Warren.

146.

Archie Frederick Warren, son of Edward (47), grandson of Maria (9), b. New Castle, Indiana November 4, 1899, d. Whitewater, Wisconsin September 21, 1971; m. place not known, 1925 Lucille Atkinson, b. Shopiere, Wisconsin July 27, 1904, d. Janesville, Wisconsin, February 21, 1994. Mr. Warren's World War I Draft Registration Card described him as tall and slender with brown hair and gray eyes. He was a student at Purdue University. His World War II Draft Registration Card noted he was 6' tall and weighed 140 pounds with brown hair and gray eyes. In 1942, Mr. Warren was employed by the Chevrolet Motor Company. In 1910, he resided in Iowa Falls, Iowa, and was employed as a machinist. By 1930, he moved to Beloit, Wisconsin, where Archie managed a clothing store. The 1940 US Census found him living in Milton, Wisconsin, where he worked as a checker. Archie and Lucille Warren were buried in Oak Hill Cemetery, Janesville, Wisconsin.

Children:

295. I. *Robert Archie Warren*, b. Janesville, Wisconsin June 19, 1928, d. Windermere, Florida, April 21, 2021. Mr. Warren graduated from Milton College and was employed as a chemist and later worked for Burgess Battery Company. Robert Warren eventually owned 46 McDonald's franchises across several states. He was married and divorced. His wife's identity is not known. He had a daughter, Kristin. Robert Warren was cremated, and the location of his remains is not known.

296. II. *James E. Warren*, b. 1935; married and had three sons: David, Mark, and Paul.

References: US Census: 1900, 1910, 1920, 1930, 1940; Wisconsin Death Index 1959-1997; Oak Hill Cemetery records, Janesville, Wisconsin; World War I Draft Registration Card 1917-18; World War II Draft Registration Card 1942; Wisconsin State Journal September 25, 1971 for Archie Warren; Obituary posted on Findagrave.com for Robert Archie Warren.

147.

Lillian F. Warren, daughter of Edward (47), granddaughter of Maria (9), b. Indiana August 21, 1902, d. San Bernardino, California February 27, 1995; m. (1) place and date not known, Robert Conway, b. Wisconsin 1892, d. Grove, Wisconsin March 5, 1936; m. (2) Riverside, California June 12, 1954 William C. Merritt, divorced Miami, Florida September 16, 1993. Robert Conway was employed as a bank cashier in Janesville, Wisconsin at the time of his death. He was buried in Emerald Grove Cemetery, Emerald Grove, Wisconsin. It is not known where Lillian Warren was buried.

Children (by first marriage):

297. I. *Jean Conway*, b. Wisconsin December 26, 1923, d. San Bernadino, California September 5, 2007; m. Riverside, California September 14, 1947, Charles Gibbs Palmer, b. Ohio June 7, 1923, d. San Bernadino, California May 13, 2005. They had three children: Christine Palmer (1943-2017), who married Steven L. Richtman, and another daughter and a son.

298. II. *Betty Ann Conway*, b. Janesville, Wisconsin, January 8, 1927, d. Janesville, Wisconsin October 7, 2013; m. November 24, 1948, Wallace H. Ebert, b. Wisconsin October 8, 1927, d. Rock County, Wisconsin March 17, 2001. Betty and Wallace Ebert were buried in Milton Lawns Memorial Park, Janesville, Wisconsin.

299. III. *Alice Conway*, Wisconsin April 14, 1928; m. Winnebago, Illinois February 18, 1950, Roger L. Sprocher; no further information.

300. IV. *Richard Warren Conway*, b. Janesville, Wisconsin November 30, 1930, b. Edgerton, Wisconsin August 16, 2011; m. September 9, 1955, Elizabeth Betty Beyer, b. 1931. Mr. Conway served in the US Military as part of the Honor Guard for General MacArthur in

Tokyo. He later served as a security guard for General Motors until getting his chiropractic degree, which he practiced until retirement in 1996. Mr. and Mrs. Warren had four children: Susan, William, Peter, and Steven.

References: US Census: 1910, 1920, 1930, 1940; Emerald Grove Cemetery records, Emerald Grove, Wisconsin; Milton Lawns Memorial Park records, Janesville, Wisconsin; WPA Birth Index 1880-1920 for Lillian Warren; California Marriage Index 1949-1959; Florida Divorce Index 1927-2001; Findagrave.com obituary for Richard Warren Conway.

148.

Richard Bryan Warren, son of Edward (47), grandson of Maria (9), b. New Castle, Indiana July 9, 1908, d. St. Paul, Minnesota March 24, 1996; m. Niles, Michigan December 22, 1934 Evelyn R. Roebeck, b. Niles, Michigan 1912, d. Michigan 2004. Mr. Warren was a teacher and later Superintendent of Schools for Niles, Michigan. They had two children: Maudella, b. 1936 and Richard C., b. 1939. Richard and Evelyn Warren were buried in Silverbrook Cemetery, Niles, Michigan.

References: US Census: 1910, 1920, 1930, 1940; Indiana Birth Certificates 1907-1940; Michigan Marriage Records 1867-1952; Silverbrook Cemetery records, Niles, Michigan.

149.

Charlotte Warren, daughter of Edward (47), granddaughter of Maria (9), b. New Castle, Indiana January 9, 1911, d. Evanston, Illinois July 21, 2004; m. place and date not known, Gordon Schieltz, b. 1910, d. 2002. Mr. Schieltz was employed as a machinist. They had one son: Gary. 1940. Charlotte and Gordon Schieltz were buried in Sunset Memory Gardens, Madison, Wisconsin.

References: US Census: 1920, 1930, 1940; Sunset Memory Gardens records, Madison, Wisconsin.

150.

Grace M. Parker is the daughter of Julia (48) and granddaughter of Maria (9), Grove, New York April 9, 1872, d. Bradford, Pennsylvania August 15, 1951; m. place and date not known, Frank Peterson, b. 1853, d. May 31, 1920. Grace resided with her parents in Dalton, New York, in 1880, but by 1900, she had married and moved to Bradford, Pennsylvania, where she spent the rest of her life. Frank Peterson was a carpenter. In 1910, Mr. Peterson was employed as an oil well pumper and worked as a carpenter until his death. Grace remained in Bradford, raising her children. She died from a cerebral hemorrhage. Grace and Frank Peterson were buried in Oak Hill Cemetery, Bradford, Pennsylvania.

Children:

301. I. ***Eva Charlene Peterson***, b. Limestone, Pennsylvania May 28, 1898, d. Sligo, Pennsylvania November 19, 1983; m. Bradford, Pennsylvania April 4, 1923, Jay Nelson Callen, b. Falls Creek, Pennsylvania February 9, 1902, d. Pennsylvania July 3, 1966, from a heart attack. Mr. Callen was a farmer in Monroe, Pennsylvania, and worked for Owens-Illinois Glass Plant in Clarion, Pennsylvania. They had three children. Eva and Jay Callen were buried in Sligo Cemetery, Sligo, Pennsylvania.

Children:

i. ***Betty Callen***; m. Frank Nichols, Jr. and resided in Warren, Pa.

ii. ***Robert J. Callen***, b. Sligo, Pennsylvania December 24, 1926, d. Sligo, Pennsylvania, September 13, 1995. His World War II Draft Registration Card described him as being 5' 11" tall, weighed 150 pounds with gray eyes and brown hair. He had a scar on his right index finger. He served with the US Navy during World War II. He never married and was buried in Sligo Cemetery.

iii. ***Thomas H. Callen***; no further information.

302. II. ***Donald Peterson***, b. Pennsylvania December 26, 1900, d.

Pennsylvania March 30, 1988. His World War II Draft Registration Card described him as being 5' 8" tall and weighing 140 pounds with brown hair and hazel eyes. He was employed with Smith Brothers, Bradford, Pennsylvania. Donald Peterson never married. He was buried in Oak Hill Cemetery, Bradford, Pennsylvania.

303.   III.   ***Bryan Frank Peterson***, b. Dalton, New York February 15, 1903, d. Bradford, Pennsylvania December 28, 1977. In the 1920s, Mr. Peterson was in a Reformatory in Huntington, Pennsylvania. He served with the US Army from September 29, 1942, to April 7, 1943. It is not known where he was buried.

304.   IV.   ***Florence Louise Peterson***, b. Pennsylvania August 22, 1908, d. Bradford, Pennsylvania, April 10, 1961, from cardiac failure. Florence never married, was employed as a housekeeper and was buried in Oak Hill Cemetery, Bradford, Pennsylvania.

References: US Census: 1880, 1900, 1910, 1920, 1930, 1940; Oak Hill Cemetery records, Bradford, Pennsylvania; Pennsylvania Birth Certificate 1906-1911 for Florence Peterson; World War II Draft Registration Card, 1942; US Department Death File 1850-2010 for Bryan Peterson; Social Security Death Index 1935-2014 for Donald Peterson; Pennsylvania Death Certificate 1906-1967 for Grace Peterson and Eva Callen; Sligo Cemetery records, Sligo, Pennsylvania; The Derrick July 5, 1966 obituary for Jay Callen.

151.

Howard Roy Parker is the son of Julia (48) and the grandson of Maria (9), Dalton, New York, November 12, 1878, d. place and date not known; m. Franklinville, New York September 17, 1903 Althea A Hussey, b. New York State July 6, 1886, d. Cleveland, Ohio October 5, 1965, divorced 1911; m. (2) Chautauqua, New York August 30, 1927 Marie Kelly Kennan, b. New York State September 11, 1892, d. Cleveland, Ohio, July 22, 1972, divorced. Roy Parker resided with his parents in Nunda, New York, and was employed as a farmer until his first marriage. Mr. Parker was listed on the 1900 US Census as single, but other records indicate he married in 1899. By 1910, Roy had moved his family to Ohio, where they resided in

Cleveland, and he worked as a clerk for a machinery company. In 1920, Mr. Parker still resided in Cleveland but was divorced and employed as a steelworker. The 1920 US Census recorded Mr. Parker resided with his ex-wife, her new husband, and their son. The 1930 US Census found that Roy Parker had remarried and was a gas station attendant. The 1940 US Census noted that he was divorced and was employed as a farmer in Gates Mills, Ohio. It is not known where he was buried. Aletta Parker remarried to Samuel Wassell. They divorced, and she later married Mr. Fleming. Samuel Wassell was buried in Acacia Masonic Memorial Park Cemetery, Mayfield Heights, Ohio. Althea was buried under the last name of Fleming in the same cemetery.

Children:

305.   I.   **Claude Jennings Parker**, b. Nunda, New York May 20, 1904; d. Gates Mills, Ohio October 21, 1976; m. Monroe, Michigan June 27, 1927, Evaden Grace Norman, b. Sandusky County, Ohio November 1, 1900, d. Cleveland Heights September 12, 1991. Mr. Parker was an attorney with the firm of Parker and Sample in Cleveland Heights. His World War II Draft Registration Card described him as 6', 200 pounds, with blue eyes and blonde hair.

Children:

    i.   **Janice Parker**, b. Ohio February 14, 1932, d. Ohio January 14, 2011; m. Harold Zimmerman, and divorced in Florida on October 10, 1994. They had two daughters: Kathy Jo and Karen.

References: US Census: 1880, 1900, 1910, 1920, 1930, 1940; New York State Marriage Index 1907-1936; Ohio Marriage Records 1774-1993 for Althea's second marriage with information on her divorce from Mr. Parker; World War II Draft Registration Card 1942; Michigan Marriage Index 1867-1952; Acacia Masonic Memorial Park Cemetery records, Mayfield Heights, Ohio; Social Security Death Index 1935-2014 for Janice Parker; Florida Divorce Index 1927-2001; New York Marriage Index 1881-1967; Ohio Death Records 1936-2018.

152.

Minerva "Minnie" Maude Christopher, daughter of Laura (49), granddaughter of Maria (9), b. Nunda, New York August 20, 1875, d. Mt. Morris, New York March 14, 1916; m. Nunda, New York November 28, 1894, William McClare Pietersen/Peterson, b. Mt. Morris, New York April 2, 1869, d. New Castle, Delaware, January 8, 1953. Mr. Peterson was a farmer in Mt. Morris, New York. By 1940 she moved with his daughter Ruth and her family to New Castle, Delaware, where he died. It is believed they were buried in a Mount Morris cemetery, but there is no confirmation of this from cemetery records.

Children:

306. I. *Howard Samuel Peterson*, b. Mt. Morris, New York October 16, 1896, d. Bishops Corner, New York December 16, 1963; m. Perry, New York, June 24, 1919 Florence Blanche Lindsay, b. place not known 1888, d. place not known, June 24, 1972. Mr. Peterson was a tinsmith by profession. The Peterson family resided in Perry, New York, where Howard owned and operated a hardware store for a time. His World War I Draft Registration Card described him as tall and slender with brown hair and eyes. He served from December 20, 1917, to June 16, 1919, with Company C, 315 Ammunition Troop, 90th Division. Howard and Florence were buried in Glenwood Cemetery, Perry, New York.

Children:

i. *Marion Peterson*, b. place not known June 30, 1920, d. place not known, November 22, 2013; m. Edgar Devitt Gilbert, b. December 21, 1909, d. November 23, 1962. They had two children: Sally Ann (1938-2015), who married twice, and had five children: Timothy, David, Bruce, Gary, Scottie, and Lawrence Wayne (1939-2020), who had two daughters and one son.

ii. *Howard Lindsey Peterson*, b. place not known March 10, 1922, d. Broward County, Florida January 21, 1995; m. (1) Betty Dorothy Pettergill, b. Maryland 1919, d.

Maryland April 3, 1991; m (2) Rhoda Irene Baughman, b. 1920, d. 1998); m. (3)) Sweden, New York May 26, 1952, Mabel Corbett, b. Brockport, New York March 19, 1927, d. Cocoa, Florida, May 12, 2008. Betty and Howard divorced in 1941. She remarried Mr. Surratt and was buried with her parents in Cedar Hill Cemetery, Brooklyn, Maryland. Howard Peterson served with the US Army from April 19, 1946, to February 27, 1958. Mr. Peterson had a son by his second marriage, Paul Franklin Peterson, b. Lexington County, South Carolina April 1, 1943, d. Columbia, South Carolina, April 4, 1963, and was married in Dunn's Chapel Methodist Church, West Columbia, South Carolina. Howard Lindsey Peterson had four children with his second wife: Kathy, Ronald, Kenneth, and Linda. Howard was buried in Hillside Cemetery, Clarendon, New York. His third wife was buried in Fountain Head Memorial Park, Palm Bay, Florida.

iii. **William J. Peterson**, b. Perry, New York February 3, 1930, d. Detroit, Michigan July 1978; m. place and date not known, Beverly J., last name not known, b. Warsaw, New York October 10, 1932, d. July 6, 1983. They had three daughters: Cheryl, Brenda, and Christy. They were buried in Glenwood Cemetery, Perry, New York.

307. II. **Ruth Agnes Peterson**, b. Mt. Morris, New York March 13, 1897, d. Warsaw, New York, February 4, 1986; m. Oswego, New York March 15, 1920, Donald Nichols, b. Grove, New York February 1899, d. Perry, New York, December 28, 1969. Donald Nicholas was an electrician by profession, and he practiced in Mt. Morris, New York, or New Castle, Delaware. Mr. Nichols World War II Draft Registration Card described him as being 6' tall, weighed 180 pounds with brown hair and blue eyes. In 1960, Ruth and Donald moved from Delaware to Silver Lake, New York. They were buried in Oakwood Cemetery, Nunda, New York. They did not have any children.

308. III. **Earle Warren Peterson**, b. Mt. Morris, New York March 16,

1900, d. Mt. Morris, New York, July 31, 1917. It is believed Earl Peterson was buried in Mt. Morris, but there is no confirmation of that from records.

309. IV. **Theodore Roosevelt Peterson**, b. Mt. Morris, New York July 29, 1903, d. Elmira, New York October 16, 1989; m. Geneseo, New York October 12, 1928, Florence Alva Prevorce, d. Manhattan, New York June 10, 1908, d. Elmira, New York, October 21, 1987. Mr. Peterson was a lineman in Mt. Morris and Southport, New York. His World War II Draft Registration The card described him as 6' tall, weighing 145 pounds, with brown hair and eyes. In 1942, Mr. Peterson was employed by New York State Electric Gas Corporation in Elmira, New York. Theodore and Florence were buried in Forest Lawn Memorial Park, Elmira, New York.

Children:

    i.   *Joyce Peterson*, b. Elmira, New York April 1, 1934; m. Cortland, New York April 2, 1955, Donald F. Mitchinson, b. Cortland, New York, May 6, 1933.

310. V. **Anna Laura Peterson**, b. Mt. Morris, New York April 9, 1905, d. Clarksville, Indiana November 2, 1985; m. New Castle, Delaware October 3, 1933, William Albert Loveless, b. New Castle, Delaware December 29, 1909, d. Jeffersonville, Indiana, February 11, 1969, from a heart condition. Mr. Loveless was employed as a welder for a steel mill in New Castle, Delaware. Later, he was a supervisor for the Jefferson Boat Company in Indiana. Anna Loveless was the owner and hostess of Samples Restaurant and Frank's Steak House in Indiana. They were buried in Walnut Ridge Cemetery, Jeffersonville, Indiana.

Children:

    i.   **William Loveless**, Delaware, December 18, 1934.

    ii.   **James Loveless**, b. Delaware March 9, 1937, d. Indiana November 12, 2016; m. Beverly J., last name not known, b. June 11, 1938. James was buried in Walnut Ridge Cemetery.

    iii.   **Barbara Loveless**, b. Delaware January 1939.

311. VI. **Ernest Alan Peterson**, b. Mt. Morris, New York June 26, 1908, d. Mineola, New York November 21, 1958; m. place and date not known, Jean, last name not known. He had a daughter, Joyce. His World War II Draft Registration The card described him as having blue eyes and brown hair. No height or weight was given. He was employed by the Cyclone Fence Company and resided in Highland Falls, New York. Ernest Peterson was buried in Long Island National Cemetery, East Farmingdale, New York.

312. VII. **Neil Christopher Peterson**, b. Mt. Morris, New York December 10, 1910, d. Mt. Morris, New York November 2, 1996; m. Mt. Morris, New York March 15, 1930 Helen Elizabeth Feigenbutz, b. Fremont Center, New York August 20, 1911, d. Mt. Morris, New York November 14, 1996. Mr. Peterson was a farmer. Neil and Helen Peterson were buried in Leicester Cemetery, Leicester, New York.

Children:

i. **Ronald N. Peterson**, b. Mt. Morris, New York, April 15, 1930.

ii. **Edwin Peterson**, b. Mt. Morris, New York, October 18, 1932.

313. VIII. **William Craig Peterson**, b. Mt. Morris, New York May 6, 1913, d. Bronx, New York June 23, 1959; m. place not known, 1943 Ola Adeline Benedict, b. Hornell, New York April 21, 1920, d. November 1984. Mr. Peterson's World War II Draft Registration Card described him as 5' 6" tall, weighing 125 pounds, with blonde hair and blue eyes. He was a PFC with the US Air Force. William Peterson was buried in Woodlawn National Cemetery, Elmira, New York. Ola remarried in 1963 to Walter Arms (1914-1964). Ola was buried in Barnard Cemetery, Corning, New York. Walter Arms was buried in Rural Cemetery, Hornell, New York.

314. IX. **Harry Maxwell Jay Peterson**, b. Mt. Morris, New York June 17, 1915, d. Marion, Florida September 4, 1997; m. New Castle, Delaware August 19, 1937, Regina E. Clymer, b. Delaware October 19, 1918, d. Ocala, Florida May 6, 1999. Mr. Peterson's World War II Draft Registration Card

described him as 5' 10" tall, weighing 133 pounds, with blonde hair and hazel eyes. He was Employed as a ferryman. It is not known where they were buried.

Children:

    i.   **Donald Peterson**, b. Wilmington, Delaware February 22, 1938, d. Delaware August 5, 2013; m. Haddon Heights, New Jersey April 1972 Marion L. Kirk.

References: US Census: 1900, 1910, 1920, 1930, 1940 New York State Census: 1915, 1925; Glenwood Cemetery records, Perry, New York; US Military Veterans Files 1925-1970; World War I Draft Registration Card 1917-18; New York State Marriage Index 1881-1967; Cedar Hill Cemetery records, Brooklyn Park, Maryland; Hillside Cemetery records, Clarendon, New York; Fountains Head Memorial Park records, Palm Bay, Florida; Dunn's Chapel Methodist Church records, West Columbia, South Carolina; Social Security Death Index 1935-2014; World War II Draft Registration Card 1942; New York State Death Index 1957-1969; New York State Birth Index 1881-1942; Forest Lawn Memorial Park records, Elmira, New York; Walnut Ridge Cemetery records, Jeffersonville, Indiana; Delaware Marriage records 1806-1933; Indiana Death Certificates 1899-2011; Long Island National Cemetery records, East Farmingdale, New York; Leicester Cemetery records, Leicester, New York; Woodlawn National Cemetery records, Elmira, New York; Barnard Cemetery records, Corning, New York; Rural Cemetery records, Hornell, New York; New Jersey Marriage Index 1901-2016; Florida Death Index 1877-1998.

153.

Ernest Warren Christopher, son of Laura (49), grandson of Maria (9), b. Brook Grove, New York May 21, 1879, d. Warsaw, New York September 5, 1953; m. New York State 1900 Ida Merloe Hamilton, b. place not known May 19, 1879, d. New York State April 1969. Ernest Christopher was a farmer in Mount Morris and Perry, New York. For a brief period in 1925 he was employed as a foundry worker in Mt. Morris. Ernest and Ida Christopher were buried in Oakwood Cemetery, Nunda, New York.

Children:

315.　I.　***Merloe H. Christopher***, b. Livingston County, New York July 31, 1901, d. Livingston County, New York May 8, 1988; m. place and date not known, Bessie M. McComb, b. Mt. Morris, New York April 14, 1891, d. Rochester, New York, December 24, 1962. It is not known if they had any children. Merloe and Bessie Christopher were buried in Oakwood Cemetery, Nunda, New York.

316.　II.　***Mildred L. Christopher***, b. place not known, 1910, d. place and date not known; m. Perry, New York June 23, 1930 Craig B. MacMillan. There is no further information on this couple.

References: US Census: 1900, 1920, 1920, 1930, 1940; New York State Census: 1915, 1925; New York State Marriage Index 1881-1967; Oakwood Cemetery records, Nunda, New York.

154.

Irene Rena Bartholomew, daughter of Cora (50), granddaughter of Maria (9), b. New York State April 20, 1880, d. Rochester, New York January 4, 1939; m. place and date not known, William Watkins b, England July 27, 1868, d. Brooks Grove, New York, November 14, 1953. Mr. Watkins was a farmer from Mt. Morris, New York. Rena and William Watkins were buried in Oakwood Cemetery, Nunda, New York.

Children:

317.　I.　***William Forrest Watkins***, b. Mt. Morris, New York May 24, 1907, d. Nunda, New York February 10, 1968; m. Mt. Morris, New York October 11, 1935, Ruth A. Andrews, b. Mt. Morris, New York November 25, 1911, d. Nunda, New York, February 3, 2010. Mr. Watkins was a teacher at both Newark Valley and Nunda, New York Public Schools. His World War II Draft Registration Card described him as being 5' 8" tall and weighing 140 pounds with brown hair and eyes. It is believed they were buried in Nunda, New York, but there are no records to confirm this.

Children:

i. **Bruce Todd Watkins**, b. April 25, 1939, d. December 12, 1988 and buried Pleasant Grove Cemetery, Ithaca, New York. He married Elizabeth A. Egan June 13, 1964 in New York State.

ii. **Barry Watkins.**

iii. **Valerie Watkins.**

iv. **Pamela Watkins.**

References: US Census: 1900, 1910, 1920, 1930, 1940; New York State Census: 1925; Oakwood Cemetery records, Nunda, New York; Pleasant Grove Cemetery records, Ithaca, New York; World War II Draft Registration Card 1942; New York State Marriage Index 1881-1967; Social Security Death Index 1935-2014.

155.

Neva Genevieve Bartholomew, daughter of Cora (50), granddaughter of Maria (9), b. Mt. Morris, New York March 1895, d. Rochester, New York October 1, 1937; m. Nunda, New York August 29, 1915 Wayne Edwin Walker, b. Nunda, New York October 11, 1895, d. Savannah, New York, October 8, 1991. Mr. Walker was a farmer and carpenter who worked in Mt. Morris and Nunda, New York. It Is unknown where they were buried, but probably at Oakwood Cemetery, Nunda, New York.

Children:

318. I. **Ethel Estelle** (Catherine E.) Walker, b. Nunda, New York August 19, 1916, d. Nunda, New York July 14, 1999; m. Mt. Morris, New York August 25, 1934, Albert John Cox, b. West Sparta, New York May 7, 1908, d. Dalton, New York April 1984. Mr. Cox was a farmer. His World War II Draft Registration Card described him as 5' 6" tall, weighing 125 pounds, with a ruddy complexion, brown hair, and blue eyes. Ethel was a nurse. They had two children: a daughter, Patricia, and a son, Jean. Ethel and Albert Cox were buried in Oakwood Cemetery, Nunda, New York.

319. II. ***Ralph Edwin Walker***, b. Nunda, New York August 16, 1920, d. North Syracuse, New York October 22, 2012; m. place and date not known, Marion Ziegler, b. Syracuse, New York May 2, 1918, d. Syracuse, New York, September 9, 2007. Mr. Walker was employed as a foreman for the New York Central Railroad and later as a tile setter for Stearns and Bergstrom, where he worked until his 1986 retirement. They had four children: Ralph, Stephanie, Wayne, and Gregory. Ralph and Marion were buried in North Syracuse Cemetery, North Syracuse, New York.

320. III. ***Laurence Warren Walker***, b. Mt. Morris, New York September 17, 1923, d. Howard, Ohio December 30, 1990; m. place and date not known, Elizabeth Anne Fitzpatrick, b. Syracuse, New York 1924, d. Cleveland, Ohio, April 13, 2020. They had six children: Laurence, Powell, James Patrick (1950-1995), Susan, and Anne. Laurence and Elizabeth were buried in St. Luke Cemetery, Danville, Ohio. Mr. Walker earned a Bronze Star and a Purple Heart with the US Army during World War II. The son Patrick was buried with them.

321. IV. ***Cora Walker***, b. Mt. Morris, New York October 11, 1930, d. Newark, New York July 21, 2017; m. Arcadia, New York April 27, 1950 Wilbur DePauw, b. Arcadia, New York December 10, 1927, d. Lyons, New York, April 8, 2013. Mr. DePauw served in Japan as the Chief Clerk to General Robert Eichelberger, the Commander of the 8th Army. Cora and Wilbur were buried in Newark Cemetery, Newark, New York.

322. V. ***David Gordon Walker***, b. New York 1926, d. Mt. Morris, New York 1934. It is not known where he was buried.

References: US Census: 1900, 1910, 1920, 1930, 1940; Oakwood Cemetery records, Nunda, New York; World War II Draft Registration Card 1942; North Syracuse Cemetery records, North Syracuse, New York; St. Luke Cemetery records, Danville, Ohio; Newark Cemetery records, Newark, New York; New York State Marriage Index 1881-1952.

157.

John Buzzard Slack, Jr., son of Mary Ellen (51), grandson of George (10), b. Philadelphia, Pennsylvania April 8, 1893, d. Glenmoore, Pennsylvania April

1974; m. Philadelphia, Pennsylvania July 29, 1914 Amelia Apfelgreen, b. Philadelphia, Pennsylvania, a. 1894, d. Voorhees, Pennsylvania September 10, 1981. His World War II Draft Registration Card described him as being 5' 8" tall, weighed 149 pounds with brown hair and eyes. He was employed by General Electric and resided in Springfield, Pennsylvania. John and Amelia Slack were buried in St. Matthew's Lutheran Cemetery, Chester Springs, Pennsylvania.

Children:

323. I. *John Buzzard Slack III*, b. Philadelphia, Pennsylvania November 25, 1917, d. December 12, 2016; m. Florence Walton Montgomery Chester, Pennsylvania January 11, 1947, b. Chester, Pennsylvania June 30, 1924, d. Dover, Delaware, April 26, 2013.

Children:

i. *John Barry Slack*, b. Lansdowne, Pennsylvania, August 2, 1950.

ii. *Susan Florence Slack*, b. Chester, Pennsylvania, July 5, 1957.

324. II. *Nadia Campbell McEldin Slack*, b. Philadelphia, Pennsylvania May 19, 1923; m. (1) Philadelphia, Pennsylvania June 1, 1946, Edward James Montgomery, b. Chester, Pennsylvania May 31, 1921, d. Media, Pennsylvania March 18, 1952; m November 6, 1952, John Rosengarten, b. March 16, 1925.

Children (by first marriage):

i. *Nadia Ellen Montgomery*, b. Drexel Hill, Pennsylvania October 20, 1948; m. Cherry Hill, New Jersey January 1972 David Albert Heller, b. Patterson, New Jersey, August 20, 1949.

Children (by second marriage):

i. *Gail Marie Rosengarten*, b. Chester, Pennsylvania, September 2, 1956.

ii. *Marilyn Jean Rosengarten*, b. Camden, New Jersey, September 25, 1961.

325. III. *Alan P. Slack*, b. Springfield, Pennsylvania April 21, 1929, d. Pennsylvania June 3, 2020; m. Charlotte Maas, b. 1925, d. 1997. Mr. Slack was the Director of Quality Assurance for the Boeing Corporation, retiring after 32 years. He was also a gifted painter who studied at the Academy of Fine Arts. They did not have any children.

References: US Census: 1900, 1910, 1920, 1930, 1940; Social Security Death Index 1935-2014; World War II Draft Registration Card 1942; St. Matthews Lutheran Cemetery records, Chester Springs, Pennsylvania.

158.

John Bradley Fuller, son of George (53), grandson of George (10), b. Philadelphia, Pennsylvania August 18, 1903, d. Pitman, New Jersey November 20, 1994; m. Pitman, New Jersey August 12, 1933 Catherine May Rihl, b. Philadelphia, Pennsylvania September 27, 1901, d. Pitman, New Jersey July 6, 2004. Mr. Fuller's World War II Draft Registration Card described him as being 6' 2" tall, weighed 190 pounds with black hair and hazel eyes. He was employed in 1942 by the Philadelphia Electric Company. John and Catherine were buried in Hillcrest Memorial Park, Hurffville, New Jersey.

Children:

326. I. *John Bradley Fuller, Jr.*, b. Philadelphia, Pennsylvania, January 5, 1935, d. October 30, 2011; m. (1)) West Chester, Pennsylvania September 7, 1957, Sylvia Jane Waltz, b. West Chester, Pennsylvania June 26, 1935; m. (2) Massachusetts 1977 Sally Luther, b. December 7, 1938, d. Acton, Massachusetts, March 22, 2009.

Children (by first marriage):

i. *Kimberly Louise Fuller*, b. Concord, Massachusetts April 2, 1963; m Andrew Bringhurst.

ii. *Amy Susan Fuller*, b. Concord, Massachusetts

March 22, 1965; m. Neil Phillip Grubb.

    iii.   *John Bradley Fuller III*, b. Concord, Massachusetts January 6, 1969; m. Vicky Lea Lakes.

327. II. *Eleanor Virginia Fuller*, b. Philadelphia, Pennsylvania November 8, 1936, d. Pittsburgh, Pennsylvania August 20, 2002; m. (1) Pitman, New Jersey September 3, 1955, Walter Hamilton Beckwith; m. (2) January 22, 1977, David Perry Rihl.

Children (by first marriage):

    i.   *Walter Hamilton Beckwith, Jr.*, b. December 14, 1956.

    ii.   *Paul David Beckwith*, b. November 17, 1958.

    iii.   *Mark Christopher Beckwith*, b. March 14, 1962.

328. III. *Douglas Berryman Fuller*, b. Philadelphia, Pennsylvania August 21, 1938; m. (1) Pitman, New Jersey August 12, 1961 Caryl JoAnn Evensen, b. Vineland, New Jersey November 30, 1938, d. Woodbury, New Jersey April 15, 1999; m. (2) Woodbury, New Jersey May 7, 2000 Pamela Anne Penrose, b. Lewes, Delaware July 3, 1946.

Children (by first marriage):

    i.   *Douglas Gregory Fuller*, b. Camden, New Jersey, January 16, 1964.

    ii.   *Eric James Fuller*, b. Camden, New Jersey, May 5, 1965.

    iii.   *Andrea Joan Fuller*, b. Camden, New Jersey, December 23, 1967.

References: US Census: 1910, 1920, 1930, 1940; World War II Draft Registration Card, 1942; Hillcrest Memorial Park records, Hurffville, New Jersey; Social Security Death Index 1935-2014.

159.

Kathryn Elizabeth Fuller, daughter of George (53), granddaughter of George (10), b. Philadelphia, Pennsylvania February 9, 1906, d. Elmer, New Jersey March 18, 1997; m. Pitman, New Jersey April 30, 1927 Enoch Francis Hoffman, divorced 1937, b. Doylestown, New Jersey August 17, 1904, d. Camden, New Jersey July 3, 1976. Mr. Hoffman was a commercial traveler for a radio manufacturing company. After their divorce Kathryn was employed as a secretary. Kathryn Hoffman was buried in Hillcrest Memorial Park, Hurffville, New Jersey with her parents. Enoch Hoffman was buried in North Cedar Hill Cemetery, Philadelphia with his mother.

Children:

329. I. ***John Francis Hoffman***, b. Quincy, Massachusetts June 26, 1931, d. Tinton Falls, New Jersey February 5, 2009; m. Elkton, Maryland July 3, 1953 Beatrice Dorothy Sheppard, b. Bridgeboro, New Jersey, September 24, 1930; Red Bank, New Jersey, January 12, 2020.

Children:

i. ***Deborah Ann Hoffman***, b. Elmer, New Jersey, January 17, 1954.

ii. ***John Francis Hoffman***, b. Heidelberg, Germany, May 29, 1959.

iii. ***Steven Lawrence Hoffman***, b. Fort Belvoir, Virginia, March 19, 1961.

iv. ***Laura Jane Hoffman***, b. North Carolina, January 30, 1965.

v. ***Linda Sue Hoffman***, Puzzuoli, Italy, November 23, 1966.

330. II. ***Baby Boy Hoffman***, b. and d. Quincy, Massachusetts June 26, 1931.

331. III. ***Kathryn Jean Hoffman***, b. and d. Philadelphia, Pennsylvania

December 12, 1935.

References: US Census: 1910, 1920, 1930, 1940; Hillcrest Memorial Park records, Hurffville, New Jersey; North Cedar Hill Cemetery records, Philadelphia, Pennsylvania; Pennsylvania Birth Certificates 1906-1913; New Jersey Death Certificates 1901-2017; Pennsylvania Death Certificates 1906-1967.

160.

Geary Vanartsdalen Fuller, son of Matthew (56), grandson of George (10), b. Philadelphia, Pennsylvania December 9, 1889, d. Pitman, New Jersey April 1, 1944; m. Delaware January 12, 1909 Elizabeth May Kirkpatrick, b. Philadelphia, Pennsylvania December 2, 1898, d. Pitman, New Jersey June 27, 1974. Mr. Fuller's World War I Draft Registration Card described him as being of medium height and weight with light hair and blue eyes. In 1917 he was employed as a bar inspector for the Pennsylvania Railroad. In 1920 Geary Fuller worked as a driver for Dupont and in 1930 as an operator for an Electric Company. Geary and Elizabeth Fuller were buried in Bethel Methodist Church Cemetery, Hurffville, New Jersey.

Children:

332. I. *Marion Elizabeth Fuller*, b. Pitman, New Jersey March 25, 1910, d. Pitman, New Jersey June 29, 1972; m. Pitman, New Jersey January 28, 1930 Leroy Hamilton Wilkerson, b. Paulsboro, New Jersey April 27, 1911, d. Volusia, Florida April 27, 1994.

Children:

i. **Leroy Geary Wilkerson**, b. Pitman, New Jersey September 21, 1936.

333. II. *Geary Vanartsdalen Fuller*, Jr., b. Pitman, New Jersey December 9, 1912, d. Pitman, New Jersey March 9, 1973; m. (1) Pitman, New Jersey May 28, 1940 Florence Ayars Mathis, b. Pitman, New Jersey May 8, 1915, d. Norristown, Pennsylvania June 4, 1963; m. (2) place and date not known, Helen Friesel, d. 1979.

Children (by first marriage):

    i.   *Elaine Nancy Fuller*, b. Pitman, New Jersey, November 25, 1942.

    ii.   *Ronald Wayne Fuller*, b. Pitman, New Jersey, August 14, 1947.

    iii.   *Elizabeth Mae Fuller*, b. Pitman, New Jersey June 4, 1952.

334.   III.   *Eleanor Clevenger Fuller*, b. Pitman, New Jersey November 5, 1914, d. Pitman, New Jersey June 23, 1975; m. Pitman, New Jersey July 3, 1935 Howard Martin Govett, b. New Jersey October 16, 1912, d. Pitman, New Jersey April 4, 1989.

Children:

    i.   *Robert Howard Govett*, b. Pitman, New Jersey March 17, 1941.

335.   IV.   *Adele May Fuller*, b. Pitman, New Jersey August 5, 1916, d. December 14, 1966; m. place and date not known, Bertram Fey, b. New Jersey 1918, d. Mantua, New Jersey April 23, 1990.

336.   V.   *Veo Jenia Fuller*, b. Pennsylvania February 14, 1918, d. Pennsylvania April 26, 1918 from spinal meningitis.

References: US Census: 1900, 1910, 1920, 1930, 1940; Bethel Methodist Church Cemetery, Hurffville, New Jersey; New Jersey Death Index 1798-1971; Pennsylvania Death Certificate 1906-1967 for Veo Fuller; Delaware Marriage Records 1806-1933; World War I Draft Registration Card 1917-18.

161.

Raymond Matthew Fuller, son of Matthew (56), grandson of George (10), b. Philadelphia, Pennsylvania June 22, 1891, d. Pitman, New Jersey November 23, 1943; m. Glassboro, New Jersey March 23, 1913 Elizabeth Jones, b. Glassboro, New Jersey August 16, 1895, d. Wenonah, New Jersey

November 5, 1968. Mr. Fuller was employed as an electric operator for an electric company (1920) and as a grounds man for an electric company (1930). His World War II Draft Registration Card noted that he was 5' 7" tall, weighed 144 pounds with gray eyes, brown hair, and a dark complexion. Mr. Fuller worked for the Atlantic Electric Company. Raymond and Elizabeth Fuller were buried in Hillcrest Memorial Park, Hurffville, New Jersey.

Children:

337. I. *Mary Virginia Williams Fuller*, b. Pitman, New Jersey April 14, 1914, d. Hammonton, New Jersey January 11, 2003; m. Elkton, Maryland August 26, 1933 Charles F. Kier, Jr.

Children:

i. *Joan Elizabeth Kier*, b. Pitman, New Jersey July 30, 1934.

ii. *Charles Fisler Kier*, III, b. Pitman, New Jersey July 3, 1936.

338. II. *Raymond Matthew Fuller*, Jr., b. Pitman, New Jersey July 25, 1916, d. India July 20, 1945; m. Pitman, New Jersey Virginia Harriet Young, b. Carney's Point, New Jersey May 24, 1917.

Children:

i. *Raymond George Fuller*, b. Philadelphia, Pennsylvania, September 23, 1942.

339. III. Jane Elizabeth Fuller, b. Pitman, New Jersey June 29, 1919, d. place and date not known; m. Williamstown, New Jersey December 18, 1939 Ralph Goldsmith Miller.

Children:

i. *Patricia Jean Miller*, b. Philadelphia, Pennsylvania, June 14, 1940.

ii. *Marilyn Sue Miller*, b. Philadelphia, Pennsylvania,

January 2, 1945.

iii. *Jacqueline Lee Miller*, b. Woodbury, New Jersey, b. April 12, 1948.

iv. *Ralph Goldsmith Miller, Jr.*, Woodbury, New Jersey, May 29, 1952.

340. IV. **William Donald Fuller**, b. Glassboro, New Jersey April 15, 1922; d. Pitman, New Jersey October 15, 2005; m. February 24, 1943 Catherine Elizabeth Ellenbrock, b. Rotterdam, Holland July 29, 1922.

Children:

i. *Barbara Jean Fuller*, b. Millville, New Jersey, September 7, 1944.

ii. *Evelyn Anne Fuller*, b. Camden, New Jersey, September 1, 1948.

341. V. **Doris Florence Fuller**, b. Glassboro, New Jersey October 9, 1924; m. Williamstown, New Jersey November 9, 1946, John Winfried Sharp.

Children:

i. *Linda Jean Sharp*, b. Woodbury, New Jersey, October 14, 1947.

ii. *John Winfried Sharp, Jr.,* b. Woodbury, New Jersey, November 29, 1948.

iii. *Janet Doris Sharp*, b. Woodbury, New Jersey, October 26, 1949.

342. VI. **Norwood Charles Fuller**, b. Williamstown, New Jersey August 24, 1927; m. Williamstown, New Jersey Irene Frances Simmermon, b. Williamstown, New Jersey August 25, 1927.

Children:

i. *Marian Carol Fuller*, b. Camden, New Jersey October 6, 1946.

ii. *Noreen Frances Fuller*, b. Woodbury, New Jersey, September 10, 1949.

343. VII. *Lorraine Dolores Fuller*, b. Pitman, New Jersey October 12, 1930; m. Williamstown, New Jersey March 22, 1940, William Norman Shimp, b. Hancock's Bridge, New Jersey August 27, 1928.

Children:

i. *William Raymond Shimp*, b. Woodbury, New Jersey, October 17, 1948.

ii. *Nancy Alberta Shimp*, b. Woodbury, New Jersey February 21, 1955.

344. VIII. *Elsie Mae Fuller*, b. Pitman, New Jersey September 18, 1933; m. Williamstown, New Jersey August 14, 1951, Warren Raymond Saul, b. Millville, New Jersey, b. May 6, 1929.

Children:

i. *Elizabeth Joyce Saul*, b. Phoenixville, Pennsylvania November 12, 1952.

ii. *Warren Raymond Saul, Jr.*, Millville, New Jersey October 13, 1955.

iii. *Cynthia Renee Saul*, b. Bridgeton, New Jersey January 6, 1957.

iv. *Edward Zachary Saul* (adopted).

v. *Robert Matthew Saul* (adopted).

References: US Census: 1900, 1910, 1920, 1930, 1940; New Jersey Death Index 1798-1971; World War II Draft Registration Card 1942; Hillcrest Memorial Park records, Hurffville, New Jersey.

162.

Henry Bickley Fuller, son of Matthew (56), grandson of George (10), b. Philadelphia, Pennsylvania June 6, 1904, d. September 23, 1937; m. Gloucester, New Jersey June 6, 1931 Mildred Coward. Mr. Fuller was a furniture store salesman at the time of his death. He was buried with his parents in Hillcrest Memorial Park, Hurffville, New Jersey.

References: US Census: 1910, 1920, 1930; New Jersey Church Birth Records 1669-2013; New Jersey Death Records 1798-1971; New Jersey Marriage Records 1670-1965; Hillcrest Memorial Park records, Hurffville, New Jersey.

163.

Esther Lillie Fuller, daughter of Edward (58), granddaughter of George (10), b. Philadelphia, Pennsylvania April 1, 1896, d. Philadelphia, Pennsylvania 1985; m. Philadelphia, Pennsylvania May 23, 1913 John Joseph Peacock, b. Darlington, England May 23, 1891, d. Woodbury, New Jersey August 12, 1962. John Peacock was employed with a cement company in Philadelphia.

Children:

345. I. ***John Joseph Peacock***, b. Philadelphia, Pennsylvania March 9, 1914, d. Collier, Florida January 4, 1987; m. (1) Wildwood, New Jersey 1939 Ethel Janet Bradley, b. Pennsylvania 1917, d. July 10, 1965; m. (2) Sylvia Cather Baker.

> Children (by first marriage):
>
> i. ***Janet Bradley Peacock***, b. Philadelphia, Pennsylvania, May 10, 1944.
>
> ii. ***John Joseph Peacock III***, b. Philadelphia, Pennsylvania, April 17, 1946.

References: US Census: 1900, 1910, 1920, 1930, 1940; Pennsylvania Marriage Index 1885-1951; Florida Death Index 1877-1998; Social Security Death Index 1935-2014.

164.

Edna Regina Fuller, daughter of Edward (58), granddaughter of George (10), b. Philadelphia, Pennsylvania February 17, 1907, d. place and date not known; m. Philadelphia, Pennsylvania June 28, 1941 James Aloysius Kelly, b. October 17, 1905, d. Upper Darby, Pennsylvania July 28, 1979. Edna resided with her aunt and uncle (Slack) in 1920, with her grandmother and mother in 1930, and with her sister in 1940. Her employment was as a clerk with a railroad steam company (1930) and as a waitress (1940).

Children:

346.   I.   ***James Aloysius Fuller, Jr.***, b. Philadelphia, Pennsylvania, January 9, 1943.

References: US Census: 1910, 1920, 1930, 1940; Pennsylvania Birth Certificate 1906-1913.

165.

Marion Anna Fuller, daughter of Edward (58), granddaughter of George (10), b. Philadelphia, Pennsylvania July 23, 1910, d. place and date not known; m. (1) July 3, 1942, Harry Dortch Lancaster, b. Wayne County, North Carolina January 15, 1911, d. West Chester, Pennsylvania April 29, 1999, divorced (?); m. (2) Philadelphia, Pennsylvania 1933 Frank Peters, b. Philadelphia, Pennsylvania May 10, 1924, d. Philadelphia, Pennsylvania, June 3, 1954, from chronic glomerulonephritis for thirteen years. Family records indicate the marriage order as stated above but the births of a son from each marriage add confusion as to the correct marriage order. Mr. Peters was a department store salesman. He was buried in Holy Cross Cemetery, Yeadon, Pennsylvania. Harry Lancaster served with the US Army from January 20, 1942, to August 4, 1945. His World War II Draft Registration Card described him as 5' 9" tall, weighing 150 pounds, with brown hair and gray eyes.

Children (by first marriage):

347.	I.	***Harry Dennis Lancaster***, b. January 6, 1948; m. Springfield, Pennsylvania September 6, 1969 Carol Ann Luchetta, b. Philadelphia, Pennsylvania, November 18, 1949.

    Children:

    i.	***Brian Dennis Lancaster***, b. Doylestown, Pennsylvania January 5, 1975.

348.	II.	***Edward Gregory Lancaster III***, b. April 4, 1951.

Children (by second marriage):

349.	I.	***Francis Peters***, d. 1954.

References: US Census: 1920, 1930, 1940; Pennsylvania Marriage Index 1885-1951 for Marion to Frank Peters; Pennsylvania Death Certificates 1906-1967 for Frank Peters; Holy Cross Cemetery records, Yeadon, Pennsylvania; US Army Veterans Death File Index 1850-2010 for Harry Lancaster; World War II Draft Registration Card 1942 for Harry Lancaster.

166.

Walter Matthew Fuller, son of Walter (59), grandson of George (10), b. Pitman, New Jersey July 10, 1921; d. 2009; m. (1) Pitman, New Jersey October 1951 Margaret F. Richter, divorced Pinellas County, Florida 1954r; m. (2) 1954 Eleanor Dolores Corrado. Mr. Fuller was an award-winning commercial artist who was employed by Kapp Studios, RCA, and Sperry-Rand. He served in the US Navy during World War II. His World War II Draft Registration Card described him as being 5' 8 ½" tall, weighed 134 pounds with a dark complexion with brown hair and hazel eyes. Walter Fuller did not have any children by either marriage. It is not known where his wives were buried. Mr. Fuller was buried in New St. Mary's Cemetery, Bellmawr, New Jersey.

References: US Census: 1930, 1940; New Jersey Death Index 1901-2017; Florida Divorce Index 1927-2001; New Jersey Marriage Index 1901-2006 for Mr. Fuller's first marriage; World War II Draft Registration Card 1942;

New St. Mary's Cemetery records, Bellmawr, New Jersey.

168.

Hannah Minnie Fuller, daughter of Walter (59), granddaughter of George (10), b. Pitman, New Jersey July 31, 1925, d. Clayton, New Jersey December 22, 1975; m. Camden, New Jersey February 12, 1943 Charles Arthur Porch, Jr., b. March 8, 1921, d. March 4, 1985. Mr. and Mrs. Porch were buried in Hillcrest Memorial Park, Hurffville, New Jersey.

Children:

350. I. *Patricia Hannah Porch*, b. Camden, New Jersey July 1, 1944; m. Elkton, Maryland February 11, 1963, Gerald J. Raines, b. Salem, New Jersey, March 9, 1941.

Children:

i. *Gerald L. Raines, Jr.*, b. Elmer, New Jersey, August 15, 1956.

ii. *Dwayne Lacy Raines*, b. Elmer, New Jersey, September 7, 1962.

iii. *Brian Charles Raines*, b. Camden, New Jersey, July 27, 1965.

iv. *Cheryl Ann Raines*, b. Camden, New Jersey, January 25, 1967.

v. *April Diane Raines*, b. Havre de Grace, Maryland, April 1, 1971.

351. II. Barbara Jean Porch, b. Camden, New Jersey June 21, 1946; m. Clayton, New Jersey January 25, 1964, Thomas Edward Reid, b. Glassboro, New Jersey December 28, 1944.

Children:

i. *Donna Lee Reid*, b. Elmer, New Jersey March 12, 1964.

> ii. **Shirley Lynn Reid**, b. Elmer, New Jersey December 9, 1965.
>
> iii. **Michelle Ann** Reid, b. Woodbury, New Jersey February 11, 1969.

352. III. **Charles Arthur Porch, Jr.**, b. Camden, New Jersey, September 13, 1947, d. February 16, 1994; m. Clayton, New Jersey March 21, 1970, Kathleen Marie Sorenson, b. Philadelphia, Pennsylvania, September 16, 1952.

> Children:
>
> i. **Susan Marie Sorenson**, b. Elmer, New Jersey August 15, 1970.
>
> ii. **Tara Lynn Sorenson**, b. Woodbury, New Jersey May 15, 1975.

353. IV. **William Allen Porch**, b. Audubon, New Jersey October 18, 1955.

References: US Census: 1930, 1940; New Jersey Death Index 1901-2016; New Jersey Marriage Index 1901-2016; Hillcrest Memorial Park records, Hurffville, New Jersey.

Appendix I
The Adams Family of Nunda, New York

Nicholas Adams was my great-great-great-great grandfather. He was born in Saratoga County, New York and resided in either Ballston or Watervliet, New York until he moved with some of his family to Livingston County, New York by the time of the taking of the 1860 US Census. It is my contention that Nicholas Adams was the son of Jesse Adams, Jr. Jesse Adams, Jr was a direct descendant of Henry Adams of Braintree, Massachusetts.

There is not a single Nicholas Adams listed in the 1898 publication *Henry Adams of Braintree, Massachusetts and His Descendants* complied by Andrew N. Adams. I will present circumstantial evidence to support my claim about Nicholas Adams. The identity of Nicholas Adams' mother remains unknown and was so stated on his death certificate in 1890. His father's name on his death certificate was listed as Jesse Adams. The only Jesse Adams listed in the Andrew N. Adams genealogy who could qualify as Nicholas Adams' father would be Jesse Adams, Jr. Nicholas Adams moved his wife and some of his children to Livingston County New York settling in Portage where Jesse Adams, Jr. had already moved with his mother, and his siblings: Abijah, Prosper, Lucy, and Zerviah. The 1898 genealogy identifies four children for Jesse Adams, Jr. However, other documents for Livingston County and Census records indicate that Jesse Adams, Jr. and his wife, Mabel Spencer Adams, had more than four children together. Two of these children, Jane and Franklin, were born after Jesse Adams, Jr. was allegedly dead sometime between 1820 and 1830. A Jesse Adams, Jr. purchased land in Illinois in 1841. Illinois was where Jesse, Jr.'s two daughters, Laura and Jane, settled after their marriages and by 1843 and

1858, respectively.

Nicholas Adams' children carried traditional Adams names such as Jesse, John, Mary Elizabeth, and Louise. It is my belief that Jesse Adams, Jr. was married before his marriage to Mabel Spencer, that an alleged unnamed first wife died and a son, Nicholas, was left behind in Saratoga County, when Jesse moved to Livingston County in Western New York. Currently it is not known where and when Jesse Adams, Jr. died.

The Adams Genealogy

1.

Henry Adams was one of the first residents of Braintree, Massachusetts, arriving in either 1632 or 1633 with his wife, eight sons, and daughter. He was given forty acres on February 24, 1639/1640. The name of his wife is unknown as are her birth and death dates. It is assumed that she returned to England with their son John and their daughter Ursula, where she died. Henry Adams died in Braintree October 6, 1646.

Children:

2.   I.   **Lieutenant Henry Adams**, b. in England, 1604; m. November 17, 1643 Braintree, Elizabeth Paine. He removed and settled in Medfield, Massachusetts in 1646. He was the first Town Clerk of Braintree and Medfield, Representative of the Town in the General Court in 1659, 1665, 1674, and 1685. He fought the Indians in the wars of 1675-76 and was killed while standing in his doorway on February 21, 1676. He was shot the same day and died February 29; they had seven children.

3.   II.   **Lieutenant Thomas Adams**, f.

4.   III.   **Captain Samuel Adams,** b. in England, 1617; m. (1) Rebecca Graves, d. October 8, 1662-4; m. (2) May 7, 1668 Esther Sparhawk, d. November 4, 1743. He removed to Concord, Massachusetts and later to Chelmsford. He was Commissioner of the Court in 1667; erected mills in east Chelmsford near present day Lowell. He had 450 acres of land granted to him on July 3, 1636 and the right to erect and run a sawmill, a grist mill, and a corn mill. He died January 24, 1688/89. He had eleven

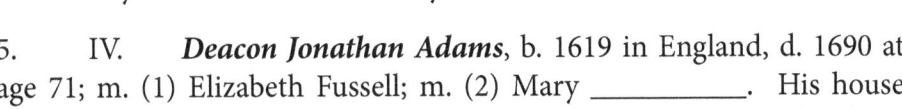

children by his first wife and four by his second wife.

5.   IV.   **Deacon Jonathan Adams**, b. 1619 in England, d. 1690 at age 71; m. (1) Elizabeth Fussell; m. (2) Mary _____. His house burned in 1676 after an Indian attack and was rebuilt on the Joseph Adams place in East Medway (Millis). He had nine children by his first marriage.

6.   V.   **Peter Adams**, b. 1622 in England, d. 1690; m. Rachel _____. He settled in Medfield in 1652. His wife and son John joined him from Braintree. His house was burned by the Indians in 1676. Peter and Rachel Adams had eleven children.

7.   VI.   **John Adams**. b. 1624 in England. Know as John of Cambridge because there is some debate about whether or not he was actually one of the sons of Henry Adams of Braintree. The debate centers on whether or not the son, John Adams, actually returned from England and settled in Cambridge, Massachusetts. In the Genealogical History of Henry Adams, John of Cambridge is considered a descendant but out of numerical order.

8.   VII.   **Joseph Adams**, b. 1626 in England, d. December 6, 1694 in Braintree; m. November 26, 1650, Abigail Baxter, d. August 27, 1692 at age 58. He was a malster, freeman (1653), and Selectman (1673). Joseph and Abigail Adams had twelve children. Presidents John Adams and John Quincy Adams are descended from Joseph Adams.

9.   VIII.   **Ensign Edward Adams**, b. 1630 in England, d. November 12, 1716 in Medfield; m. (1) in 1652 Lydia Rockwood, d. March 3, 1676; m. (2) in 1678 Abigail Ruggles, d. 1707; m. (3) January 6, 1709/10 Sarah Taylor. He settled in Medfield, Massachusetts where he served as an Ensign, Selectman, and was Medfield's representative in the General Court in 1689, 1692, and 1702. He was the last of the original settlers of Medfield at the time of his death. Edward and Lydia Adams had fourteen children.

3.

Lieutenant Thomas Adams, b. 1612 in England d. July 20, 1688, age 76, in Chelmsford; m. Mary _____, d. March 23, 1694/5 at age 82. Thomas

Adams removed to Concord, Massachusetts with his brothers Samuel and John in 1646. Thomas and Samuel later moved to West Cambridge (Arlington) sometime between 1650 and 1654. He was chosen chief Sergeant of the military in 1659. He was not confirmed by the County Court until 1660, because of his religious view. He was chosen Ensign in 1678 and Lieutenant in 1682 in the company where his brother Samuel served as Captain. He held the additional offices of Town Clerk, Selectman, Commissioner or Representative to the General Court. Thomas Adams' will exist and identifies family members.

Children:

10. I. *Mary Adams*, b. July 24, 1643 Braintree, Massachusetts, died soon after birth.

11. II. *Jonathan Adams*, a twin, b. January 6, 1646 Concord, Massachusetts, d. November 25, 1712; m. Leah Gould or Goole, d. 1718. Jonathan Adams was a farmer in Littleton, Massachusetts. They had eight children.

12. III. *Pelatiah Adams*, a twin, b. January 6, 1646 Concord, Massachusetts, d. April 29, 1725 Chelmsford; m. Ruth _____, d. September 18, 1719. They had nine children.

13. IV. *Timothy Adams*, b. February 15 or April 2, 1648, Concord, d. Chelmsford July 1, 1708; m. Mary _____. They had five children.

14. V. *George Adams*, b. March 29, 1650 concord, died young.

15. VI. *Samuel Adams*, f.

16. VII. *Edith Adams*, b. February 21, 1655 Chelmsford, died unmarried.

17. VIII. *Rebecca Adams*, b. September 18, 1657 Chelmsford, died young.

18. IX. *Elizabeth Adams*, b. October 21, 1658/9 Chelmsford, died

young.

19. X. ***Thomas Adams***, b. July 22, 1660 Chelmsford, d. November 20, 1660.

20. XI. ***Mary Adams***, b. October 29, 1664 Chelmsford; m. _____ Cooper.

15.

Samuel Adams, b. Chelmsford between 1652 and 1653, d. November 26, 1727 Canterbury, Connecticut; m. Mary _____, d. March 28, 1718 Canterbury, Connecticut. He was a millwright who moved first to Charlestown, Massachusetts and later to Canterbury, Connecticut. Samuel was one of the first board of selectmen in Canterbury, chosen May 31, 1699. Samuel and Mary Adams reputedly had twelve children, five of whom died young. His will was made, signed, and probated at Plainfield December 4, 1727. The will mentions three sons and four daughters, but only identifies two sons and two daughters by name.

Children:

21. I. ***Abigail Adams***, b. Chelmsford, Massachusetts, d. unknown; m. July 26, 1709, Paul Davenport of Dorchester, Massachusetts. b. January 30, 1683, d. unknown.

22. II. ***Captain Joseph Adams***, f.

23. III. ***Henry Adams***, b. a. 1684 Chelmsford, d. unknown; m. Sarah Adams, b. March 8, 1683, d. April 16 1758.

24. IV. ***Thomas Adams***, b. a. 1688 Chelmsford, d. unknown; m. Abigail Davenport, b. March 10, 1693, d. June 3, 1733.

25. V. ***Samuel Adams***, Jr., b. a. 1690 Chelmsford, d. unknown; m. Mary Cady, d. February 11, 1735/6.

26. VI. ***Susanna Adams***, b. March 13, 1692 Chelmsford, d. unknown; m. James Bradford (as his second wife).

27. VII. ***Katharine Adams***, b. May 27, 1695 Chelmsford, d. August

2, 1733, age 38; m. David Adams, b. September 3, 1692, d. August 29, 1753.

28. VIII. *Margaret Adams*, b. Canterbury, Connecticut, d. unknown, but will was made in 1733; m. Samuel Adams, b. February 25, 1684/5, d. April 24, 1742. No known children. Children of her sister Katharine were appointed executors.

29. IX. *Rebecca Adams*, b. Canterbury, Connecticut, d. July 5, 1709.

22.

Captain Joseph Adams, b. a. 1682/3 Chelmsford, d. March 8, 1752, age 70; m. (1) July 23, 1708 Ennice Spalding, d. April 5, 1726; m. (2) April 4, 1728, Mrs. Susanna Woodward Adams, b. 1693, d. April 29, 1790, buried Baldwin Cemetery, South Canterbury, Connecticut. Joseph was a larger land owner in Canterbury and referred as Joseph Adams, Esquire.

Children (by first marriage):

30. I. *Joseph Adams*, b. June 10, 1709 Canterbury, Connecticut, d. September 7, 1709.

31. II. *Captain Samuel Adams*, b. September 4, 1710 Canterbury, Connecticut, d. December 27, 1700 Canterbury, Connecticut.; m. (1) 1731 Sarah Cady, d. January 1736; m. (2) 1739 Abigail Dams, b. November 12, 1712, d. 21 August 1809, age 89, Coventry, Connecticut. Abigail remarried to Deacon Richard Hale, father of Captain Nathan Hale.

32. III. *Eunice Adams*, b. July 25, 1713, d. unknown; m. Thomas Bradford, b. November 13, 1712. They resided in Canterbury, Connecticut.

33. IV. *Lieutenant Joseph Adams*, f.

34. V. *Mary Adams*, b. August 5, 1719 Canterbury, d. unknown; m. _____ Leach.

35. VI. *Parker Adams*, b. April 18, 1722 Canterbury, d. unknown; m. May 9, 1745, Freelove Fanning.

Children (by second marriage):

36. VII. *Susanna Adams*, b. January 19, 1728/9, Canterbury, Connecticut, d. October 8, 172?

37. VIII. *Elihu Adams*, b. June 11, 1731 Canterbury, d. December 22, 1804, age 74; m. Jerube Adams March 6, 1753, b. August 24, 1729, d. January 24, 1815.

38. IX. *Captain Thomas Adams*, b. July 31, 1734 Canterbury, Connecticut, d. April 22, 1815; m. (1) Susanna Peck March 7, 175? d. February 13, 1780; m. (2) Mary Mudge January 4, 1732, d. September 27, 1814, age 77.

33.

Lieutenant Joseph Adams, b. December 6, 1713 Canterbury, Connecticut, d. December 6, 1780, age 65; m. Sarah Bradford 1738, b. August 27, 1720, d. March 20, 1807, age 86.

Children:

39. I. *William Adams*, b. March 4, 1740 Canterbury, Connecticut, d. July 5, 1739.

40. II. *Samuel Adams*, b. March 30, 1742 Canterbury, Connecticut, d. April 11, 1820; m. Mrs. Sarah Willsby. There was no issue of this marriage.

41. III. *John Adams*, b. February 17, 1743/4 Canterbury, Connecticut, d. November 25, 1810 age 66, Fly Creek, Otego County, New York; m. Submit Butts December 21, 1765.

42. IV. *Joseph Adams*, b. Canterbury, Connecticut February 2, 1745/6, d. September 25, 1824, age 79; m. (1) Elizabeth Chapman November 25, 1773, d. April 16, 1785, age 38; m. (2) Lydia Chapman June 19, 1788 (niece of his first wife), d. February 22, 1852, age 90. Joseph Adams and his second wife are buried in Westminster Parish, Connecticut.

43. V. *James Adams*, b. June 7, 1748 Canterbury, Connecticut, d.

June 28, 1805; m. Jerusha Knight February 16, 1772, b. March 22, 1742, d. July 26, 1829.

44. VI. **Sarah Adams** (twin of James), b. June 7, 1748 Canterbury, d. a widow 1834/5; m. a.1770 David Hale or Hyde.

45. VII. **John Bradford Adams**, b. June 11, 1750 Canterbury, Connecticut, d. June 30, 1829; m. April 6, 1780 Sarah Davenport, b. October 24, 1759, d. August 30, 1815, age 36. John Bradford Adams served as a private in Captain Obadiah Johnson's Company from May 10 to December 15, 1775.

46. VIII. *Jesse Adams*, b. December 7, 1752 Canterbury, died young.

47. IX. **Elisha Adams** (twin of Jesse Adams), b. December 7, 1752 Canterbury, d. January 12, 1753.

48. X. **Mary Adams**, b. Canterbury, Connecticut December 5, 1755, d. 1776 with an infant child; m. 1774 Samuel Barstow, b. January 1749, d. unknown.

49. XI. *Jesse Adams*, f.

50. XII. **Tryphena Adams**, b. Canterbury, Connecticut July 17, 1760, d. unknown; m. a. 1786 Joseph Safford, b. September 29, 1788, d. unknown.

49.

Jesse Adams, b. Canterbury, Connecticut July 17 or February 6, 1757, d. 1812, age 55, Pawlet, Vermont; m. Zerviah Cady November 30, 1780. Jesse Adams removed to Lebanon, Connecticut and later to Pawlet, Vermont where he died. His family resettled in Nunda, New York. In the 1790 U.S. Federal census Jesse Adams and his family resided in Pawlet. The family numbered seven members with three being males under 16, one male over 16, and three females. In the 1800 Federal census the Jesse Adams family of Pawlet numbered nine with one male under ten, 1 male aged 10-15 years, 2 males aged 16-25 and one male over 26. There was one female under 10, two females between the ages of 10-15, and one female over 26.

In 1810 the Jesse Adams family still resided in Pawlet. However, Jesse's first name has been transcribed as "Jesfe Adams." There are eight family members with two males being aged 16-25, 1 male aged 26-44, and one male over 45. There was one female between the ages of 10-15, two females from 16-25 and one female over 45. Jesse Adams, Sr. died in Pawlet, Vermont on February 28, 1812. He was buried in Old Pawlet Cemetery, Pawlet, Vermont. For a century it was claimed that his wife, Zerviah, was buried with him, but that is incorrect. Zerviah Cady Adams, born June 24, 1757, Canterbury, Connecticut, died in 1818 in Livingston County, New York and is buried in that County. The burial location is unknown. Jesse Adams, Sr.'s tombstone reads: In Memory of Jesse Adams who died 28 February 1812, aged 55 years and 22 days. His generous heart that felt for human woe. His dauntless soul, that fear'd no human pain, made him the friend of good, of vice the foe, Hath on this path integrity his guide.

References: Andrew N. Adams 1898 genealogy; Old Paulet Cemetery Records, Pawlet, Vermont; Livingston County, New York death records.

Children:

51. I. **Abijah Adams**, b. October 3, 1781 Lebanon, Connecticut, killed July 1824 or 1832 Portage, New York while raising a barn for Nathaniel Olney. He died unmarried.

52. II. **Olney Adams**, b. January 8, 1783 Lebanon, Connecticut, d. July 14, 1783. Her name may have been Lucy.

53. III. **Festus Adams**, b. Lebanon, Connecticut May 31, 1784, drowned about 1845 Brighton, Monroe County, New York; m. Julia Parsons October 12, 1813 Benson, Vermont, b. February 23, 1796, d. October 1847.

54. IV. **Prosper Adams**, b. Lebanon, Connecticut November 27, 1785, d. April 4, 1839 Alma, New York; m. Polly Robinson September 8, 1811, b. June 15, 1798, d. November 6, 1873. Prosper Adams came to Portage/Nunda in 1816 and was the first innkeeper and supervisor of the town. His mother, Zerviah Cady Adams, came with him and brought all of her children. They moved to Alma, New York where they are buried in the

Sunnyside Cemetery. He was the great-grandfather of Anna Georgiana Storms, kindergarten teacher at Allentown Union School, Allentown, New York. She was both my kindergarten teacher as well as my brother's. My grandfather, Leo C. Root, always indicated we were related to Miss Storms but he never explained how we were related.

55.   V.   ***Sarah Adams***, b. September 13, 1787 Pawlet, Vermont. No further information.

56.   VI.   ***Lucy Adams*** (Twin of Sarah Adams), b. September 13, 1787 Pawlet, Vermont, d. a. 1851 Portage, New York; m. (1) _____Dana; m. (2) John Patterson of Portage, New York. She had a daughter, Laura, by her first husband and four sons by her second husband.

57.   VII.   ***Sybil Adams***, 1780 Pawlet, Vermont; m. David Clark. They had one son, Aaron, and resided in Westport, New York.

58.   VIII.   ***Jesse Adams***, Jr., f.

59.   IX.   ***Zerviah Adams***, b. Pawlet, Vermont October 16, 1796, d. August 10, 1830; m. Elisha Smith February 24, 1820, b. May 12, 1784, Preston, Connecticut, d. March 5, 1861, from drowning in Canaseraga Creek. They had two sons, Prosper, who married a sister of Roderick Spencer and died at Genesee Falls, and William, who became a prominent teacher and afterward a soldier of the Civil War. Elisha Smith saw service in the War of 1812.

58.

Jesse Adams, Jr., b. Pawlet, Vermont, October 19, 1792. His death date is not known, but it was claimed to be before the 1830 federal census; m. (2) Mabel Spencer, b. a. 1796, Pawlet, Vermont, settled in Gainesville, Wyoming County, New York, d. Mt. Morris, New York January 9, 1863. Prosper Adams, Jesse's older brother, moved to Nunda in 1816. Jesse, his mother, and most of his siblings moved to the Nunda/Portage area later that same year. The Spencer family moved to the Nunda area in 1817. Jesse Adams, Jr. and Mabel Spencer were married by 1818, the year of their first child's birth. In the 1820 federal census Jesse and his family resided in Gainesville, Wyoming County, New York. He had three sons and two daughters. In the 1830 federal census Mabel Adams lived in Sparta, Livingston County, with two sons, one aged 5 to 10 years, a second son between the ages of 10-15, and a daughter aged 10-15. Mabel Adams does not appear in the 1840 and 1850 federal census records. The 1855 New York State Census recorded Mabel Adams residing in Nunda, New York with her daughter, Jane, and son, Franklin. In the 1860 federal census Mabel Adams resided in Nunda, New York with her daughter Jane Adams, age 24, who was a school teacher. However, this data has some problems because the ages of Jane and Franklin Adams in the 1860 federal census mean they were born after their father's assumed death.

It is unclear how many children Jesse and Mabel Adams had. The genealogy about the descendants of Henry Adams of Braintree identified four children: Clark, Ralph, George, and Laura. The Centennial History of Nunda, New York identifies four: Clark, George, Jane, and Frank. It is my contention that Jesse Adams, Jr. was married before his union with Mabel Spencer and that this marriage produced at least one child, a son, Nicholas Adams, born in Saratoga County, New York in the years 1812 to 1814. Saratoga County was a natural migration point for New Englanders from Vermont traveling west to take advantage of land sales in western New York. It is also my assumption that Jesse Adams, Jr.'s first wife died and the son, Nicholas, was left with maternal grandparents or other relatives to be raised.

There was a Jesse Adams, Jr. who purchased land in Illinois on July 31, 1841. This could be Jesse Adams, Jr. of Gainesville, New York because his eldest daughter, Laura, moved to Illinois after her marriage and by 1843 and because Laura's son, Albert Burr Clark, Jr. was born in Illinois and his youngest daughter, Jane, and her family also moved to Illinois. However, the land purchase would have been after Jesse Adams, Jr.'s assumed death. There was a Jesse Adams born in Vermont in 1792, the same year as Jesse Adams, Jr., residing in Iowa with the Noel Adams family. It is less clear if this Jesse Adams in Iowa is the same Jesse Adams, Jr. of Gainesville, New York. It remains unknown where Jesse Adams, Jr. died and when. Did he and Mable Spencer Adams, his wife, separate? There is no documentation to currently answer these questions, but if the Jesse Adams, Jr. who purchased land in Illinois in 1841 is the Jesse Adams, Jr. of Gainesville, New York, then this solidifies the claim that both Jane Adams and Franklin Adams were his children.

The assumption that Jesse Adams, Jr. died before 1830 was probably based on the US Census for 1830 listing Mabel Adams as the head of the household in Livingston County, New York with three children. However, Mabel Adams had four living children by 1830. Where is the fourth child and third son? The 1830 US Census does list a Jesse Adams residing in Franklin, Illinois with a wife and six children. This could be Jesse Adams, Jr. because a Jesse Adams, Jr. later purchased forty acres of land in Illinois in 1841. Four of the children listed in this Census record correspond in age to Jesse and Mabel's known children. There were two additional daughters listed. The 1820 US Census does list an additional daughter who must have died in comparing the 1820 and 1830 US Census records. Jesse Adams, Jr. had to be alive after 1830 because he fathered two more children: Jane and Franklin Spencer Adams. Mabel Adams died at the home of her son, Clark B. Adams, a Mt. Morris attorney in 1863. It is not known where Mabel and Jesse Adams, Jr. were buried.

Children: (by a first marriage)

60. I. **Nicholas Adams**, f.

Children: (by marriage to Mabel Spencer)

61. I. **Laura Adams**, f.

62. II. **Clark B. Adams**, f.

63. III. **Ralph H. Adams**, f.

64. IV. **George Jesse Adams**, f.

65. V. **Jane Adams**, f.

66. VI. **Frank S. Adams**, f.

References: Vermont Vital Records 1720-1908 for Jesse Adams, Jr.'s birth; US Census: 1820 for Jesse, Jr., 1830 for Mabel Adams, 1830 US Census for

Jessee Adams in Illinois, 1860 for Mabel Adams; New York State Census: 1855 for Mabel Adams; Illinois Public Land Purchase Records 1813-1909 for Jesse Adams, Jr.; Mt. Morris, New York Register of Deaths, 1863 for Mabel Adams; Centennial History of Nunda, New York.

60.

Nicholas Adams, b. between 1811 and 1814, Saratoga County, New York, d. June 10, 1890 Nunda, New York, from an accidental suicide from a laudanum overdose; m. place and date not known, Mary Ann Herald, b. a. 1810 Saratoga County, New York, d. June 21, 1890 Nunda, New York from cancer of the face. Mary Adams was the daughter of Elias and Phebe Herald from Saratoga County, New York. The evidence for Nicholas Adams being the son of Jesse Adams, Jr. is circumstantial. His death certificate identifies his father as Jesse Adams; mother unknown. He settled in the Portage section of Nunda where known Adams family descendants resided and were recorded in the Centennial History of the Town of Nunda. Several of their children were given traditional Adams first names including Louise, Mary Elizabeth, John, and Jesse. Nicholas and his wife were buried in unmarked graves in Oakhill Cemetery in a lot next to that of Jesse Adams, his son. These are large lots and are able to accommodate at least four family members.

Nicholas Adams first appears in Census records in 1840 residing in Ballston, Saratoga County, New York. He had three sons under five years of age and two daughters between the ages of 5 and 9. He farmed. Nicholas Adams and his family cannot be found on the 1850 US Census, but they are listed on the 1855 New York State Census residing in Watervliet, Albany County, New York. One of his sons and one of his daughters appear to be dead by 1855, but two more sons and two more daughters were born after the 1840 US Census. In the 1860 federal census Nicholas, transcribed Nchabes, Adams resided in Mt. Morris, Livingston County, New York with his wife and three children: Mary Elizabeth, John, and Jesse. Nicholas farmed. The 1865 New York State Census found Nicholas Adams employed as a laborer in Mt. Morris with daughter Louisa and sons, John and Jesse, residing with him. In the 1870 federal census Nicholas and Mary Adams moved to Hume, Allegany County, New York living with their daughter and son-in-law, Francis and Louise Sargent. However, Mary Adams' age is incorrect. In the 1875 New York State Census and the 1880 US Census Nicholas and Mary Adams were farming at Nunda Station, lived alone, on a farm next to their son, Jesse Adams.

In 1880 the Nicholas Adams farm tilled three acres of land with another two acres in other farm use. The farm value was $4000 and the farm implements were valued at $100 with livestock valued at $300. Farm income for 1879 was listed as $500. There were three cows and 100 pounds of cheese were made. Both peaches and potatoes were harvested and sold, but in small amounts. The farm appears to be on a downward decline given the agricultural statistics and this may be due to the age of Nicholas Adams working a farm by himself.

Nicholas Adams was an accidental suicide on Tuesday morning June 10, 1890 at 5 a.m. because of an overdose of laudanum. Mr. Adams had purchased two ounces of laudanum at Robinson's drug store (Nunda) on Monday and took about half of it near noon. He went into a drowsy stupor about 3 p.m. when a daughter discovered that something was wrong and sent for Doctors Alley and Ostrander. Nicholas Adams died peacefully the next morning. He was 79 years of age and lived on Oakland Road. A son, identified as D. C. Adams, probably Dewitt Clinton Adams, lived in the next house. His 80-year-old wife was suffering from cancer of the face. He may have purchased the laudanum for her use and probably took it himself in a moment of despondency. Mr. Adams was not a drinking man, had no reason to wish to die, and had everything to make his home comfortable. Mrs. Adams died June 21, 1890 from cancer of the face. They were buried in Nunda's Oakhill Cemetery but no markers are in evidence.

When Nicholas Adams died in 1890, four of the six adult children of Jesse Adams, Jr. and Mabel Spencer Adams were already dead. Laura Adams Clark had died in 1877 in Illinois, Ralph H. Adams had died in Cincinnati, Ohio in 1864, George C. Adams had died in Ceres, Pennsylvania in 1862, and Clark B. Adams committed suicide in Mr. Morris, New York in 1869. There are no documents from these four potential half-siblings of Nicholas Adams to confirm his descent from Jesse Adams, Jr. Franklin S. Adams died in 1900 in an insane asylum and Jane died in 1913 in Illinois.

Appendix I : The Adams Family of Nunda, New York

By the time of Nicholas Adams' death his line of descent was the only Adams line still in Livingston County potentially descended from Henry Adams of Braintree. Nicholas Adams' grandson, Frank Carter, and his great-grandson, Allen Carter, were both committed to insane asylums. Both Carters were the son and grandson of Mary Elizabeth Adams Carter, Nicholas' daughter. It cannot be confirmed that mental illness is hereditary but it could be a possible family trait. When Nicholas Adams moved to Livingston County, New York he resided in Mt. Morris, Portageville, and Nunda, New York where children and grandchildren of Jesse Adams, Jr. and Mabel Spencer Adams then resided.

Children:

67. I. **Alta A. Adams**, b. a. 1835 Saratoga County, New York. She was listed on the 1855 New York State Census, but further information is unavailable.

68. II. **Cortland Adams**, b. a. 1837 Saratoga County, New York. He was listed on the 1855 New York State Census, but further information is unavailable.

69. III. **Dewitt C. Adams**, f.

70. IV. **Louise Adams**, f.

71. V. **Mary Elizabeth Adams**, (see listing under Daniel Carter).

72. VI. **John N. Adams**, b. a. 1847 Saratoga County, New York. He was listed on the 1855 New York State Census, but further information is unavailable.

73. VII. **Jesse Adams**, f.

References: US Census: 1840, 1860, 1870, 1880; New York State Census: 1855, 1865, 1875; Oakhill Cemetery Records, Nunda, New York; NYS Death Index 1880-1956 for Nicholas Adams; Nunda News, June 14, 1890 and June 28, 1890; Town of Nunda, Nunda, New York Death Certificate for Nicholas Adams; Centennial History of Nunda, New York.

61.

Laura Spencer Adams, b. a. 1818 New York State, died Galesburg, Illinois 1877; m. probably New York State, date not known, Albert Burr Clark, Sr., b. Manchester, Vermont February 23, 1817, d. Galesburg, Illinois February 10, 1882. Laura Adams Clark's first two children were born in New York State. When their third child, Albert Burr Clark, Jr., was born on October 1843, they had moved to Galesburg, Illinois where they resided until their respective deaths. Albert Clark, Sr. was employed as a carpenter his entire life. Laura Spencer Adams Clark and her husband, Albert, were buried in Hope Cemetery, Galesburg, Illinois

Children:

74.   I.   ***George Adams Clark***, f.

75.   II.   ***Florence Clark***, f.

76.   III.   ***Albert Burr Clark, Jr.***, f.

77.   IV.   ***Laura Clark***, Galesburg, Illinois 1848, d. Galesburg, Illinois 1849 and was buried in the family plot in Hope Cemetery, Galesburg, Illinois.

78.   V.   ***Laura Elizabeth Clark***, b. Galesburg, Illinois February 15, 1850, d. Decatur, Michigan, July 25, 1927. She resided in Galesburg through 1910 until she moved to Michigan, where she resided with a niece, Jennie Clark Hunt. Laura never married and no employment was listed for her. She was buried in Hope Cemetery in Galesburg in the Clark family plot.

79.   VI.   ***Frederick B. Clark***, b. Galesburg, Illinois 1852, d. February 1860, from scarlet fever after suffering for five days. He was buried in Hope Cemetery, Galesburg, Illinois, in the Clark family plot.

80.   VII.   ***Infant Son Clark***, b. and d. Galesburg, Illinois, 1855, and buried in Hope Cemetery, Galesburg, Illinois.

81.   VIII.   ***Frank M. Clark***, b. Galesburg, Illinois 1856, d. Galesburg, Illinois, 1872, and was buried in Hope Cemetery in Galesburg in the Clark

family plot.

82. IX. *Mabel Clark*, f.

References: US Census: 1830, 1850, 1870, 1880; Hope Cemetery Records, Galesburg, Illinois.

62.

Clark B. Adams, b. Gainesville, New York September 12, 1820 (a twin), d. Mt. Morris, New York December 9, 1869; m. place and date not known, Alma Thompson, b. place not known, a. 1827, d. place and date not known. In the 1850 US Census Clark Adams was listed as an attorney residing in Mt. Morris, New York with his wife and mother-in-law. Clark Adams' law practice was located on 1 Main Street in Mount Morris. His land value was $400. They continued to reside in Mt. Morris based on the 1855 New York State Census, the 1860 US Census, and the 1865 New York State Census. Their first son was born in 1864 and two more sons were born after 1865. Clark Adams committed suicide by cutting his throat. It is not known where he was buried. In 1870 Mrs. Adams resided in Trumansburg, New York with her oldest and youngest son. The middle child must have died. She resided with Henry Barto, a banker, and his family who may have been related as one of her sons had Barto as a middle name. It is not known where Clark and Alma Adams were buried.

Children:

83. I. *Richard Vernon Adams*, f.

84. II. *Henry Barto Adams*, b. Mt. Morris, New York May 2, 1865, baptized St. John's Church in Mt. Morris, New York October 29, 1865, d. before the 1870 US Census. His burial location is not known.

85. III. *Frederick Clark Adams*, f.

References: US Census: 1850, 1860, 1870; New York State Census: 1855, 1865; US Federal Census Mortality Schedules 1850-1885; Watertown Daily Times January 6, 1870; New York Episcopal Diocese of Rochester, New York Church Records 1800-1970 for Henry B. Adams.

63.

Ralph H. Adams, b. Gainesville, New York September 12, 1820 (a twin), d. Cincinnati, Ohio March 14, 1864; m. Portageville, New York February 6, 1845 Almira Elmer, b. Ceres, New York September 12, 1845, d. Mandan, Wisconsin 1925. At the time of his marriage Ralph Adams' occupation was listed as a merchant with the military rank of major. No military documentation can currently be found for this military rank. His wife was the daughter of Elijah Elmer, Esquire, an attorney residing in Portage, New York. At the time of the 1850 US Census, Ralph Adams and his family resided in Genesee Township, New York with his wife and two eldest children. He was a lumberman. In the 1855 New York State Census Ralph and Almira had three children: Allen, Sarah, and Henry and still resided in Genesee Township in Allegany County, New York. At the time of the 1860 US Census Ralph Adams had moved his family to Rochester, New York. Ralph Adams died unexpectedly after arriving in Cincinnati, Ohio. The cause of death remains unknown. Mr. Adams had appeared in good health until his sudden death. It is not known where Mr. and Mrs. Adams were buried.

Children:

86 I. ***Allen Adams***, f.

87. II. ***Sarah Alice Adams***, f.

88. III. ***Henry Adams***, f.

References: US Census: 1850, 1860; New York State Census: 1855; Rochester Daily Advertiser February 22, 1845; Onion and Advertiser March 15, 1864; New York Wills and Probate Records 1659-1999.

64.

George Jesse Adams, b. Gainesville, New York January 1826, d. Ceres, Pennsylvania June 15, 1862; m. place and date not known, Ann, last name not known. George Adams resided in Ceres, Pennsylvania where he was listed as a merchant and a lumberman. He died young and further information about his wife and career are currently not known. He was buried in Evergreen Cemetery, Ceres, Pennsylvania.

References: US Census: 1850, 1860; Evergreen Cemetery Records, Ceres, Pennsylvania.

65.

Jane "Jennie" Adams, b. New York State January 9, 1838; d. Galva, Illinois May 7, 1913; m. Galva, Illinois July 26, 1871 Oscar A. Hempstead, b. 1837, d. Galva, Illinois January 2, 1912. There is some confusion about Jane Adams' birthdate. The 1900 US Census gives the date as January 1845. Her younger brother, Franklin Adams, was also born in 1838 according to some records, but in August. However, Franklin's birth year is variously given as 1837, 1838, and 1839. Jane was known as Jennie and taught school in Mt. Morris. She moved to Illinois where her older sister, Laura, resided and married there. Jennie had one child who died in infancy according to the 1900 US Census. She raised her husbands three children: Edwin, Winifred, and Josephine, from his first marriage to Josephine Lloyd Hempstead who died in 1870. Jane and Oscar Hempstead were buried in Galva Cemetery, Galva, Illinois.

References: US Census: 1850, 1860, 18880, 1900, 1910; New York State Census: 1855, 1865; Galva Cemetery Records, Galva, Illinois; Illinois Marriage Index 1860-1920.

66.

Franklin Spencer Adams, b. Nunda, New York August 23, 1838, d. Jacksonville, Illinois September 9, 1900. There is a dispute about the birthdate of Franklin Adams. His death certificate provided the date of August 23, 1838, which would have meant that he was born seven and one-half months after his sister Jane. It could have been possible, but risky in that era for two births so close together. Various Census records indicate that the age difference between Franklin and Jane made him one to three years younger than his sister. In 1855 he resided in Nunda with his mother and sister Jane and was employed as a clerk. In 1860 Franklin Adams had moved to Olean, New York where he also worked as a clerk. He enlisted August 16, 1862 into the US Army at Portage, New York as a Second

Lieutenant. He was promoted to First Lieutenant on October 1, 1862 with Company I, New York 1st Calvary Regiment. Lieutenant Adams was mustered out on June 20, 1865 at Cloud's Mills, Virginia. It is not known where he resided between 1865 and 1900 when he was committed to the Hospital for the Insane in Morgan, Illinois where he died on September 9, 1900. His commitment papers indicate he was divorced, but there is no record of marriage or knowledge of children born to a marriage for him at this time. Franklin Adams was buried in Jacksonville East Cemetery, Jacksonville, Illinois.

References: US Census: 1860, 1900; New York State Census: 1855; Jacksonville East Cemetery Records, Jacksonville, Illinois; Illinois Wills and Probate Records 1772-1999 for his commitment; Illinois Death Index 1877-1916; Civil War Soldier Records and Profiles 1861-1865; New York Town Clerks' Registers of Men who served in the Civil War 1861-1865.

69.

Dewitt Clinton Adams, b. New York State March 1838, d. New York State 1915; m. Margaret Jane Clarkson Williams, b. New York State 1840, d. New York State 1918. Dewitt Adams resided in Saratoga County and later Watervliet as a young boy. He moved with his parents to Mt. Morris in Livingston County where he farmed. In 1870 Mr. Adams moved his wife and children to Poughkeepsie New York where he either worked as a laborer, master roofer, or famer. Their two sons, George Washington Adams and William Adams, were baptized at St. Paul's Church in Poughkeepsie on March 20, 1870. They continued to reside in Duchess County, New York in Wappinger, New York until their respective deaths. However, the obituary of Nicholas Adams, the father of Dewitt Adams, states that Dewitt farmed the neighboring property in 1890. There is no surviving 1892 New York State Census for Livingston County to verify this. Dewitt and Margaret Adams were buried in Fishkill Rural Cemetery, Fishkill, New York. They had three children: George Washington Adams, born 1859, William Adams, born 1864, and Susan Francis Adams, born 1880 who married a Mr. Pulling and died in 1962. Susan was buried with her parents.

References: US Census: 1850, 1860, 1870, 1880, 1900, 1910; New York State Census: 1855, 1865, 1892; Fishkill Rural Cemetery Records, Fishkill, New York; New York Episcopal Diocese of New York Church Records 1767-1970.

70.

Louis/Lois/Louise Adams, New York State May 1847, d. Bolivar, New York July 18, 1904; m. place and date not know, Francis Wagland Sargent, b. Nunda, New York September 7, 1835, d. Milwaukee, Wisconsin April 4, 1913; believed divorced or separated. Lois or Louise Adams resided with her parents until her marriage on Oakland Road. In the 1870 US Census she and her husband resided in Hume, New York where they ran a lodging house and her parents, Nicholas and Mary Adams resided with them. Lois could not be found on the New York State Census for 1875 probably because she had already moved to Titusville, Pennsylvania by 1880 where she was employed as a domestic servant. Her husband could not be found in any future documents. In the 1892 New York State Census Lois Sargent was residing in Bolivar, New York where she operated a boarding house. Her nephew, Willie Adams, lived with her. In 1900 Lois Sargent continued to reside in Bolivar, New York with her nephew, but her boarding house was coming under increasing scrutiny because several of the women who resided with her were arrested in Olean, New York for prostitution. The 1900 US Census listed Lois as married, but the whereabouts of her husband are unclear. Lois Adams Sargent died July 18, 1904 from heart disease at the age of 57. Her obituary records that she came to Bolivar during the oil boom and operated a shady resort in a building on Railroad Avenue where she died. Bolivar police raided her residence over several years, but the last five years of her life that police action had stopped. It is not known who her survivors were since her nephew, William N. Adams, had died a few months earlier and her siblings were either deceased or living in eastern New York State. Lois Sargent was taken to Oakhill Cemetery in Nunda for burial, probably in her parent's lot. There is no marker in evidence. Her estate was valued at $5000, which today would amount to $143,632.85. This was a sizeable inheritance and who benefited from it is not known. Her residence on Railroad Avenue was sold to the W. H.

Benson family by August 4, 1904.

Frederick Wagland Sargent enlisted with the 33rd New York Volunteers, Company F in Nunda, New York May 30, 1861. His enlistment papers described him as being 5' 9" tall with a dark complexion. He was employed as a carpenter. He was discharged May 30, 1863 because his term of service had expired and his vision was severely impaired. After discharge he married Lois Adams and they resided in Hume, New York until they separated. From 1886 to 1905, Mr. Sargent was admitted twelve times to various National Homes for Veterans from Leavenworth, Kansas; Danville, Illinois; Johnson City, Tennessee; Togus, Maine; Marion, Indiana; Bath, New York and Milwaukee, Wisconsin. Francis W. Sargent died in Milwaukee, Wisconsin April 4, 1913 and was buried in the Wood National Cemetery there. A marker is in evidence.

References: US Census: 1850, 1860, 1870, 1880, 1900; New York State Census: 1855, 1865, 1892; Oakhill Cemetery Records, Nunda, New York; Bolivar Breeze, February 25, 1904, July 21, 1904, August 4, 1904; NYS DI 1880-1956. US National Homes for Disabled Volunteer Soldiers 1866-1938; New York Civil War Muster Roll Abstracts 1861-1900; Wood National Cemetery Records, Milwaukee, Wisconsin.

73.

Jesse Adams, b. New York State a. 1852, d. New York State, date not known but by 1892; m. place and date not known, Mary F., last name not known, b. a. 1852, d. date and place not known but by 1892. Jesse Adams was employed as a farmer working in Mt. Morris, Nunda Station, Granger township, and Bolivar, New York. The 1880 New York State Census indicated that he farmed the property next to his father's property on Oakland Road. I assume both Jesse and his wife were deceased by 1892, because their only child, Willie Adams, was living in Bolivar, New York with his maternal aunt, Lois Sargent. The obituary of their son, William Nicholas Adams, in 1904 states that both Jesse and Mary F. Adams were deceased. It is believed that Jesse and Mary Adams were buried in Oakhill Cemetery, Nunda, New York in the plot they purchased next to his parents. No markers are in evidence.

Children:

89. I. ***William Nicholas Adams***, f.

74.

George Adams Clark, b. New York State March 1840, d. Decatur, Michigan July 6, 1873; m. place and date not known Sarah L. Williams, b. Galesburg, Illinois a. 1846, place of death and date of death not known. Mr. Clark enlisted in the Civil War August 14, 1861 and was discharged with a disability in St. Louis, Missouri December 6, 1862. He served as a Sergeant in Company E, 23rd Illinois Infantry. He was described as being 5' 6" tall with light hair and blue eyes. Mr. Clark was employed as a farmer before enlistment. He moved to Decatur, Michigan where he died. George Adams Clark was buried in Hope Cemetery, Galesburg, Illinois. Further information on his wife is not currently available. They had two children: Jennie E. Clark and William C. Clark.

Children:

90. I. ***Jennie Clark***, f.

91. II. ***William C. Clark***, f.

References: US Census: 1850, 1860, 1870; Headstones for Deceased Civil War Veterans 1861-1904; Illinois Data Bases, Veterans Index 1775-1995; Hope Cemetery Records, Galesburg, Illinois; Undocumented family tree on Ancestry.Com; Illinois Wills and Probate Records 1772-1999 for Albert Burr Clark, Jr.; Michigan Death Records 1867-1952 for George Clark.

75.

Florence Clark, b. Rochester, New York October 15, 1843, d. Sao Paulo, Brazil April 4, 1927; m. Knox County, Illinois March 9, 1863 William Byrnes/Byrns, b. Angelica, New York 1838, d. Galesburg, Illinois June 10, 1875. William Byrnes was a medical doctor and served in the Civil War as a Captain with Company B, 1st Michigan Infantry. He was buried in Hope Cemetery, Galesburg, Illinois. Florence remained in Galesburg residing with various relatives including her father. She had no occupation other than "Capitalist" on the Census records. She traveled with the Carl W.

Cooper family to Sao Paulo, Brazil where Mrs. Clark applied for residency on December 10, 1915 and it was given. Her income was from a Civil War pension. Her death was caused by a heart attack, acute indigestion, and old age. She was buried in The Blossom Home Cemetery in Sao Paulo. There is a grave maker for her in the Clark burial plot, but it is not clear if her remains were transferred from Brazil to Illinois. Florence and William Byrnes had one son, Albert Clark Byrnes, but his whereabouts were unknown at the time of her death in Brazil and her nearest kin was a Clark cousin in Galesburg, Illinois.

Children:

92. I. ***Albert C. Byrnes***, f.

References: US Census: 1850, 1860, 1880, 1900, 1910; U.S. Consular Registration Certificates 1907-1918; Reports of Deaths Abroad of American Citizens Abroad 1835-1974; Headstones for Deceased Union Veterans 1861-1904; Hope Cemetery Records, Galesburg, Illinois; The Blossom Home Cemetery, Sao Paulo, Brazil; Illinois Marriage Records 1800-1940.

76.

Albert Burr Clark, Jr., b. Hamilton County New York March 1840, d. Galesburg, Illinois January 10, 1914. Albert, Jr. never married. He resided at the family home in Galesburg and then as a bachelor. He was employed as a druggist. Mr. Clark briefly served in the Civil War enlisting in Galesburg May 14, 1864 and being mustered out October 28, 1864 serving with Company D of the 139th Illinois Infantry as a private. His probated will left his estate to be divided between his surviving sisters Florence Clark Byrnes and Laura E. Clark and his nieces Jennie Clark Hunt and Emma W. Byrnes and his nephew William C. Clark.

References: USI Census: 1850, 1860, 1870 1880, 1900; Illinois Wills and Probate Records 1772-1999; Hope Cemetery Records, Galesburg, Illinois; Headstones for Deceased Union Veterans 1861-1904.

82.

Mabel Clark, b. Galesburg, Illinois December 12, 1858, d. Oneida, Illinois September 24, 1885; m. Galva, Illinois December 6, 1882 Lyman Baxter Shedd, b. Farmington, Illinois March 20, 1857, d. Oneida, Illinois December 1, 1905. Mabel Clark Shedd was buried in Hope Cemetery, Galesburg, Illinois. Lyman Shedd remarried to Flora Belle Hosler in Oneida, Illinois October 4, 1892, b. Brownsville, Ohio April 19, 1863, d. Oneida, Illinois July 22, 1941 and was buried in Ontario Cemetery. It is not known where Lyman Shedd was buried. He had two children by his second marriage: Clarence Ezra Shedd, b. December 24, 1893 in Oneida, Illinois and died in Oneida March 1980 and Lucille Evelyn Shedd, b. Oneida, Illinois February 26, 1901, d. Oneida April 1985.

References: US Census: 1860, 1870, 1880; Illinois Marriage Records 1851-1900; Illinois Death Records 1916-1947; Ontario Cemetery Records for Flora Hosler Shedd; Hope Cemetery Records, Galesburg, Illinois.

83.

Richard Vernon Adams, b. Trumansburg, New York November 11, 1858, d. Chicago, Illinois August 1, 1928; m. a. 1879 Rose Coggins, b. October 1852/1857, d. Milwaukee, Wisconsin July 26, 1948. Richard Adams resided in Trumansburg, New York after his father's death in 1869 and through the 1880 US Census. He was employed as a railroad express agent. He moved his family to Manitowoc, Wisconsin where he continued to work for the railroads as a billing clerk, a clerk for the railroad commission, and a rate clerk for the railroad commission. In 1910 the Adams family had moved to Watertown, Wisconsin and in 1920 to Chicago where he died. After his death, his widow ran a boarding house in Madison, Wisconsin. Richard and Rose Adams were buried in Resurrection Cemetery, Madison, Wisconsin.

Children:

93.   I.   **Vernon C. Adams**, f.

References: US Census: 1860, 1870, 1880, 1900, 1910, 1920; Resurrection Cemetery Records, Madison, Wisconsin.

85.

Frederick Clark Adams, b. Mt. Morris, New York July 12, 1868, d. Kansas City, Missouri March 29, 1944; m. 1898 May D., last name not known, b. Chicago, Illinois September 7, 1873, d. Kansas City, Missouri June 5, 1966. The 1900 US Census recorded that Frederick Adams and his wife did not have any children. He was employed as a railroad cashier in Kansas City, Missouri where they resided the rest of their lives. Mr. Adams was also employed as a Vice-President of a Storage Transfer Company. They were buried in Mt. Washington Cemetery, Kansas City, Missouri.

References: US Census: 1870, 1880, 1900, 1910, 1920, 1930, 1940; New York State Census: 1875; Mt. Washington Cemetery Records, Kansas City, Missouri.

86.

Allen Adams, b. Ceres, New York September 12, 1845/December 1847, d. Mondovi, Wisconsin July 15, 1925; m. probably Wisconsin, a. 1875 Rose Etta Bangle, b. Augusta, Wisconsin March 19, 1851, d. Minneapolis, Minnesota March 1, 1920. Allen Adams resided in Ceres or Genesee Township in Allegany County, New York until 1860 when the family moved to Rochester, New York. After the death of his father, Allen Adams briefly lived with a paternal uncle, Clark B. Adams, in Mt. Morris, New York. Mr. Adams moved to Wisconsin after 1870 and remained in that state for most of his life where he farmed in Bridge Creek and Cleveland, Wisconsin. In 1910 he took his family to Minneapolis, Minnesota where they ran a boarding house. They had five children all of whom grew to adulthood. Allen Adams died at his daughter's residence from stomach cancer. Allen and Rose Adams were buried in Riverside City Cemetery, Mondavi, Wisconsin.

Children:

94. I. **Ray Adams**, f.

95. II. **LeRoy Edward "Roy" Adams**, f.

96. III. Ralph Adams, b. Eau Claire, Wisconsin January 10, 1880, d.

Auburn, California November 8, 1911 and buried Placer County Hospital Cemetery, Auburn, California. Cause of death not known.

97. IV.   *Ruby Marion Adams*, f.

98. V.   *Rusk Adams*, f.

References: US Census: 1850, 1860, 1870, 1880, 1900, 1910, 1920; New York State Census: 1855, 1865; Riverside City Cemetery Records, Mondavi, Wisconsin; Wisconsin State Census: 1895, 1905; Placer County Hospital Cemetery Records, Auburn, California.

87.

Alice Adams, b. Ceres, New York November 1848, d. Wyoming County, New York September 4, 1936; m. New York State a. 1869 Edwin Stebbins, b. New York State August 1848, d. Tonawanda, New York August 7, 1907. Alice resided with her parents until her father's death. For a time, she resided with her mother and younger brother with a maternal uncle in Hume, New York until her marriage to Edwin Stebbins. During their married years Alice and Edwin Stebbins lived in Portageville, New York, Genesee Falls, New York, and Attica, New York where he was employed as a carpenter. During the Civil War, Mr. Stebbins served with Company F, 33rd New York Infantry from May 22, 1861 to June 2, 1863. For the last twenty-five years of his employment history, Mr. Stebbins worked for the Erie Railroad as a bridge foreman. Alice and Edwin Stebbins were buried in Forest Hill Cemetery in Attica, New York.

Children:

99. I.   *Ralph A. Stebbins*, b. May 1870, d. Lyons, New York, December 2, 1913. He was employed as a carpenter and bridge builder, and he resided with his parents until his death. He did not marry and was buried in Forest Hill Cemetery, Attica, New York.

100. II.   *Nellie Stebbins*, f.

101. III. *Carl Stebbins*, b. March 1877, date and place of death not known. He was employed as a railroad carpenter and was single when last

on a US Census. Further information is not currently available.

102. IV. *Edwin Stebbins*, b. New York State 1878, d. Attica November 3, 1893, and was buried in Forest Hill Cemetery, Attica, New York.

103. V. *Myra Stebbins*, b. Wyoming County, New York July 1889, d. Buffalo, New York, September 29, 1900, and was buried in Forest Hill Cemetery, Attica, New York.

References: US Census: 1850, 1860, 1870, 1880, 1900, 1910, 1920, 1930; New York State Census: 1855, 1865; Forest Hill Cemetery Records, Attica, New York; North Tonawanda the Evening News August 7, 1907 obituary.

88.

Henry Adams, b. Hume, New York April 1852, d. after 1915; m. probably Wyoming County, New York a. 1879, Rose, last name not know, b. New York State a. 1862, d. probably Paterson, New Jersey November 15, 1916. Henry Adams was employed as a railroad freight agent most of his life working in Genesee Falls, New York, Patterson, New Jersey, and New York City. The 1900 US Census recorded that Henry and Rose Adams had been married 21 years and they had had two children with only one living. However, the 1880 US Census records a first-born son born in 1879. It is not currently known where Henry Adams was buried. Rose Adams was buried in Cedar Lawn Cemetery, Paterson, New Jersey.

Children:

104. I. *John Q. Adams*, b. New York State 1879 and recorded on the 1880 US Census, but no further record on this son survives.

105. II. *Ralph Henry Adams*, b. Genesee Falls, New York May 31, 1880, d. Paterson, New Jersey, April 17, 1927. Mr. Adams was employed as a musician and as a railroad Agent. It appears he never married. Where he was buried is unknown, but Presbyterian Church Records list Paterson, New Jersey.

106. III. *John Elmer Adams*, b. Genesee Falls, New York February 1889, d. 1904 and buried in Cedar Lawn Cemetery, Paterson, New Jersey.

References: US Census: 1860, 1870, 1880, 1900, 1910; New York State Census: 1855, 1865, 1915; New Jersey State Census: 1895, 1905; Cedar Lawn Cemetery Records, Paterson, New Jersey; New Jersey Death Index 1901-2017 for Ralph H. Adams; US Presbyterian Church Records 1701-1970 for Ralph H. Adams.

89.

William Nicholas Adams, b. Nunda, New York either August or October 1879, d. Whitesville, New York from a nitroglycerine explosion February 16, 1904. Willie Adams resided with his parents until their death on a farm on Oakland Road in Nunda, New York. He briefly attended Nunda High School. From 1892 until his 1904 death, Mr. Adams resided with his aunt, Lois Sargent, in Bolivar, New York. He was regarded as an expert oil well shooter and was employed by the Van Curen High Explosives Company, Bolivar, New York. He was known as a quiet young man, very careful with his work, who had many friends. On a Tuesday morning, he left Bolivar with a two-horse team and sleigh carrying 190 quarts of nitroglycerine. The sleigh tipped over and the explosion occurred. Nothing remained of the sleigh. Only a few small body parts could be found for Willie Adams. A house and barn fifteen rods away were destroyed. Windows in homes over a half-mile away were broken. Windows in Greenwood, New York were shaken and several students at the Marsh School were found unconscious from the blast. A hole eight feet deep and fifteen feet long was blown into the frozen ground. William Adams' obituary was found in the poetry book of his cousin, Belle Fuller Root. William Adams was buried in Oakwood Cemetery, Nunda, New York instead of in the family plots in Oakhill Cemetery. The Bolivar Breeze for February 25, 1904 carried a card of thanks from his aunt, Mrs. Louis Sargent.

References: US Census: 1880, 1900; New York State Census: 1892; Bolivar Breeze February 18, 1904 and February 25, 1904; The Livingston Democrat, February 24, 1904; The Greenwood Times, February 1904; The Belmont Courier, March 1, 1904; The Truth of Nunda, February 19, 1904; The Whitesville News, March 24, 1910; Oakwood Cemetery Records, Nunda, New York.

90.

Jennie E. Clark, b. Galesburg, Illinois November 18, 1866, d. Battle Creek, Michigan September 3, 1947; m. Galesburg, Illinois December 19, 1890 Reuben William Hunt, Jr., b. Salerlong, Illinois October 6, 1866, d. Decatur, Illinois December 14, 1926. Reuben Hunt was a successful truck farmer. He died from angina. Jennie and Reuben Hunt did not have any children and were buried in Lakeside Cemetery, Decatur, Illinois.

References: US Census: 1870 1880, 1900, 1910, 1920, 1930, 1940; Lakeside Cemetery Records, Decatur, Michigan; Illinois Marriage Records 1860-1920; Michigan Death Records 1867-1952; The News Palladium, September 4, 1947 obituary for Jennie Clark Hunt.

91.

William C. Clark, b. Galesburg, Illinois March 1869, d. place and date not known.; m. 1895 Ella, last name not known, b. June 1871, place and date of death not known. The 1900 US Census noted William Clark's occupation as a bookkeeper. In 1910 Mr. Clark was employed as a milliner and in the 1920 and 1930 US Census records, he was a lumber salesman. They had two sons: Albert Warren born about 1902 and Theodore born about 1905. Further information on this line is not currently available.

References: US Census: 1900, 1910, 1920, 1930.

92.

Albert Clark Byrnes, b. Galesburg, Illinois Mary 1868, place and date of death not known; m. Christian, Illinois 1898 Emma E. Wilson, b. Faubourg, Illinois June 3, 1865, d. Normal, Illinois May 20, 1935. Based on the 1910 US Census, Emma Wilson Byrnes was a widow. It is not known when Albert Byrnes died. Records on his mother's death indicate she did not know what happened to him. In 1910 Emma Byrnes was employed as a hotel proprietor in Pontiac, Michigan. In 1920 she and her daughter, Florence, continued to reside in Pontiac where Emma was employed as a dressmaker and Florence was a teacher. In the 1930 US Census they moved to Peoria, Illinois where Emma resided with her daughter, son-in-law, and grandson. It is not currently known where Emma Byrnes was buried.

Children:

107.   I   *Florence Byrnes*, b. Galesburg, Illinois January 8, 1900, d. Normal, Illinois March 18, 1981; m. place and date not known, Thomas T. Linden, b. 1905, d. Bloomington, Illinois August 22, 1964. Mr. Linden was employed as an enameller in a washing machine factory and as a salesman. Florence and Thomas Linden were buried in Park Hill Cemetery in Bloomington, Illinois. They had two sons: Thomas Richard Linden born about 1923 and William Linden born about 1931. Further information on this line is not currently known.

References: US Census: 1880, 1900, 1910, 1920, 1930, 1940; Park Hill Cemetery Records, Bloomington, Illinois

93.

Vernon Clark Adams, b. Java Center, New York June 15, 1884, d. Madison, Wisconsin July 9, 1953, m. place and date not known Irma Whittman, b. Manitowoc, Wisconsin August 30, 1886, d. Beloit, Wisconsin January 9, 1975. From 1900 until his death Mr. Adams resided in Wisconsin. His World War I Draft Registration Card described him as being tall and slender with blue eyes and light hair. Vernon Adams was employed as a railroad rate commission clerk in Madison. Mr. Adams' World War II Draft Registration Card describe him as being 6' tall and weighing 197 pounds with blue eyes, gray hair, and a ruddy complexion. He had a scar on the right finger of his right hand. Vernon Adams was employed as a US Government Inspector for the railroads. His entire employment career was with the railroad industry. Vernon and Irma Adams had two sons, seven grandchildren and 1 great-grandchild. They were buried in Evergreen Cemetery, Manitowoc, Wisconsin.

Children

108.   I.   *Richard F. Adams*, f.

109.   II. *Robert Clark Adams*, f.

References: US Census: 1900, 1910, 1920, 1930, 1940; Evergreen Cemetery Records, Manitowoc, Wisconsin; World War I Draft Registration Card 1917-18; World War II Draft Registration Card 1942; Social Security Death Index.

94.

Ray Hartley Adams, b. Augusta, Wisconsin December 5, 1877, d. Sioux Falls, South Dakota January 9, 1914; m. Nobles, Minnesota May 27, 1902 Emma Josephine "Josie" Colvin, b. Minnesota February 6, 1877, d. Minneapolis, Minnesota November 15, 1942. Ray Adams resided in Bridge Creek and Fairchild, Wisconsin until he was twenty. An August 1898 local newspaper indicated that Mr. Adams was the pitcher for the Fairchild baseball team. In 1900, Ray Adams had moved to Minneapolis, Minnesota where he was employed as a lumber grader. He was single until his 1902 marriage. After his marriage and the birth of his son, the Adams family relocated to Magnolia, Minnesota and in 1910 was employed as a cashier at a bank. On January 9, 1914, Ray Adams committed suicide while at the Cataract Hotel (Room 70). The cause was not made known. Ray Adams was buried in Maplewood Cemetery in Luverne, Minnesota. Josephine Adams worked as a bank teller after her husband's death and continued to reside in Minneapolis. She was buried in Lakewood Cemetery, Minneapolis, Minnesota.

Children:

110.   I.   *Cedric Malcolm Adams*, f.

References: US Census: 1880, 1900, 1910, 1920; Maplewood Cemetery Records, Luverne, Minnesota; Lakewood Cemetery Records, Minneapolis, Minnesota.

95.

LeRoy Edward "Roy" Adams, b. Eau Claire, Wisconsin June 19, 1879, d. Minneapolis, Minnesota October 15, 1962; m. Willmar, Minnesota July 13, 1921 Ethel M. Gates, b. Wisconsin September 9, 1902, d. Minneapolis, Minnesota January 26, 1986. Roy Adams resided in Wisconsin until after the 1900 US Census where he was employed as a laborer. After moving to Minneapolis, Minnesota Mr. Adams was employed as a railroad switchman with the Great Northern Railroad. Both his World War I and World War II Draft Registration Cards describes him as being 5' 10" tall, weighing 148 pounds with brown eyes and brown hair. They had four daughters, one of whom died soon after birth. Roy and Ethel Adams were buried in Riverside City Cemetery, Mondovi, Wisconsin.

Children:

111.   I.   *Female Adams*, b. and d. 1922. Burial location is not known.

112.   II.   *Rosetta Ethel Adams*, b. Minnesota 1924, d. Roseville, Minnesota February 24, 2012; m. Ralph E. Henrikson, b. May 7, 1923, d. March 4, 2009, and buried in Roselawn Cemetery, Roseville, Minnesota. They had five children: Rose-Jean, Roxanne, Randy, Russ, and Roy.

113.   III.   *Barbara Adams*, b. Minneapolis, Minnesota December 18, 1926, place and date of death not known; m. Minneapolis December 27, 1945, Donald H. Kelly, divorced October 10, 1972. They had at least one daughter.

114.   IV.   *Dona Jean Adams*, b. Minneapolis, Minnesota October 10, 1928, d. Minneapolis, Minnesota September 14, 2019; m. Thomas Lee Grady, b. October 3, 1928, b. November 17, 2008. He served as a Corporal in the US Army. They were buried in Fort Snelling National Cemetery, Minneapolis, Minnesota.

References: US Census: 1880, 1900, 1910, 1920, 1930, 1940; Riverside City Cemetery Records, Mondovi, Wisconsin; World War I Draft Registration Card 1917-1918; World War II Draft Registration Card, 1942; Wisconsin Birth Index 1820-1907; Minnesota Death Index 1908-2002.

97.

Ruby Marion Adams, b. Bridge Creek, Wisconsin, d. Mondovi, Wisconsin January 25, 1951; m. place and date not known, James Arthur Harvey, b. 1881, d. 1967. Mr. Harvey was a farmer. They were buried in Oak Park

Cemetery, Mondovi, Wisconsin.

Children:

115. I. **Leland LeRoy Harvey**, b. Mondovi, Wisconsin August 30, 1909, d. Mondovi, Wisconsin October 28, 1996; m. September 20, 1930, Frances Lulu Helwig, b. Mondovi, Wisconsin April 19, 1910, d. Mondovi, Wisconsin October 28, 1996. They were buried in Oak Park Cemetery, Mondovi, Wisconsin.

116. II. **James N. "Jimmie" Harvey**, b. Mondovi, Wisconsin October 23, 1911, d. Spokane, Washington February 16, 1998. He served in World War II and the Korean War and was buried in Oak Park Cemetery, Mondovi, Wisconsin.

117. III. **Allen Alfred Harvey**, b. Mondovi, Wisconsin February 24, 1914, d. Spokane, Washington November 29, 2000; m. Fannie C. Kent, b. Mondovi, Wisconsin October 16, 1922, d. Spokane, Washington April 18, 1999. They were buried in Greenwood Memorial Terrace, Spokane, Washington.

118. IV. **Robert Joseph Harvey**, b. Mondovi, Wisconsin September 13, 1915, d. Waukegan, Illinois February 12, 1963; m. Myra N., last name not known, b. 1915, d. 1972. They were buried in Avon Center Cemetery, Grayslake, Illinois.

119. V. **Marian Harvey**, b. Mondovi, Wisconsin March 28, 1917, d. Lindenhurst, Illinois July 16, 2008; m. Charles F. Clow, b. Grayslake, Illinois November 26, 1918, d. Libertyville, Illinois August 28, 2000. Mr. Clow served with the US Navy during World War II in the Pacific for two years. They had two sons: Robert and Charles, Jr. and seven grandchildren. They were buried in Warren Cemetery, Gumee, Illinois.

120. VI. **Anne Jane "Annie" Harvey**, b. Mondovi, Wisconsin December 30, 1918, d. Eleva, Wisconsin June 24, 1999; m. Colonel Nyre, b. Naples, Wisconsin October 23, 1916, d. Strum, Wisconsin January 19, 1991. They had at least one Child, Jerry A, Nyre, b. 1939, d. 1940. All three were buried in Oak Park Cemetery, Mondovi, Wisconsin.

121. VII. ***Shirley Lynn Harvey***, b. Eau Clarie, Wisconsin December 12, 1926, d. Durand, Wisconsin April 1, 2017; m. Eleva, Wisconsin August 10, 1946, Melvin Richard Pederson, b. Drammen, Wisconsin February 6, 1918, d. Eleva, Wisconsin November 25, 2000. Mr. Pederson served with the US Army in World War II, rising to the rank of Staff Sergeant. He was a dairy farmer. They had four children: Roger, Mary, Jim, and Robert, ten grandchildren, and twelve great-grandchildren. They were buried in Oak Park Cemetery, Mondovi, Wisconsin.

References: US Census: 1900, 1910, 1920, 1930, 1940; Wisconsin Birth Index 1820-1907; Wisconsin Marriage Index 1820-1907; Oak Park Cemetery Records, Mondovi, Wisconsin; Greenwood Memorial Terrace Cemetery Records, Spokane, Washington; Avon Center Cemetery Records, Grayslake, Illinois; Warren Cemetery Records, Gumee, Illinois.

98.

Rusk Adams, b. Wisconsin February 1886; d. Lima, New York September 2, 1948; m. 1931 Estella Mattern, b. Rush, New York September 11, 1980, d. Lima, New York June 24, 1960. Estella was previously married to Chauncey Burkhart (1893-1919) by whom she had three children. Rusk and Estella did not have any children. Rusk Adams was an electrical engineer. His World War II Draft Registration Card described him as being 5' 11" tall, weighing 260 pounds with brown eyes, black hair and a ruddy complexion. They were buried in Honeoye Falls Cemetery, Honeoye Falls, New York.

References: US Census: 1900, 1910, 1920, 1930, 1940; Honeoye Falls Cemetery Records, Honeoye Falls, New York; World War II Draft Registration Card 1942; NYS Death Index 1852-1956.

100.

Nellie Stebbins, b. New York State May 1873, d. Canton, Ohio 1953; m. a. 1894 Elton D. Oakes, b. place and date not known, d. Canton, Ohio December 1, 1929. Mr. Oakes was employed as a railroad ticket agent in Wheeling, West Virginia and Canton, Ohio. It is not known where Elton Oakes was buried but Nellie Stebbins Oakes was buried in North Lawn Cemetery, Canton, Ohio with two of her four daughters.

Children:

122. I. **Alice E. Oakes**, b. Canton, Ohio, September 1896. No further information.

123. II. **Esther M. Oakes**, b. 1904, d. Canton, Ohio, 1988 and buried in North Lawn Cemetery, Canton, Ohio. No further information.

124. III. **Mary Oakes**, b. 1908 and was a teacher. No further information.

125. IV. **Elinor I. Oakes**, b. 1917, d. Canton, Ohio, 1998, and buried in North Lawn Cemetery, Canton, Ohio. No further information.

References: US Census: 1900, 1910, 1920, 1930; North Lawn Cemetery Records, Canton, Ohio; Ohio Death Index for Elton Oakes.

108.

Richard F. Adams, b. Wisconsin July 11, 1914, d. San Pedro, California September 4, 2001; m. place and date not known Elizabeth Millard Wisconsin September 21, 1915, d. Los Angeles, California July 15, 1997. Richard Adams' World War II Draft Registration Card described him as being 5' 11" tall and weighing 155 pounds with blue eyes and blonde hair. He was employed with the motor vehicle department. It is not currently known how many children they had. Richard and Elizabeth Adams were buried in Green Hills Memorial Park, Rancho Palo Verde, California.

References: US Census: 1920, 1930, 1940; World War II Draft Registration Card 1942; Green Hills Memorial Park Records, Rancho Palo Verde, California; Social Security Death Index.

109.

Robert Clark Adams, b. Wisconsin June 4, 1922, d. Beloit, Wisconsin April 22, 1988; m. place and date not known, Helen Mae Hellwig, b. La Crosse, Wisconsin May 11, 1928, d. Beloit, Wisconsin June 2, 1987. Robert Adams served with the US Army from January 5, 1943 to February 19, 1946. His World War II Draft Registration Card described him as being 5' 11 ½ "tall and weighing 130 pounds with brown eyes and blonde hair. It is not currently known how many children they had or where they are buried.

References: US Census: 1930, 1940; World War II Draft Registration Card 1940-47; US Army Records; Social Security Death Index.

110.

Cedric Malcolm Adams, b. Adrian, Minnesota May 27, 1902, d. Austin, Minnesota February 18, 1961; m. Roberts, South Dakota April 25, 1931 Bernice Lenont, b. Virginia, Minnesota July 7, 1910, d. Borrego Springs, California January 22, 1987. Cedric Adams was a newspaper columnist, radio personality, newscaster, variety show emcee and was known in the 1930s, 1940, and 1950s throughout the upper Midwest for his folksy humor, infectious laugh, and provincial style. At one point he did 54 radio shows, eight television broadcasts, and 15 newspaper columns a week. He was a regular fill-in for Arthur Godfrey on CBS television. His World War II Draft Registration Card described him as being 5' 11" tall, weighing 200 pounds with blue eyes and brown hair. At the time of his draft registration Mr. Adams was employed with the Maple Star Journal. He was buried in Lakewood Cemetery, Minneapolis, Minnesota with his wife. Mrs. Adams remarried in 1963 to Harry Arby Tinker (1903-1989). Harry Tinker was buried with his first wife, Margaret Schultz Tinker (1908-1962) in Lakewood Cemetery as well.

Children:

126. I.   *David Adams*, no further information.

127. II. *Cedric Adams*, Jr., f.

128. III. *Stephen Adams*, f.

References: US Census: 1910, 1920, 1930, 1940; World War II Draft Registration Card 1942; Findagrave.com obituary; Lakewood Cemetery Records, Minneapolis, Minnesota.

127.

Cedric Lenont "Ric" Adams, b. Minneapolis, Minnesota May 7, 1936, d. Phoenix, Arizona March 22, 1998; m. (1) Roberts, South Dakota March 22, 1957 Carolyn Thill, divorced June 9, 1977; m. (2) Lelyla F. Bauley. Mr. Adams had two children by his first wife: Cedric Adams III and Ann Lenont Adams. Further information is not currently available.

References: South Dakota Marriage Index 1905-2013; Minnesota Marriage Index 1958-2001; Minnesota Divorce Index 1935-2002; Social Security Death Index 1935=2014.

128.

Stephen Adams, b. Minnesota 1937; m. (1) Virginia Susan Ridgway, deceased; m. (2) name not known; m. (3) name not known; m. (4) Denise Rhea. Mr. Adams has four children by his first wife: Stephen Marcus Adams, Mark Charles Adams, Kent Ridgway Adams, and Scott Learned Adams. Stephen Adams is an American businessman, private equity investor, and philanthropist. His holdings include Good Sam Enterprises and Adams Outdoor Advertising. His previous holdings included operators of television and radio stations, print publishers, cola bottlers, and community banks. Stephan Adams graduated from Yale University and Stanford Graduate School of Business. His son Mark had founded Adams Publishing Group headquartered in Greeneville, Tennessee.

References: Internet Encyclopedias.

APPENDIX II:
The Carter Family of Nunda, New York

Introduction

I am a great-great-great grandson of Daniel Carter. My line of descent is through his eldest daughter Edith Estella Carter. In the decade since my last updating of this genealogical line, I still find myself unable to take Daniel Carter's family history beyond the identification of his parents. I found more documents to provide additional biographical details for Daniel Carter and his four brothers, but nothing has been found about his sisters. This genealogical research has been complicated by the fact that Daniel Carter's first and last name were also names of other residents of Livingston County, New York. The same would be true for his brothers. Therefore, considerable time was spent on close examination of the information on each Carter brother to be sure it was appropriate for that person. The same proved true for Daniel Carter's parents. The following narrative is what I have learned since my last attempt to update this line ten years ago.

The Carter Genealogy

1.

John Carter, b. a. 1795 in Delaware County, New York, d. probably in Ohio between the 1850 and 1860 federal censuses; m. Mary Polly Parrish, b. a. 1796 in Saratoga County, New York, d. after the 1860 federal census. In the 1830 federal census John Carter and his wife resided in Mt. Morris, Livingston County, New York. They had one son under the age of 5, three sons between the ages of 5 to 9, one son between the ages of 15 to 19, two daughters under the age of five, and one daughter between the ages of 15 to 19. In the 1840 federal census the Carters had moved to nearby Castile in Genesee County. There were two sons under the age of 5, two sons between the ages of 5 to 9, and one son between the ages of 15 to 19. In addition, there were two daughters between the ages of 10 to 14. Between 1830 and 1840 at least one daughter and two sons must have died and two more sons were born. Of the six sons born to John and Mary Carter, the identities of five are known. Of the three daughters of John and Mary Carter, none of their identities are known. According to the 1850 federal census the Carters moved to Gorham in Fulton County, Ohio where they farmed. Residing with John and Mary Polly Carter were four sons ranging in age from 12 to 20. It is possible that the two surviving daughters either married or died between the 1840 and 1850 federal census. In the 1850 federal census the four sons of John and Mary Carter living at home were Daniel, Chester, Owen, and Bradford. A fifth son George W. Carter had relocated to Michigan. Why the Carter family moved to Ohio and then back to New York State is not known. By 1860 Mary Carter and her son Daniel were once again living in Mt. Morris. It is assumed that John Carter had died. Daniel Carter was employed as a farmer. Chester and Owen Carter returned to Livingston County New York while Bradford Carter moved to Michigan. At this time, it is not known who the parents of either John Carter or Mary Polly Parish Carter were. It is Daniel Carter who married into the Adams family of Nunda, New York and is the subject of this genealogical narrative on the Carter family. It is not known where John and Mary Polly Carter were buried.

    Children:

2.   I.   **Daniel Carter**, f.

3.   II.   **George W. Carter**, f.

4.   III.   **Chester Carter**, f.

5.   IV.   **Owen Carter**, f.

6.   V.   **Bradford Cordon Carter**, f.

Appendix II: The Carter Family of Nunda, New York

References: US Census: 1830, 1840, 1850, 1860; New York State Census: 1855.

2.

Daniel Carter, b. 1830, Mt. Morris, New York, d. October 19, 1884, Nunda, New York; m. Mary Elizabeth Adams April 16, 1863, b. 1842 Albany County, New York, d. April 30, 1904, Nunda, New York. In the 1860 federal census Daniel Carter lived with his mother, Mary Carter, age 68 in Mt. Morris Township where he farmed. In June 1863, Daniel Carter, age 33, registered for the Civil War draft. His registration papers indicated he farmed and was married. There are no records to learn if Daniel Carter actually served. By the time of the 1870 census Daniel Carter was married, had four children, and was employed as a painter in Nunda. Ten years later in the 1880 federal census Daniel Carter and his family still resided in Nunda where he continued to work as a painter. Four years later he was dead. Oakwood Cemetery records indicated that a Daniel Carter was buried in Section D-12, but there is no evidence of a marker. On a Carter family gravestone in the newer section, N-4, is listed a Daniel Carter born 1833 and died 1866. The dates do not correspond to the Daniel Carter described above. Whoever this Daniel Carter was, he was buried with two of Daniel and Mary Elizabeth Carter's children! The death dates for Daniel and Mary Elizabeth Carter came from a paper found in a small bible that once belonged to Leo C. Root. The paper also lists the birth dates for each one of the Carters four children. It is not known who the Bible's original owner was, but it could have been either Edith or her daughter Belle. Oakwood Cemetery records now indicate both were buried there in unmarked graves. Daniel Carter became insane and was taken to the county asylum before he died in 1884.

Children:

7. I. **Edith Estelle Carter**, f.

8. II. **John Franklin Carter**, f.

9. III. **Alta May Carter**, f.

10.   IV.   ***Lois Annette Carter***, f.

References: US Census: 1850, 1860, 1870, 1880; New York State Census: 1855, 1865, 1875; Family Bible with paper recording marriage date of Daniel and Mary Adams, their respective death dates, and the birth dates of their four children; US Civil War Draft Registration Record 1863-1865; Nunda News, September 20, 1884; Oakwood Cemetery Records, Nunda, New York.

3.

George Washington Carter, b. New York State December 30, 1830, d. Ithaca, Michigan August 30, 1893; m. Fairfield, Michigan February 18, 1854 Maryette Burdick February 18, 1854, b. Fairfield, Michigan December 23, 1836, d. Crystal, Michigan March 3, 1917. George Carter moved out of the family home by 1850 and resided in Medina, Michigan where he was employed as a laborer. His Civil War Draft Registration Records indicate he was a carpenter by trade and married by 1863. The Carters had three children. Mr. Carter was a farmer in Fairfield, Michigan. In the 1870 Federal Census his farm was valued at $1400 and the farm equipment at $150. Mr. Carter died from a nervous disability. After the death of George Washington Carter, Maryette remarried to her brother-in-law, Bradford Carter. George Washington Carter and his wife were buried in Fulton Center Cemetery, Perinton, Michigan.

Children:

11.   I.   ***Amanda Carter***, f.

12.   II.   ***Mary Carter***, f.

13.   III.   ***John Anderson Carter***, f.

References: US Census: 1850, 1860, 1870, 1880; US Civil War Draft Registration Records 1863-65; Michigan Death Record 1867-1952 for George Carter; Fulton Center Cemetery Records, Perinton, Michigan.

4.

Chester Carter, b. a. 1834 Allegany County, New York, place and date of death not known; m. Jane, last name not known, b. a. 1839 in Michigan, d. place and date of death not known. Chester Carter resided with his parents in both Nunda, New York and Gorham, Ohio. In the 1855 New York State Census he continued to reside with parents and oldest brother, Daniel. In the 1860 US Census Chester Carter had married and had one son. The Carters resided in Nunda, New York where Chester was employed as a carpenter. Mr. Carter must have resided for a time in Michigan because his wife was from that state and their son was born in Michigan. They had one child, a son, Franklin S. Carter, b. a. 1859. Chester Carter enlisted in Nunda, New York on August 4, 1862 as a private with the First Dragoons. He was mustered out with a disability on August 22, 1864. There is no further information on this line of decent.

Children:

14.   I.   ***Franklin Carter***, b. Michigan 1859; no further information.

References: US Census: 1850, 1860; New York State Census: 1855; US Civil War Soldiers Records and Profiles 1861-1865.

5.

Owen Volney Carter, b. New York State June 25, 1835, d. Bradford, Pennsylvania 1898; m. Anna, last name not known, b. a. 1830 New York State, death date unknown. Owen Carter was listed under several different first names. They include Loron Owen Carter, Volney Owen Carter, and Owen Carter. As Volney Owen Carter he enlisted April 22, 1861 in the 33rd Infantry, Company F, New York Volunteers during the Civil War. Mr. Carter was mustered out April 30, 1862 at Yorktown, Virginia for desertion. He enlisted a second time on September 4, 1863 as a private with Company K, 16th cavalry, New York Volunteers. He deserted October 15, 1863. His Civil War Registration Papers noted his employment as a joiner who was 5' 9" tall with blue eyes, light hair, and a light complexion. In the 1870 US census and 1875 New York State census Owen and his wife Anna resided in Gainesville, Wyoming County, New York where he was employed as a carpenter. In the 1880 federal census Owen and Anna Carter lived in Duke Center, McKean County, Pennsylvania where he continued to find work as a carpenter. It does not appear that Owen and Anna Carter had any children. Owen Carter was buried in Oak Hill Cemetery, Bradford, Pennsylvania. It is not currently known where Anna Carter was buried.

References: US Census: 1850, 1870, 1880; New York State Census: 1875; Oak Hill Cemetery Records, Bradford, Pennsylvania; US Civil War Soldier Records and Profiles 1861-1865; Civil War Muster Rolls 1861-1900; New York Town Clerks' Registers of Men Who Served in the Civil War 1861-1865.

6.

Bradford Cordon Carter, b. Mt. Morris, New York August 10, 1837, d. Ithaca, Michigan October 26, 1909; m. (1) place and date not known, Eleanora/Elnora Barstow, b. a. 1841, d. Ithaca, Michigan June 22, 1893; m. (2) Ithaca, Michigan June 19, 1894 Maryette Burdick Carter, b. Fairfield, Michigan December 23, 1836, d. Crystal, Michigan March 3, 1917. Bradford Carter's second marriage was to his brother Chester's widow. In the 1850 federal census Bradford Carter resided with his parents and brothers in Gorham, Ohio. He was not found in the 1860 federal census. Mr. Carter enlisted and served during the Civil War with the First Michigan Engineers, Company K. His was discharged for a disability in 1862, but he reenlisted December 22, 1863. He was mustered out with the rank of Corporal. In the 1870 federal census Bradford Carter resided in Vermontville, Michigan with his first wife and four children, two sons and two daughters. In the 1880 federal census the family resided in Pine River, Michigan where Bradford Carter was employed as a carpenter. All four children continued to reside at home. In the 1900 federal census Bradford Carter had moved to Ithaca, Michigan and remarried to his sister-in-law. Bradford and Elnora Carter had six children, two of whom died in infancy. There were no children from Bradford Carter's second marriage. Bradford Carter died from heart disease and bronchitis. Bradford and Elenora were buried in Ithaca Cemetery, Ithaca, Michigan. Maryette was buried with her first husband.

Children: (by first marriage)

15. I. **Charles Bradford Carter**, f.

16. II. **Dora A. Carter**, f.

17. III. **Eugene Henry Carter**, f.

18. IV. **Rena May Carter**, f.

19. V. **Frankie Carter**, b. Vermontville, Michigan 1875, d. Michigan April 24, 1875, age 3 months and 14 days from Whooping Cough. He was buried in Welch Cemetery, Sunfield, Michigan.

20. VI. **Jessie Carter**, Otisco, Michigan May 6, 1877, d. Michigan 1878 and believed buried in Ithaca Cemetery, Ithaca, Michigan.

References: US Census: 1850, 1870, 1880, 1900; Michigan Death Record 1897-1929 for Bradford Carter; Michigan Birth Index 1867-1911 for Jessie Carter; Michigan Marriage Record 1867-1952 for Bradford Carter's second marriage; Welch Cemetery Records, Sunfield, Michigan; Ithaca Cemetery Records, Ithaca, Michigan; US Civil War Soldier Records and Profiles 1861-1865; 1890 Veterans Schedule, US Federal Census.

7.

Edith Estelle Carter, b. September 13, 1865, Nunda, New York, d. October 22, 1911 Binghamton, New York from an obstruction of the bowels; m. (1) Nunda, New York April 19, 1880 Albert James Fuller, b. Nunda, New York July 10, 1864, d. Kalamazoo, Michigan June 8, 1944 from old age, divorced, place and date not known; m. (2) Binghamton, New York April 19, 1902 Lemuel Deyo Stalker, b. Binghamton, New York May 1855, d. Dickinson, New York September 6, 1931. Edith Carter first appears in the 1870 federal census with her parents, Daniel and Mary Elizabeth Adams Carter and her three siblings. In the 1880 federal census, Edith Carter appears twice. She was listed with her parents and siblings in Nunda, New York and, also, as a servant in the William C. Fuller household, Nunda. In 1880 she married the youngest son of William C. Fuller, Albert "Abbie" James Fuller. There is no surviving record for the Livingston County, New

York 1892 New York State Census. Sometime in the mid-1890s Albert and Edith Fuller separated. In the 1900 federal census Edith Carter Fuller resided in Olean, New York with her daughter Belle Fuller Root, her son-in-law Ernest Root, two grandchildren, Leo C. and Nordica Root, and her other daughter, Louise, and son Jesse. A document of divorce between Edith and Albert Fuller has not been found. In the 1900 federal census for Kalamazoo, Michigan Albert Fuller had remarried to Nancy B. Larrabee on May 19, 1897. Albert Fuller's marriage application with Nancy Larrabee states that he had never been married before and that his birthplace was Buffalo, New York, both of which are untrue. Albert Fuller had a son, Donald, by his second wife. Donald Fuller's children were stunned to learn about his marriage to Edith Carter. Albert Fuller's second wife committed suicide. He remarried a third time to Lula May Bailey, a woman 34 years younger than himself. Curiously, Earnest Root appears twice in the 1900 federal census. The first time was with his wife, children, and in-laws in Olean, New York, and a second time in the 1900 US Census for Smethport, Pennsylvania. It is possible that Ernest and Belle had already separated.

Edith Carter Fuller, her son Jesse, daughters Louise and Belle, and her Root grandchildren moved to Binghamton sometime after the 1900 federal census. Lemuel Deyo Stalker was first listed in the 1870 federal census with his parents and siblings in Nanticoke, Broome County, New York. In the 1880 federal census L. D. Stalker was married with three children residing in Lisle, Broome County, New York and was employed as a carpenter. In the 1900 federal census L. D. Stalker was a resident of Binghamton, New York living with his wife, two of his children, Fred Stalker, his daughter, Lula, and son-in-law Andrew Johnson, widower of Lena Stalker Johnson, and his two Johnson grandchildren. L. D. Stalker's first wife died in Binghamton, New York June 24, 1901. In the 1910 US Census Lemuel and Edith Stalker resided in Binghamton. The 1920 US Census L. D. Stalker resided in Union, Broome County, New York with his son, daughter-in-law, and grandson. At the time of the 1930 federal census L. D. Stalker was a resident at the Broome County Alms House.

Edith Carter Fuller Stalker was buried in Floral Park Cemetery in an unmarked grave next to her youngest daughter Louise Fuller Hungerford in the Hungerford family plot. There are no tombstones for anyone in that lot. Albert Fuller was buried in Riverside Cemetery in Kalamazoo, Michigan with his third wife. Lemuel Deyo Stalker was buried in Floral Park Cemetery, Binghamton, New York with his first wife, Mary Johnson Stalker (1858-1901).

Children: (by first marriage)

21.   I.   **Belle Fuller**, f.

22.   II. **Jesse Fuller**, f.

23.   III. **Louise Fuller**, f.

References: US Census: 1870, 1880, 1900, 1910, 1920, 1930; New York State Census: 1865, 1875, 1905, 1915, 1925; 1898 Fuller Family History; NYS Marriage Index 1881-1967 for Edith's second marriage; Edith Stalker obituary, Binghamton, New York October 23, 1911; Edith Stalker Funeral Notice, Binghamton, New York, October 24, 1911; New York State Death Certificate October 22, 1911 for Edith Stalker; Lemuel Stalker Funeral Notice, September 10, 1931, Binghamton, New York; Binghamton City Directories 1902, 1906, 1908; Floral Park Cemetery Records, Johnson City, New York; Riverside Cemetery Records, Kalamazoo, Michigan; Michigan Marriage Records May 19, 1897 for Albert Fuller's second marriage.

8.

John Franklin (Frank) Carter, b. Nunda, New York November 27, 1866, d. Nunda, New York July 6. 1926, a suicide by shooting; m. probably Nunda, New York, a.1888 Carrie H. Angier, b. New York State November 1862, d. Nunda, New York October 28, 1933. There is some confusion about Frank Carter's birth date. His death certificate and obituary say November 16, 1867, the federal census says October 1868, and a family bible says November 27, 1866. Mr. Carter was self-employed for a number of years and later the owner of a meat market in the Derx block in Nunda village. He opened this business November 7, 1896. Frank Carter later sold the business to purchase the Cole farm in Nunda Township. In the 1900 federal census Frank Carter was listed as a junk dealer living in Portage, NY with his wife and son. In the 1910 federal census Frank Carter and his family lived at 148 Center Street, Nunda. He and his son, Allen J. Carter, owned and operated a freight line between Nunda and Dalton. Their line was one of the first to carry both mail and passengers. The fare was 25 cents.

Frank Carter suffered from a number of illnesses. The Nunda News reported on May 16, 1896 that Mr. Carter was very ill with typhoid fever and had become violently insane and was removed to the Ovid Asylum. He later recovered. The death of Frank Carter's son apparently affected his health. On August 23, 1910 he was declared insane and was regarded as mentally unbalanced for the rest of his life. In the 1920 census Frank Carter was a tenant farmer living with his wife. Frank Carter committed suicide by putting a revolver to his heart before his family could take him to the Rochester, New York state hospital for treatment and commitment.

Carrie, his wife, was the daughter of John and Mary Rockafellow Angier. Her father was a prominent farmer in Nunda and a deacon of the Nunda Baptist Church. In widowhood she resided at the home of Mr. and Mrs. William Gelser. Both Carrie and Frank Carter were buried with their son in Nunda's Oakwood Cemetery in the same lot as the mysterious Daniel Carter b.1833, d. 1866.

Children:

24.   I.   **Allen J. Carter**, f.

References: US Census: 1870, 1880, 1900, 1910, 1920, 1930; New York State Census: 1875, 1905, 1915, 1925; Oakwood Cemetery Records, Nunda, New York, NYS Death Certificate July 6, 1926; The Nunda News Mary 16, 1896 and November 3, 1933.

9.

Alta May/Mae Carter, b. Nunda, New York November 18, 1867, d. Binghamton, New York December 21, 1956; m. probably Nunda, New York 1882 James Palmer, b. Binghamton, New York June 1853, d. Binghamton, New York April 15, 1940. Alta was named for her mother's sister, Alta Adams. Alta Carter married James Palmer when she was fourteen years old. James Palmer was 29 years of age at the time. Their first son was born in Nunda, therefore, if James and Alta Palmer did not meet in Binghamton, then work brought James Palmer to Nunda where they met. James Palmer resided with his parents and siblings in both the 1870 and 1880 federal censuses in Nanticoke, Broome County, New York. The Palmers resided in Binghamton, NY where James Palmer was employed as a painter after the birth of their three eldest sons. In the 1900 US Census they resided at 142 1/2 Clinton Street. In both the 1910 and 1920 US Censuses the Palmers lived at 19 Dickson Avenue in Binghamton. Each census indicates the Palmers either took in at least one boarder or had several sons and grandchildren living with them.

Alta Palmer was Leo C. Root's great-aunt. Leo resided with the Palmer family after his mother's death in 1914. He remained in frequent contact with her until her death in 1956. I have a few pieces of correspondence between them that relates to the Floral Park Cemetery lots where Leo's mother and uncle, Jesse Fuller, were buried. Leo's daughter, Nordica Root Anderson, was in frequent contact with Alta Palmer, but none of that correspondence survives. For several decades I tried, along with my mother, Dorothy Root Paquette, to locate the Palmer burial site. Diligent searches of Binghamton, New York cemeteries turned up nothing. It was assumed that because the Palmers resided in Binghamton most of their married lives, they would be buried in either Binghamton or Johnson City's Floral Park Cemetery where Alta's sister, Edith Carter Fuller Stalker, and her sister's family were buried. After much sleuthing, it was learned that Alta and James Palmer were buried in the Vestal Park Cemetery in Vestal, New York. The lot was transferred to them in 1940 by a James Rice. The Vestal Park Cemetery caretakers could not provide an answer why such longtime residents of Binghamton would have been buried such a distance from that city. None of the Palmer children or their descendants were buried a Vestal Park.

Children:

25. I. ***Arthur N. Palmer***, f.

26. II. ***Frank J. Palmer***, f.

27. III. **Cortland Palmer**, f.

28. IV. **James H. Palmer**, f.

References: US Census: 1870, 1880, 1900, 1910, 1920, 1930, 1940; New York State Census: 1875, 1905, 1915, 1925; NYS Death Index 1867-1956; Vestal Park Cemetery Records, Vestal, N.Y.

10.

Lois Annette Carter b. Nunda, New York December 18, 1868, d. Nunda, New York May 26, 1942 from a coronary thrombosis; m. place not known, May 26, 1886 Charles David Foose, b. Union, NY October 1858, d. Geneseo, New York January 18, 1948 from chronic myocardial disease in a nursing home. Lois or "Louie" or "Lottie" died on her 56th wedding anniversary at the home of her daughter, Mary Foose Tackach on Massachusetts Street in Nunda. She was also referred to as "Nettie" by some family members. She was named for her mother's sister, Lois Adams Sargent. At the time of the 1900 federal census the Fooses lived in Cuba, New York where Charles Foose managed an insurance business. They had three children: George, Lottie, and Harry. By 1910 the Fooses had moved to Dansville, New York where Charles was employed as a traveling salesman for a drug company. By this time Carlotta had married and the Fooses had a second daughter, Mary. In 1920 the Fooses resided in Buffalo, New York. For a brief time, they took in their great-niece Nordica Root based on the 1915 New York State census. Charles Foose was employed as a traveling salesman selling paints and oils. Their children, Mary and Harry, still lived at home. The Fooses lived in Fillmore, New York in 1930 managing a hotel there. They lived with their daughter Mary, her second husband, and a grandson. Charles David Foose also managed hotels in Belfast and the Hotel St. John on Portage Street in Nunda. Charles Foose was a member of the IOOF Lodge of Union, NY and received a 50-year membership award prior to his death. Both Charles and Nettie Foose were buried in Oakwood Cemetery in Nunda in the Carter lot, section N-4. They had four children but only three survived them. By the time of Charles Foose's death in 1948 there were five grandchildren and six great-grandchildren.

Charles Foose was listed on the 1860 federal census for Mount Morris,

Livingston County, as David C. Foose. In 1860 he resided with his parents Samuel and Jane Foose and four siblings. In the 1870 census for York, Livingston County, he continued to reside with his parents and four siblings. This time the four siblings are: Isabella, Laura, Frank, and William. In the 1860 census they were: Isabel, Thomas, George, and Laura and he is listed as David Foose. Still listed as David Foose in the 1880 federal census for Mount Morris, he continued to live with his parents and youngest brother, William. David Foose was employed as a day laborer.

Children:

29. I. *George Bain Foose*, f.

30. II. *Carlotta Foose*, f.

31. III. *Harry Foose*, f.

32. IV. *Mary Foose*, f.

References: US Census: 1860, 1870, 1880, 1900, 1910, 1920, 1930, 1940; New York State Census: 1875, 1905, 1915, 1925; Oakwood Cemetery Records, Nunda, New York; Nunda News, 5/29/1942; Mt. Morris Enterprise, 6/3/1942; Picket Line Post, 1/23/1948.

11.

Amanda Carter, b. Fairfield, Michigan January 25, 1855, d. Crystal, Michigan October 2, 1920, from cancer of the stomach; m. Fairfield, Michigan August 17, 1873 John H. Orcutt, b. Lenawee County, Michigan December 24, 1847, d. Crystal, Michigan, April 22, 1923. Amanda Carter resided with her parents until her marriage. John Orcutt was a carpenter by trade and was later a manager of a hardware store in Crystal, Michigan. They had three children. Amanda and John Orcutt were buried in Crystal Cemetery, Crystal, Michigan.

Children:

33. I. *Charles Ezra Orcutt*, b. Lenawee County, Michigan December 14, 1875, d. Carson City, Michigan, September 7, 1944 from

cancer of the larynx; m. Montcalm, Michigan August 15, 1903 Carrie Ellen Braid, b. Carson City, Michigan January 15, 1884, d. Michigan September 17, 1955. Mr. Orcutt was a baker. It is not known if they had any children. Charles and Carrie Orcutt were buried in Carson City Cemetery, Carson City, Michigan.

34. II. **Clarence George Orcutt**, b. Fairfield, Michigan October 31, 1877, d. Fairfield, Michigan November 5, 1948; m. Crystal, Michigan September 16, 1898 Louella Munn, b. Crystal, Michigan August 19, 1879, d. Crystal, Michigan September 9, 1941. Clarence Orcutt was a harness maker by trade. They were buried in Crystal Cemetery, Crystal, Michigan.

  Children:

  i. **Otho John Orcutt**, b. Crystal, Michigan December 24, 1902, d. Fenton, Michigan November 18, 1957; m. Ruth Irene Ogreen, b. Montcalm County Michigan March 20, 1904, d. Grand Blanc, Michigan June 18, 1994. They were buried in Crestwood Memorial Cemetery, Grand Blanc, Michigan. It is not known if they had children.

35. III. **Sarah Orcutt**, b. Michigan October 30, 1886, d. Newark, Michigan November 2, 1886 from congestion of the lungs. It is not known where she was buried.

References: US Census: 1860, 1870, 1880, 1900, 1910, 1920, 1930, 1940; Michigan Death Records 1867-1952; Michigan Marriage Records 1867-1952; Crystal Cemetery Records, Crystal, Michigan; Carson City Cemetery Records, Carson City, Michigan; Crestwood Memorial Cemetery Records, Grand Blanc, Michigan.

12.

Mary Carter, b. Lenawee County, Michigan November 12, 1863, d. North Star, Michigan May 21, 1900 from complications of child birth; m. Fairfield, Michigan September 27 1880 Irvine George Willetts, b. Fairfield, Michigan February 26, 1858, d. Detroit, Michigan August 14, 1944. Mr. Willetts was a farmer by profession. Mary Carter Willetts died from pernicious anemia and the problems of a premature birth. They were buried in North Star Cemetery, North Star, Michigan.

Children:

36. I. **Bessie Elmira Willetts**, b. Michigan March 16, 1882. No further information.

37. II. **Elmer John Willetts**, b. 1884, d. 1953; m. Jane Potter. They were buried in North Star Cemetery. No further information.

38. III. **Leamon Leroy Willetts**, b. 1887, d. 1930; m. Nellie E. Selfridge, b. 1880, d.1960. They had two daughters and one son. They were buried in North Star Cemetery.

39. IV. **May Willetts**, b. 1889, d. 1905 and buried in North Star Cemetery.

40. V. **Ruth Amanda Willetts**, b. 1895, d. date not known; m. Arthur J. Gough, b. 1892, d. 1953. They had two sons.

41. VI. **Bernice Allice Willetts**, b. 1898, d. 1980. Married three times and had one daughter.

42. VII. **Female Infant Willetts**, b. May 14, 1900, d. Mary 23, 1900 and buried in North Star Cemetery.

References: US Census: 1870, 1880, 1900, 1910, 1920, 1930, 1940; Michigan Death Index 1867-1995; North Star Cemetery Records, North Star, Michigan; Michigan Marriage Index 1867-1952

13.

John Anderson Carter, b. Lenawee County, Michigan February 14, 1866, d. Arcada, Michigan January 26, 1948; m. North Star, Michigan September 20, 1886 Mary Lucinda Johnson, b. Michigan March 1857, d. Michigan 1953. John Carter was a long time Michigan farmer. He resided in Newark, Michigan and later spent the rest of his life in Arcada. They had three children: Merle, Claude, and Alice. Some census records incorrectly identify Claude as Clara resulting in the incorrect listing of a fourth child.

John and Mary Carter were buried in Ithaca Cemetery, Ithaca, Michigan.

Children:

43. I. **Merle George Carter**, b. Michigan October 1, 1887, d. Michigan July 1963; m. Ithaca, Michigan August 6, 1910 Augusta Olive Farrington, b. Ithaca, Michigan August 6, 1894, d. Columbus, Ohio December 17, 1970. Mr. Carter was a farmer in Arvada continuing the tradition of employment of his father. His widow removed to Ohio for reasons not currently clear where she died. Merle and Augusta Carter were buried in Ithaca Cemetery, Ithaca, Michigan. They had eight children. The identities of seven are currently known. They raised their grandson, Theodore Carter, illegitimate son of their daughter Ada Carter who died soon after Theodore was born.

Children:

i. **Alta May Carter**, b. Arcada, Michigan August 7, 1911, d. Ann Arbor, Michigan from pneumonia and issues arising from childbirth, February3, 1932. Miss Carter's son, Theodore Carter, was raised by her parents and resided with them. The boy's father was Bruce Clark. Alta Carter was buried in Ithaca Cemetery, Ithaca, Michigan. Theodore, b. January 12, 1932, d. August 1989; m. Anna M., last name not known, b. 1924, d. 2003. Theodore and Anna Carter were buried in Pine Grove Cemetery, Ithaca, Michigan.

ii. **Earnest Claud Carter**, b. Ithaca, Michigan July 4, 1913, d. Flint, Michigan August 20, 1940 when a truck rolled back while he was cranking a loader and crushed his head.; m. Ashley, Michigan March 19, 1932 Lena McDonald, b. Michigan May 13, 1913, d. Flint, Michigan January 31, 1941 from a lung abscess caused by an automobile accident. Earnest Carter was employed as a laborer by the WPA. They had three children: Norma, b. 1933, Gerald, b. 1936, d. 2011, and Geraldine, b. 1939. Mr. and Mrs. Carter were buried in Collier Cemetery, Pompeii, Michigan.

Appendix II: The Carter Family of Nunda, New York

iii. ***Carl B. Carter***, b. Michigan January 2, 1914, d. Michigan September 27, 1914 from acute enteritis. He was buried in Ithaca Cemetery, Ithaca, Michigan.

iv. ***Alice Eugenia Carter***, b. 1916, d. 1977; m. (1) Alma, Michigan June 17, 1934 Fred Van Horn, divorced Lowell, Michigan October 23, 1944 for extreme cruelty; m. (2) Alma, Michigan Claude Edward Phelps September 4, 1948, b. 1910, d. 1978. Jennie had two sons by her first marriage: Lester, born 1936 and Freddie, born 1939. Mr. and Mrs. Phelps were buried in Riverdale Cemetery, Riverdale, Michigan.

v. ***Myrtle Merline Carter***, b. Michigan April 25, 1916, d. Michigan May 20, 1916 from a congenital heart defect. She was buried in Ithaca Cemetery, Ithaca, Michigan.

vi. ***Hazel Irene Carter***, b. Michigan April 26, 1917 d. Michigan September 27, 1917 from extreme colitis. She was buried in Ithaca Cemetery, Ithaca, Michigan.

vii. ***Jesse Clifford Carter***, b. Gratiot, Michigan August 22, 1919, d. Carson City, Michigan August 21, 1996; m. Ithaca, Michigan November 29, 1947 Dorothy Dunckel, b. 1927, d. 1996. They had at least one child. A son, Earnest Clifford Carter was born Flint, Michigan February 11, 1949 and died Flint, Michigan March 30, 1948. The son was buried at Graceland Cemetery, Flint, Michigan. Jesse and Dorothy Carter were buried in Pine Grove Cemetery, Ithaca, Michigan.

44. II. ***Claud Noble Carter***, b. Newark, Michigan December 8 1894, d. Ithaca, Michigan January 1969. Mr. Cater never married and resided with his parents while they were alive employed as a farm laborer in Arcada, Michigan. His World War II Draft Registration Card described him as being 5' 11" tall, weighing 150 pounds with blue eyes, red hair, and light complexion. Claud Carter was buried in Ithaca Cemetery, Ithaca, Michigan.

45. III. **Alice Carter**, b. Newark, Michigan February 1, 1904, d. Alma, Michigan February 15, 1996; m. Newark, Michigan June 16, 1926 Fred Towersey, b. Champaign, Illinois September 14, 1899, d. Alma, Michigan April 28, 1976. Fred Towersey was employed by the telephone company in the maintenance department. They had four children including twin sons. Alice and Fred Towersey were buried in Riverside Cemetery, Alma, Michigan.

Children:

i. **Jane M. Towersey**, b. Michigan June 14, 1927, d. place and date not known; m. Leon H. Schmelzer, b. Indiana February 10, 1927, d. Alma, Michigan June 9, 1951. Further information not currently available.

ii. **Sarah Evelyn Towersey**, b. Alma, Michigan November 4, 1928, d. Michigan October 5, 2004; m. Alma, Michigan December 1, 1951 Raymond Carl Alexander, b. 1929, d. place and date of death not known. Further information not currently available.

iii. **Darrell F. Towersey**, b. Alma, Michigan December 30, 1930, d. Alma, Michigan June 10, 2016; m. Alma, Michigan June 6, 1964 Patricia Wood, b. Ithaca, Michigan July 28, 1933, d. Alma, Michigan June 6, 2014. Darrell and his twin brother founded Towersey Brothers Sales and Service in Alma. Darrell and Patricia had two daughters: Christine Towersey Eaton and Karen Towersey Whittaker, eight grandchildren, and three great-grandchildren. They were buried in Riverside Cemetery, Alma, Michigan.

iv. **Delbert Towersey**, b. Alma, Michigan December 30, 1930; m. Sandy, last name not known. Further information is not currently available.

References: US Census: 1870, 1880, 1900, 1910, 1920, 1930, 1940; Michigan Death Records 1867-1952; Michigan Marriage Records 1822-1940; World War I Draft Registration Card, 1917-1918; World War II

Draft Registration Card 1942; Ithaca Cemetery Records, Ithaca, Michigan; Riverside Cemetery Records, Alma, Michigan; Pine Grove Cemetery Records, Ithaca, Michigan; Social Security Death Index 1935-2014; Graceland Cemetery Records, Flint, Michigan; Michigan Divorce Records 1897-1952; Collier Cemetery Records, Pompeii, Michigan.

15.

Charles Bradford Carter, b. Marshall, Michigan July 7, 1859, d. Grand Rapids, Michigan February 10, 1903 from acute gastritis; m. Detroit, Michigan October 1, 1882 Linda Kinney/Cooney, b. Haterla, New York February 11, 1861, d. St. Louis, Michigan April 24, 1936 from a left hernia causing strangulation. Mr. Carter was a barber by profession. They were buried in Greenwood Cemetery, Grand Rapids, Michigan.

Children:

46. I. ***Ray B. Carter***, b. January 1884, d. place and date not known. He was employed as a barber in Grand Rapids, Michigan in 1903. No further information.

47. II. ***Ethel E. Carter***, b. Saginaw, Michigan February 12, 1888, d. Chicago, Illinois May 29, 1945; m. (1) Grand Rapids, Michigan November 18, 1910, divorced January 5, 1922 for extreme cruelty; m. (2) Henry B. Sweet, b. Detroit, Michigan July 10, 1884, d. Chicago, Illinois December 28, 1943. Ethel had a son born in 1912 by her first marriage, Charles Rider, who was adopted by her second husband. She had two children by her second marriage: Ethelind, b. 1924 and Duwain b. 1927. Ethel and Henry Sweet were buried in Ridgewood Cemetery, Des Plaines, Illinois.

References: US Census: 1860, 1870, 1880, 1900, 1910, 1920, 1930, 1940; Greenwood Cemetery Records, Grand Rapids, Michigan; Ridgewood Cemetery Records, Des Plaines, Illinois; Michigan Death Records 1867-1952; Michigan Marriage Records 1867-1952; Michigan Divorce Records 1897-1952.

16.

Dora A. Carter, b. Eaton County, Michigan, d. Newark Michigan June 5, 1897; m. North Star, Michigan September 1887 Frank A. Orcutt, b. Ohio July 5, 1868, d. Crystal, Michigan September 10, 1924. Dora Carter resided with her parents until her marriage. She was buried with her parents in Ithaca Cemetery, Ithaca, Michigan. Frank Orcutt was employed as a farm laborer who resided with his mother after the death of his wife and in 1920 with the Roy Munn family in Crystal, Michigan. His death was caused by acute nephritis and general dropsy. Mr. Orcutt never remarried and was buried in Crystal Cemetery, Crystal, Michigan.

References: US Census: 1870, 1880, 1900, 1910, 1920; Michigan Marriage Records 1867-1952; Michigan Death Index 1867-1995; Ithaca Cemetery Records, Ithaca, Michigan; Crystal Cemetery Records, Crystal, Michigan.

17.

Eugene Henry Carter, b. Vermontville, Michigan August 19, 1866, d. Grass Lake, Michigan May 26, 1929; m. Ithaca, Michigan March 13, 1893 Jennie Eunice Brown, b. Michigan 1872, d. Michigan 1956. Mr. Carter was employed as a barber in the 1900 and 1920 US Census records and as a printer in a paper office e in the 1910 US Census. Eugene and Jennie had eight children. They are buried in Grass Lake East Cemetery, Grass Lake, Michigan.

Children;

48.   I.   ***Bradford Cordon Carter***, b. Ithaca, Michigan July 25, 1893, d. Jackson, Michigan May 5, 1939; m. (1) Grass Lake, Michigan June 17, 1916 Amelia Irene Rohrer, b. May 12, 1888, d. Grass Lake December 5, 1917 in child birth. The baby was born and died December 5, 1917; m. (2) Urania, Michigan June 30, 1921 Ruth Cook, b. Delhi, Louisiana March 26, 1898, d. Northville, Michigan September 13, 1983. They had four children: Bradford C. (1922-1993), Roberta Ruth (1924-2010), Fred Eugene (1927-2008), and Ann (1931-?). Mr. and Mrs. Carter were buried in Grass Lake East Cemetery, Grass Lake, Michigan.

49. II. **Matie Marguerite Carter**, b. Ithaca, Michigan June 8, 1895, d. Santa Barbara, California November 5, 1991. Miss Carter never married and was a career teacher in Flint, Michigan. She graduated from Eastern Michigan University. Matie Carter was buried in Pacific View Memorial Park, Corona del Mar, California.

50. III. **Wilma Eunice** Carter, b. Ithaca, Michigan December 20, 1897, d. Fort Collins, Colorado November 15, 1999; m. Grass Lake, Michigan May 30, 1923 Archibald Edwards, b. Guernsey, England January 3, 1896, d. Saginaw, Michigan Juen 25, 1955. Wilma attended Eastern Michigan University for two years. Her husband moved to the United States in 1914 and served with the US Army in World War I. He was a buyer for wholesale hardware company. They had one daughter, Marjorie, b. 1924 who married Hugh Daniell (1925-2014) and had two children. Mr. and Mrs. Edwards were buried in Roselawn Memorial Gardens, Saginaw, Michigan.

51. IV. **Devere Eugene Carter**, b. Ithaca, Michigan March 31, 1900, d. Knox, Indiana December 4, 1952; m. place and date not known Viola Solomon, b. Chicago May 1,1909, d. Denham Springs Louisiana July 4, 1964. Mr. Carter was a truck driver for an ice cream company in Chicago. They had one daughter, Shirley Mae who was born in Chicago December 20, 1926, died in Chicago December 21, 1927 and was buried in St. Lucas Cemetery, Chicago. They had a son, Charles, b. 1928. It is not known where Mrs. Carter was buried.

52. V. **Isadore Jennie Carter**, b. Ithaca, Michigan April 2, 1902, d. Dayton, Ohio July 23, 1996; m. Grass Lake, Michigan March 3, 1928 Horace S. McColgan, b. Grass Lake, Michigan October 11, 1901, d. Kettering, Ohio July 16, 1997. Mr. McColgan was a farmer and also worked for the Crescent Printing Company. It is believed that Mr. McColgan was previously married to a Helen Capen who died but left him with a daughter Leona (1923-2003). Jennie had two daughters by her marriage: Barbara Jean (1928-2011) and Marion (1931-2002). Mr. and Mrs. McColgan were buried in Valley View Memorial Gardens, Xenia, Ohio.

53. VI. **Della Brown Carter**, b. St. Louis, Michigan May 24, 1909, d. Phoenix, Arizona February 19, 1997; m. Steuben, Indiana March 14,

1934 Roger Stone Ervin, b. 1909, died 1997. They had three children: John Ervin (1934-1934), Richard Ervin (1936-?), and Sally Jane Ervin (1940-2000). Mr. and Mrs. Ervin were buried in Greenwood Memory Lawn Cemetery, Phoenix, Arizona.

54.   VII.   *Frederick Jack Carter*, b. St. Louis, Michigan June 9, 1913, d. Alma, Michigan May 23, 2009; m. September 14, 1940 Vivian M. Leach. Mr. Carter was employed for many years by Sears and later as a tool and die maker in Saginaw. They had two sons: Clifford and John. Mr. and Mrs. Carter were buried in Roselawn Memorial Gardens, Saginaw, Michigan.

55.   VIII.   *Elizabeth Irene Carter*, b. Michigan September 4, 1915, d. Santa Barbara, California February 14, 1996; m. Flint, Michigan October 19, 1935 Warren Borgquist, b. Serier, Utah November 26, 1910, d. Santa Barbara, California July 16, 1996. Warren was a draftsman. They had two children: Nancy, b. 1937 and Bruce, b. 1938. It is not known where Elizabeth and Warren were buried.

References: US Census: 1870, 1880, 1900, 1910, 1920, 1930, 1940; Grass Lake East Cemetery Records, Grass Lake, Michigan; Pacific View Memorial Park Records, Corona del Mar, California; Roselawn Memorial Gardens Records, Saginaw, Michigan; St. Lucas Cemetery Records, Chicago, Illinois; Valley View Memorial Gardens Records, Xenia, Ohio; Greenwood Memory Lawn Cemetery Records, Saginaw, Michigan.

18.

Rena May Carter, b. Michigan April 11, 1869, d. Carsonville, Michigan May 6, 1921 from epilepsy; m. Ithaca, Michigan December 14, 1893 Frank Elbert Deline, b. Michigan August 24, 1867, d. St. Louis, Michigan July 21, 1915 from asthma and pyorrhea. Rena and Frank each resided with their parents until their marriage. Frank Orcutt was employed as a farmer, a barber, and lastly as a city clerk for St. Louis, Michigan. Rena and Frank Orcutt were buried in Oak Grove Cemetery, St. Louis, Michigan.

Children:

56.   I.   *Verna F. Deline*, b. Toledo, Ohio September 6, 1895, d. St.

Louis, Michigan November 25, 1969. Verna was an English Teacher who never married. She was buried with her parents in Oak Grove Cemetery, St. Louis, Michigan.

References: US Census: 1870, 1880, 1900, 1910, 1920, 1930, 1940; Oak Grove Cemetery Records, St. Louis, Michigan; Michigan Marriage Records 1822-1940; Michigan Death Records 1867-1952.

21.

Belle Fuller, b. Nunda, New York April 16, 1881, d. Binghamton, New York December 14, 1914 from cancer; m. Olean, New York February 19, 1898 Ernest Jerome Root, b. Bolivar, New York July 15, 1873 Bolivar, New York, d. Bolivar, New York July 23, 1904, a suicide. Belle Fuller Root was a direct descendant of Mayflower passengers Edward Fuller, his wife, and son, Samuel Fuller. In 1898 Belle was a student at a private school in Olean, New York. It was in Olean that Belle met Ernest Root. Ernest Root worked as a blacksmith for his brother, Earls L. Root, in Olean. In 1900 Ernest worked in Smethport, Pennsylvania. It is not known if this was the time of their separation. Belle and Ernest Root were living apart at the time of his death in 1904. He still lived in Smethport and Belle had gone to live in Binghamton taking her children with her sometime after the 1900 US Census. Ernest Root was an alcoholic and was physically abusive to his wife and children. In Binghamton, New York Belle operated a dress shop with Jenny J. Cox, a milliner. She resided at 28 Court Street, Binghamton and was first listed in the Binghamton City Directory in 1905. Belle suffered from cancer for five years. She had planned to remarry to William Stone of Binghamton, but the disease's progress prevented a wedding. William Stone remained at Belle's side until her death. Conversations with the late Nordica Root Wylie, Belle's daughter, indicated that Belle and Ernest Root might have had a third child that died either at birth or was a stillborn in either 1900 or 1901. Belle was buried in Johnson City's Floral Park Cemetery, but the birth year on the tombstone is incorrect. Custody of her children was given to her brother, Jesse Fuller, but her son, Leo, resided with Belle's aunt, Alta Carter Palmer in Binghamton, New York and Nordica resided in Buffalo, New York with Belle's aunt, Nettie Carter Foose, after her death. The photographs of Belle Root epitomize the beauty of the "Gibson Girl" look of that era.

Children:

57.   I.   ***Leo Cassar Root***. See Root Family History for descendants.

58.   II.   ***Nordica Thelma Root***. See Root Family History for descendants.

References: US Census: 1900, 1910; New York State Census: 1905; Floral Park Cemetery Records, Johnson City, New York; New York State Death Certificate December 14, 1914; Binghamton, New York City Directory 1905.

22.

Jesse Nicholas Fuller, b. Nunda, New York January 24, 1883, d. Binghamton, New York January 24, 1934 from angina pectoris; m. Binghamton, New York June 6, 1906 Emma Graf, b. Pennsylvania May 30 1886, d. Clearwater, Florida January 15, 1978 from natural causes. Jesse Fuller was named for two members of the Adams family, his maternal grandfather, Nicholas Adams and his maternal great-grandfather, Jesse Adams. In the 1905 New York State Census Jesse Fuller resided with Dr. William Wilson for whom he drove a team of horses. It was on his rounds for Dr. Wilson that Jesse met his future wife, Emma Graf. His World War I Draft Registration Card described him as being of medium height and build with brown eyes and dark black hair. Mr. Fuller was employed with the Endicott Johnson Shoe Company as a shoe worker. The Fullers had no children. They were given custody of Leo and Nordica Root, Belle's children, but their nephew and niece did not always reside with them. Leo Root's daughter, Nordica Root Anderson, made annual trips to Johnson City to visit Emma Fuller until Emma moved to Clearwater Florida in the late 1960s. The correspondence between the two no longer exists. Emma Fuller was employed by Endicott-Johnson Shoe Company for 43 years. She was a member of the St. Paul's Lutheran Church, Johnson City, the O.E.S. Chapter #14, Binghamton, the White Shrine of Jerusalem #8 Binghamton, the Greenbriar Club in Clearwater, Florida and the W. and SL. Club of Greenbriar, Clearwater. Before her move to Florida, Emma resided at 599 Main Street in Johnson

City. I have a set of monogrammed Brazilian silver flatware that belonged to Jesse and Emma Fuller, a rocking chair that belonged to Jesse Fuller, and a number of items embroidered and tatted by Emma Fuller. Emma Fuller's remains were cremated and returned to Floral Park Cemetery from Florida for burial with Jesse Fuller in the Fuller-Root lot.

References: US Census: 1900, 1910, 1920, 1930, 1940; New York State Census: 1905, 1915, 1925; Floral Park Cemetery Records, Johnson City, New York; Obituary January 18, 1978 Binghamton, New York newspaper, WWI Draft Registration Card 1917-1918.

23.

Louise Fuller, b. Nunda, New York February 1884, d. Binghamton, New York March 15, 1904 Binghamton, New York from pneumonia after a five-day illness; m. Binghamton, New York November 20, 1901 Charles Elisha Hungerford, b. Broome County, New York August 15, 1880, d. Conklin, New York April 28, 1942. Louise contracted pneumonia from her mother by taking care of her and sleeping with her during the mother's illness. She was buried in an unmarked grave in Johnson City's Floral Park Cemetery in the Hungerford family lot with her husband's parents and brother. Louise's mother was later buried next to her where Charles Hungerford was to have been buried. There are no markers for any members of the Hungerford family. I have in my possession a large hand colored photograph of Louise Fuller Hungerford. It is the only known photograph of her. Charles Hungerford resided with his parents before his marriage to Louise Fuller and after her death. He was employed as a cigar maker. Charles married two more times, first to Bessie Prentice in 1906, by whom he had a son, Sheridan Everett Hungerford, born in Binghamton, March 15, 1907. This marriage ended in divorce and Charles Hungerford resided with Hungerford family members based on the 1915 New York State Census. The 1920 and 1930 US Census recorded Charles Hungerford as single. He remarried a third time after 1930 to Margaret Haley, born 1888, d. December 8, 1941. Charles Hungerford's World War I Draft Registration Card described him as being tall, stout, with blue eyes and dark brown hair. Charles Hungerford and his third wife were buried in Calvary Cemetery, Johnson City, New York. Charles' son, Sheridan, did not marry until late in life. His World War II Draft Registration Card described Sheridan Hungerford as being 5' 6" tall, weighing 150 pounds with blue eyes and light brown hair. He wore glasses, had a scar over his left hand and was very lame. In 1940 Sheridan was serving prison time in Waterbury, Connecticut. By 1942 he had married Hazel J., last name not known, and was employed as a tool maker in New Haven, Connecticut. He died in 1978.

References: US Census: 1900, 1910, 1920, 1930, 1940; New York State Census: 1905, 1915, 1925; World War I Draft Registration Card 1917-1918; World War II Draft Registration Card, 1942 for Sheridan Hungerford; Calvary Cemetery Records, Johnson City, New York; Social Security Death Index 1935-2014 for Sheridan Hungerford; Press and Sun Bulletin, Binghamton, New York for April 27, 1942; NYS Marriage Index 1881-1967 for marriage of Louise Fuller and Charles Hungerford; NYS Death Index 1852-1956 for Louise Fuller Hungerford; Floral Park Cemetery Records, Johnson City, New York.

24.

Allen Jesse Carter, b. Nunda, New York August 1889, d. Rochester, New York May 28, 1910 at the Rochester, NY state hospital. Allen Carter was described in his obituary as a popular young businessman who was well liked by all who knew him. He had been in business with his father conducting the Dalton Stage Line and later operating the meat market in Nunda village. A few months prior to his death, Allen Carter went west on a visit and upon his return suffered from organic brain trouble which caused his death. He was buried in the Carter lot in Nunda's Oakwood Cemetery. It is unclear if Allen Carter's illness could have been hereditary from his Adams ancestry.

References: US Census: 1900, 1910; New York State Census: 1905; Oakwood Cemetery Records, Nunda, New York; The Nunda News June 4, 1910.

25.

Arthur Nicholas Palmer, b. Nunda, New York June 12, 1885, d. Johnson City, New York October 1, 1885; m. Binghamton, New York July 18, 1914 Florence Mason, b. Franklin, Pennsylvania April 27, 1895, d. Binghamton, New York February 1, 1991. Arthur's middle name was the first name of his maternal great-grandfather Nicholas Adams. In both the 1900 and the 1910 federal censuses, Arthur resided with his parents and was employed as a painter. He enlisted in the New York State Guard April 17, 1912 and served with Battery C, 1st Battalion. After his marriage Arthur was employed as an assembler with a camera factory in Binghamton. They resided at 68 Grant Avenue in Johnson City. Arthur continued to work in a camera factory rising to the position of foreman by the 1940 US Census. Arthur Palmer was best man for his cousin Jesse Fuller at Jesse's wedding to Emma Graf. Arthur and Florence Palmer were buried in Riverhurst Cemetery, Endicott, New York.

Children:

59.   I.   *Robert Arthur Palmer*, f.

60.   II.   *Douglas Robert Palmer*, f.

References: US Census: 1900, 1910, 1920, 1930, 1940; New York State Census: 1905, 1915, 1925; New York State Birth Index 1881-1942; New York State Marriage Index 1881-1967; Social Security Death Index 1935-2014; New York Guard Service 1906-1918; Riverhurst Cemetery Records, Endicott, New York.

26.

Frank J. Palmer b. Alexander, New York December 12, 1886, d. Binghamton, New York July 1978. Frank resided at home with his parents through the 1940 US Census. He was employed at ashoe factory and as a Nailer at a washer factory in Binghamton. His World War I Draft RegistrationCard described him as being of medium build, slender with brown eyes and brown hair. Mr. Carter's World War II Draft Registration Card noted that he worked for the Truitt Shoe Company, was 5' 5 ½ "tall and weighed 120 pounds, and continued to reside with his mother in Binghamton. Mr. Carter was probably named for his mother's brother, Franklin Carter. Frank Palmer never married. It is not currently known where he was buried.

References: US Census: 1900, 1910, 1920, 1930, 1940; New York State Census: 1905, 1915; New York State Birth Index 1881-1942; Social Security Death Index 1935=2014; World War I Draft Registration Card 1917-1918; World War II Draft Registration Card 1942.

27.

Cortland Daniel Palmer b. Perry, New York June 10, 1890, d. Binghamton, New York July 5, 1965; m. (1) Binghamton, New York April 9, 1917 Lillian M. Graebner, b. Binghamton, New York April 9, 1891, d. Binghamton, New York October 22, 1926; m. (2) Endicott, New York September 17, 1934 Altha Winnifred Stafford, b. Nunda, New York May 7, 1901, d. Binghamton, New York March 29, 1968. Mr. Palmer was named for his great-uncle, Cortland Adams, and his maternal grandfather, Daniel Carter. His World War I Draft Registration Card described him as short and slender with blue eyes and light brown hair. He was employed as a painter working with his father. Cortland Palmer's World War II Draft Registration Card noted he was employed as an elevator operator with Security Mutual Life Insurance Company. He was described as being 5' 6" tall, weighed 120 pounds with blue eyes and brown hair. He was hard of hearing in his right ear. In the 1920 federal census Cortland Palmer resided with his father-in-law, George Graebner, at 17 Hotchkiss Street in Binghamton. Cortland Palmer was employed as a floor manager at a shoe factory in Binghamton in 1920. He had previously worked as a paper hanger. After his first wife's death Mr. Palmer resided with his parents with his two children from his first marriage. Cortland Palmer had six more children by his second marriage. It is not currently known where Cortland Palmer and his first wife were buried. Cortland Palmer's obituary stated burial was in Spring Forest Cemetery, Binghamton, but this cannot be confirmed. Altha Palmer was buried in Chenango Valley Cemetery, Binghamton, New York. Mrs. Palmer had an illegitimate son, Nelson LeRoy Stafford (1925-1985) before her marriage. Nelson Stafford was buried in the same cemetery with his

Appendix II: The Carter Family of Nunda, New York

wife and mother.

Children (by first marriage):

61.   I.   **Harold George Palmer**, b. Walton, New York March 3, 1918, d. Binghamton, New York June 25, 1996; m. Binghamton, New York December 31, 1954 Florence N. Corey, b. 1906, d. Binghamton, New York August 4, 1986. Mr. Palmer's World War II Draft Registration Card described him as being 5'7" tall, weighed 130 pounds with brown hair and brown eyes. He had a scar inside of his right wrist. In 1942 Harold Palmer was employed with the Barnard Bake Shop in Binghamton. It does not appear that there were any children. Harold and Florence Palmer were buried in Riverside Cemetery, Endicott, New York.

62.   II.   **Raymond Courtland Palmer**, b. New York state June 15, 1921, d. Oxford, New York January 19, 2016; m. Binghamton, New York June 1945 Beverly L. Smith, b. New York state May 2, 1925, d. New York state September 28, 2012. Mr. Palmer's Draft Registration Card described him being 5' 10" tall, weighed 138 pounds with brown hair and brown eyes. H was employed with Sears Roebuck. Mr. Palmer served with the US Army in World War II and held the rank of corporal. They had one son, David Palmer, and one grandson, Robert Palmer. They were buried in Vestal Hills Memorial Park, Endicott, New York.

Children (by second marriage):

63.   I.   **David George Palmer**, b. Johnson City, New York February 12, 1936, d. Binghamton, New York February 10, 2012; m. Endicott, New York April 24, 1965 Martha L. Maher, b. New York 1939, d. New York State July 26, 1992. They had at least five children: Kira, David, Todd, Wendy, and Craig. David and Martha Palmer were buried in Calvary Cemetery, Johnson City, New York.

64.   II.   **Richard S. Palmer**, b. Johnson City, New York June 19, 1937, d. Binghamton, New York October 30, 2002; m. Binghamton, New York March 27, 1963 Nancy Ann Kasmarcik, b. Binghamton, New York March 8, 1944, d. Hartford, New York January 20, 2017. Mr. Palmer served in the US Navy. It is not known if they had any children. Mrs. Palmer was

previously married and may have had two children by her first marriage. Richard and Nancy Palmer were buried in Floral Park Cemetery, Johnson City, New York.

65.   III.   **Roberta J. "Bobbie" Palmer**, b. Niagara, New York April 25, 1934, d. Binghamton, New York July 1983. Miss Palmer never married and was employed as a clerk at Montgomery Wards for many years. It is not known where she was buried.

66.   IV.   **Dorothy E. Palmer**, b. Binghamton, New York December 24, 1940, d. Johnson City, New York May 31, 2008; m. Binghamton, New York September 7, 1957 David W. Starks. Undocumented sources imply Dorothy Palmer was married at least three times. It is not clear how many children she had and by whom. She was buried in Calvary Cemetery, Johnson City, New York and her tombstone will be shared with one of her sons: Kevin Thomas.

67.   V.   **Courtland Daniel Palmer, Jr.**, place and date of birth not known; m. Binghamton, New York October 25, 1958 Millie J. Canniff. No further information.

68.   VI.   **Joel S. Palmer**, b. Binghamton, New York February 20, 1944; m. Binghamton, New York September 30, 1967 Mary J. White.

References: US Census: 1900, 1910, 1920, 1930, 1940; New York State Census: 1905, 1915, 1925; Floral Park Cemetery Records, Johnson City, New York; Calvary Cemetery Records, Johnson City, New York; NYS Birth Index 1881-1942; NYS Death Index 1935-2014; NYS Marriage Index 1881-1967; Riverside Cemetery Records, Endicott, New York; Vestal Hills Memorial Park, Endicott, New York; Chenango Valley Cemetery Records, Binghamton, New York; World War I Draft Registration Card 1917-18; World War II Draft Registration Card 1942; Courtland Palmer obituary Binghamton, New York July 7, 1965.

28.

James Harold Palmer b Binghamton, New York September 20 1903, d. Binghamton, New York March 1980; m. (1) Binghamton, New York June

2, 1926 Mary Ann Griffin, b. Grand Rapids, Michigan January 31, 1906, d. Binghamton, New York November 28, 1955 from cirrhosis of the liver after a ten-year battle with the disease; m. (2) place and date not known, Anna L. Simko Szewczak, b. Binghamton, New York January 25, 1915, d. Binghamton, New York October 12, 1996. James Palmer resided with his parents based on the 1910, 1920, and 1930 federal censuses. In the 1930 federal census his wife Mary, his daughter Beverly, b. a. 1928, and a son Gerald, b. a. 1929, were living with him at his parent's home. James Palmer's World War II Draft Registration Card described him as being 5' 10 ½ "tall, weighed 140 pounds with brown hair and brown eyes. He had a mole under his right eye and a scar on his left hand. Mr. Palmer was employed as a truck driver and later as an assistant foreman for a camera factory. Mary Palmer was buried in Vestal Hills Memorial Park, Vestal, New York. Anna Palmer was previously married to Arthur F. Szewczak who died October 1, 1947 and by whom she had at least two children. James and Anna Palmer were buried in Calvary Cemetery, Johnson City, New York.

Children (by first marriage):

69. I. **Beverly Jean Palmer**, b. Binghamton, New York June 16, 1926, d. Loughman, Florida December 10, 1982; m. place and date not known, Charles Edward White, born Johnson City, New York July 27, 1927, d. Douglas County, Georgia October 9, 2012. They had at least one child. It is not currently known where they were buried.

70. II. **Gerald Thomas Palmer**, b. Johnson City, New York July 1, 1929, d. Raleigh, North Carolina August 30, 2016; m. (1) Binghamton, New York Mildred Miller, b. June 3, 1930, d. Raleigh, North Carolina February 19, 2007, divorced Wake, North Carolina March 23, 1977; m. (2) place and date not known, Margaret Morgan, b. 1940, d. Raleigh, North Carolina 2013. It is not known how many children Gerald Palmer had by his first wife because his obituary lists both his children and step-children together. James Palmer was employed as an IBM Designer. Mildred Palmer was buried in Raleigh Memorial Park, Raleigh, North Carolina. James and Margaret Palmer were buried together in the same cemetery.

71. III. **Ronald James Palmer**, b. Binghamton, New York April 12, 1932, d. December 3,1950 in Korea. Mr. Palmer's body was never recovered. His death date was his MIA date of disappearance. He served with Company C, 32 Medical Infantry, Seventh Division.

References: US Census: 1910, 1920, 1930, 1940; New York State Census: 1915, 1925; Vestal Hills Memorial Park Records, Vestal, New York; Calvary Cemetery Records, Johnson City, New York; Raleigh Memorial Park Records, Raleigh, North Carolina; World War II Draft Registration Card, 1942; North Carolina Divorce Index 1958-2004; Social Security Death Index 1935-2014.

29.

George Bain Foose b. Nunda, New York January 16, 1889, Buffalo, New York November 8, 1918; m. Buffalo, New York December 16, 1914 Agnes H. Haft, b. Buffalo, New York May 14, 1891, d. Buffalo, New York January 1, 1921. Mr. Fosse's World War I Draft Registration Card described him as being tall and slender with blue eyes and black hair. He was employed as a merchant with his father. George and Agnes Haft resided at 633 Masten Street in Buffalo. Agnes Foose was employed as a hairdresser and during her widowhood did housework. She moved back in with her parents after Mr. Foose died. It is not known what they died of as such young ages. George and Agnes Foose were buried in Forest Lawn Cemetery, Buffalo, New York. They did not have any Children.

References: US Census: 1900, 1910, 1920; New York State Census: 1905, 1915; World War I Draft Registration Card 1917-1918; Forest Lawn Cemetery Records, Buffalo, New York; NYS Death Index 1880-1956.

30.

Carlotta (Lottie) Eula/Evelyn Foose, b. Mt. Morris, New York February 5, 1891, d. Nunda, New New York November 22, 1949; m. (1) North Dansville, New York September 6, 1908 Edwin A. Hall, b. Dansville, New York December 6, 1866, d. Chicago, Illinois August 3, 1935, divorced; m. (2) Franklin, Arkansas October 21, 1939 Auguste P. Ferrier, b. New Orleans, Louisiana August 5, 1891, d. World War II February 28, 1944. Edwin Hall was previously married and had a son, Wilmot (1895-1963). Carlotta and Edwin Hall had four children, two of whom died young. Edwin Hall was buried in Graceland Cemetery, Chicago. He had been employed as a grocer in New York, Washington, and Illinois states. The Halls moved from New York State to Chehalis, Washington by the 1920 US Census. Auguste Ferrier served in World War I in France from March 16. 1918 to January 15, 1919 with the US Marine Corps rising to the rank of Sergeant. At the time of his marriage to Carlotta, Mr. Ferrier was employed with the merchant marine. He died in World War II in a civilian capacity with the merchant marine and was buried in Honolulu at the National Memorial Cemetery of the Pacific. Carlotta resided with her daughter, Dorothy, in Uniontown, Pennsylvania in 1940 and later in Nunda, New York where she died. Carlotta was buried in Greenmount Cemetery, Dansville, New York.

Children (by first marriage):

72. I. ***Edwin Hall***, b. Dansville, New York September 2, 1909, d. Buffalo, New York March 2, 1917 and was buried in Greenmount Cemetery, Dansville, New York.

73. II. ***Charles Lansing Hall***, b. Dansville, New York October 7, 1911, d. place and date not known; m. Clara B., last name not known. He worked with the WPA in Washington state. He served with the US Marines and was described as 5' 6" tall, weighed 129 pounds with blue eyes and brown hair. No further information.

74. III. ***Jane A. Hall***, b. Dansville, New York April 1913, d. Dansville, New York June 6, 1913 and was buried in Greenmount Cemetery, Dansville, New York.

75. IV. ***Dorothy Eula Hall***, b. Dansville, New York April 8, 1914, d. Perry, New York July 30, 1996; m. date and place not known Herman Baxter Blankenship, b. Illinois December 31, 1900, d. Greenville, Illinois November 1980. Mr. Blankenship was buried in Graceland Cemetery, Chicago with his first wife, Ester Blankenship, who died in 1937 from diphtheria along with his two children from the first marriage. Herman was a grocer by profession and while in Pennsylvania in 1940 was employed

as a foreman for a drainage engineering company. Dorothy Blankenship was buried in Greenmount Cemetery with her mother and siblings.

Children:

i. **Richard Blankenship** of Perry, New York. No further information.

ii. **Lois Blankenship Smith**; m. Ronald Smith and resided in Nunda, New York. No further information.

iii. **Joyce Blankenship Heiland**; m. Gary Heiland and reside in Aurora, Colorado. No further information.

iv. **Rita Kay Blankenship**, b. Ohio September 21, 1943, d. Perry, New York March 23, 2009; m. (1) Nunda, New York July 22, 1960 Dalene E. Langdon, b. Bliss, New York May 2, 1938, d. Perry, New York May 26, 2006, divorced; m. (2) place and date not known Dean Barrows, b. Perry, New York January 13, 1922, d. Mt. Morris, New York May 3, 2011. Dean Barrows was buried in West Perry Cemetery, Perry, New York and Rita was buried in Greenmount Cemetery, Dansville, New York. They had seven grandchildren and 4 great-grandchildren.

Children (by first marriage):

a. **Brian Langdon**

b. **Deborah Langdon Synder**

c. **Stephanie Langdon Eichenseer**

d. **Rhonda Langdon**

v. **Marty E. Blankenship**, b. Dansville, New York October 27, 1946, d. Muscoda, Wisconsin February 28, 2007; m. July 5, 1980 Cheryl Gauva, b. August 24, 1955. Marty was employed as a union carpenter in Madison, Wisconsin. He had four daughters, three sons, 14 grandchildren, and one great-grandchild. He was buried in St. John's Cemetery, Muscoda, Wisconsin.

References: US Census: 1900, 1910, 1920, 1930, 1940; New York State Census: 1905, 1915; Greenmount Cemetery Records, Dansville, New York; Graceland Cemetery Records, Chicago, Illinois; St. John's Cemetery Records, Muscoda, Wisconsin; NYS Marriage Index 1881-1967 for Carlotta's firs marriage; Arkansas Marriage Index 1837-1957 for Carlotta's second marriage; Dansville Breeze newspaper obituary November 24, 1949 for Carlotta Ferrier; US National Cemetery Interment Control Forms 1928-1962 for Auguste Ferrier; World War II Draft Registration Card 1942; Honolulu, Hawaii National Memorial Cemetery of the Pacific 1941-2011; US National Homes for Disabled Volunteer Soldiers 1866-1938

31.

Harry Warren Foose b. Nunda/ Cuba, New York April 22, 1896, d. Ventura, California December 16, 1954; m. (1) Fillmore, New York August 18, 1934 Leola Beatrice van Dyke, b. Hunts, New York June 1, 1914, d. Magalia, California February 10, 1986, divorced; m. (2) Ventura, California December 31, 1945, Lois Louis Vest, b. Buffalo, New York November 16, 1917, d. Atascadero, California May 9, 2018. In the 1920 federal census, Harry Foose resided with his parents and was employed as a traveling salesman for a chemical company. In the 1930 federal census Harry moved to Belfast, New York. He was employed as a newspaper promoter in 1930 and the time of death as mail clerk. His World War I Draft Registration Card recorded that he worked as a stock clerk at the Curtis Aeroplane Company in Buffalo, New York. He was described as tall and slender with blue eyes and light hair. He served from May 26, 1917, to December 12, 1917, with the Machine Gun Company of the 108th Infantry. Mr. Foose was mustered out with a 33 1/3 % disability. Mr. Fosse's first wife remarried on April 27, 1952, to John Armour Ericson. Harry Foose was buried in Ivy Lawn Memorial Park, Ventura, California. His daughter and grandson were also buried there. Lois Vest Palmer was married four times.

Children (by first marriage):

76. I. ***Douglas B. Foose***, b. Nunda, New York a. 1936. He served in the US Army at the time of his father's death. No further information.

Children (by second marriage):

77. II. ***Sharon Ann Foose***, b. Oxnard, California October 26, 1946, d. Oxnard, California February 24, 1991; m. February 27, 1965, Garry Leon Johnson, b. San Francisco, California July 7, 1944, d. Weaverville, California March 10, 2000, divorced February 13, 1990.

Children:

i. ***David Leon Johnson***, b. Oxnard, California August 20, 1965, d. Pine Creek County, California February 6, 1981, falling from a cliff. He was buried in Ivey Lawn Cemetery, Ventura, California with his mother.

References: US Census: 1900, 1910, 1920, 1930, 1940; NYS Marriage Index 1881-1967 for Harry Fosse's first marriage; World War I Draft Registration Card 1917-18; World War II Draft Registration Card 1942; Ivy Lawn Memorial Park Records, Ventura, California; US Headstone Applications for Military Veterans 1925-1963; New York Abstracts of National Guard Service WWI 1917-1919; Ventura County Star-Free Press newspaper obituary December 18, 1954.

32.

Mary Elizabeth Foose, b. Cuba, New York May 21, 1903, d. Oxnard, California May 16, 1951; m. (1) m. a. 1921 Louis Paul Schubert, b. Budapest, Hungary August 31, 1900, d. Fort Meade, Florida July 22, 1969, divorced; m. (2) place not known, 1926 Frank Edmond Trent, b. place not known, July 12, 1898, d. place not known, March 31, 1961, divorced; m. (3) place and date not known, a Mr. Takach; m. (4) place and date not known, a Mr. Wiseman. Mary Elizabeth Foose was named for her maternal grandmother, Mary Elizabeth Adams Carter. She resided with her parents in Cuba, New York (1905), North Dansville (1910), Buffalo, New York (1915), and Buffalo, New York (1920). In 1930 Mary resided with her parents, second husband, and her son from her first marriage in Fillmore, New York where her parents operated the hotel and her then husband was employed as a cook. In 1935 she lived in New Brunswick, New Jersey and by 1940 was married a third time and resided with her mother and son in Fillmore, New York. At the time of her death Mary had remarried a fourth time. The identities of her third and fourth husbands are not known. It is not known where she was buried.

Children (by first marriage):

78.   I.   **Louis Paul Schubert, Jr.**, b. Warsaw, New York October 19, 1922, d. Bakersfield, California June 15, 1999; m. place and date not known, Dorothy M. Bubel, b. Rochester, New York November 1, 1922, d. Bakersfield, California August 28, 2004. Mr. Schubert enlisted in the US Army in World War II serving from February 9, 1943 to December 24, 1945 as a skilled mechanic and repairman. In Oxnard he owned and operated Custom TV. They had two children. The identity of only one is currently known. It is not known where they were buried.

Children:

i..   **Kenneth L. Schubert**, b. Nunda, New York January 12, 1943, d. Las Vegas, Nevada April 8, 2001; m. March 29, 1973 Suellen Comeau. He had four children by his first marriage and one child by a second marriage. Further information is not currently available.

References: US Census: 1910, 1920, 1930, 1940; New York State Census: 1905, 1915; Evergreen Cemetery Records, Fort Meade, Florida; World War II Draft Registration Card, 1942; US Social Security Applications and Claims Index 1936-2007; California Death Index 1940-1997.

33.

Robert Arthur Palmer, b. Johnson City, New York April 14, 1918, d. Norwich, New York February 14, 1982; m. place and date not known Elizabeth Marie Boerl, b. Herrick Center, Pennsylvania January 4, 1918, d. Norwich, New York June 1995. Robert Palmer served in the US Army during World War II from July 10, 1942 to November 12, 1945. His World War II Draft Registration Card described him as being 5' 10 ½ "tall, weighing 145 pounds, with brown eyes and black hair. He wore glasses. He worked for Agfa Ansco. There is currently no record that they had any children. Robert and Elizabeth Palmer were buried at Riverhurst Cemetery, Endicott, New York.

References: US Census: 1920, 1930, 1940; New York State Census: 1925; World War II Draft Registration Card 1942; Riverhurst Cemetery Records, Endicott, New York.

34.

Douglas Robert Palmer, b. Johnson City, New York June 7, 1920, d. Johnson City, New York July 11, 1993; m. Binghamton, New York April 15, 1942 Lillian Arlene Murphy, b. Johnson City, New York April 22, 1923, d. Johnson City, New York June 12, 2012. They had four children. Douglas and Arlene Palmer were buried in Riverhurst Cemetery, Endicott, New York.

Children:

79. I. ***Sally Palmer Chamberlain***, no further information.

80. II. ***Debbi Palmer Osenni***, no further information.

81. III. ***Robert Palmer***, no further information.

84. IV. ***Craig Alan Palmer***, b. Johnson City, New York February 27, 1948, d. Johnson City, New York August 19, 1991. He served as a Sergeant with the US Marine Corps in Vietnam. Mr. Palmer was buried in Glenwood Cemetery, Dickinson, New York.

References: US Census: 1920, 1930, 1940; New York State Census: 1925; Glenwood Cemetery Records, Dickinson, New York; Riverhurst Cemetery Records, Endicott, New York; New York State Birth Index 1881-1942; New York State Death Index 1935-2014; US Obituary Index.

APPENDIX III:
Lists of Photographs

Photographs of the Fuller Family of Nunda, New York for the 19th century, are not currently available. An extensive search of different family lines failed to find Fuller images. The Nunda Historical Society did not have any Fuller images either. The same result turned out to be true for the Adams and Carter family lines presented in this publication. I found this unusual given the Fuller family's prominence. Grave stones must serve as the visual record for Fuller, Adams, and Carter family members. Unfortunately, many tombstones are also missing. All of the images for this book belong to the author or were taken by the author with the exception of the Open-Source images of Burnham Hoyt and three of his architectural designs and for the images of descendants of Albert J. Fuller's second marriage. A special thank you to Teddi Kella (Fuller) for those family photographs. (*Photographs belonging to the author are Copyrighted and cannot be used or reproduced without permission.*)

1. Nunda, New York: 1870 Nunda Village map showing the residence of Joshua Fuller on Massachusetts Street.

2. Nunda, New York: 1900, State Street commercial district.

3. Nunda, New York Universalist Church founded by Joshua Fuller.

4. Nunda, New York intersection of Fuller Road with Paine Road where the Fuller farms were once located.

5. Nunda, New York Oakwood Cemetery where Fuller graves are located on the extreme front left side of the cemetery.

6. Nunda, New York Oakwood Cemetery: Graves for Joshua and Marcy Fuller and John B. Payne (Paine), their son-in-law.

7. Humphrey, New York Chappellsburg Burying Ground: Grave of Pliny Brewer Fuller, son of Joshua Fuller and his first wife, Polly Brewer.

8. Nunda, New York Oakwood Cemetery: Graves for William C. and Louisa Guy Fuller.

9. William C. Fuller 1870 signed check.

10. 1861 image of William H. Guy (1830-1895), brother of Louisa Guy Fuller.

11. Nunda, New York Oakwood Cemetery: Graves of Henry and Esther Barker Fuller, son and daughter-in-law of William C. Fuller.

12. Nunda, New York Oakwood Cemetery: Grave of Arthur Fuller, son of William C. Fuller.

13. Nunda, New York Oakwood Cemetery: Grave of Charles Fuller, son of William C. Fuller.

14. Kalamazoo, Michigan Riverside Cemetery: Grave of Martha Fuller Drury Cragin Underwood, daughter of William C. Fuller.

15. Kalamazoo, Michigan Riverside Cemetery: Grave of George C. Fuller, son of William C. Fuller.

16. Kalamazoo, Michigan Riverside Cemetery: Graves of Albert Fuller, son of William C. Fuller, with Albert's third wife.

17. Sandy Creek, New York Woodlawn Cemetery: Grave of Mary Fuller Paine Slater Rolison, daughter of William C. Fuller.

18. Nunda, New York Oakwood Cemetery: Grave of Alfred Goldthwait, son-in-law of Joshua Fuller, married to Clarissa Caroline Fuller. No marker for Clarissa.

Appendix III: Photographs

19. Nunda, New York, Oakwood Cemetery: Grave for Norton Goldthwait, Civil War veteran, grandson of Joshua Fuller and his wife, Jane.

20. Madison, Wisconsin, Forest Hill Cemetery: Graves of Sophie Fuller Chittenden, daughter of Joshua Fuller, and her husband, Dr. Nelson Chittenden and their children.

21. Dr. Charles Curtis Chittenden (1842-1905), son of Sophie Fuller Chittenden.

22. Vicksburg, Michigan, Clement Cemetery: Graves of James Fuller and his wife Sarah. James was the son of Joshua Fuller.

23. Brochure for the Northern Queen Manufacturing Company founded by George Pliny Fuller, grandson of Joshua Fuller.

24. Washboard invented by George Pliny Fuller with helpful instructions.

25. Advertising for Northern Queen Washboard manufactured in Kalamazoo, Michigan.

26. Burnham Hoyt (1887-1960), internationally known architect and husband of Mildred Fuller (1892-1978), great-granddaughter of Pliny B. Fuller.

27. Hoyt designed 4th Church of Christ Scientist, Denver Colorado.

28. Hoyt designed Red Rocks Amphitheater, Denver, Colorado.

29. Hoyt designed Riverside Church, Manhattan, New York City.

30. Bradford Carter (1837-1909), brother of Daniel Carter.

31. Ithaca, Michigan, Ithaca Cemetery: Grave of Bradford Carter.

32. Nunda, New York advertisement for the Frank and Alan Carter Bus Line.

33. Carter genealogical information written down and found in a New Testament belonging to Edith Carter Fuller Stalker.

34. Nunda, New York, Oakwood Cemetery: Marker for Carter graves in the back of the cemetery.

35. Nunda, New York, Oakwood Cemetery: probable burial location for Daniel Carter and his wife, Mary Elizabeth Adams Carter.

36. Nunda, New York, Oakwood Cemetery: Grave for Frank J. Carter.

37. Nunda, New York, Frank Carter farm: Jesse Fuller standing with his aunt, Nettie Carter Foose and seated, his aunt, Carrie Angier Carter (Mrs. Frank Carter).

38. Nunda, New York, Oakwood Cemetery: Grave of Carrie Angier Carter.

39. Nunda, New York, Oakwood Cemetery: Grave of Allen J. Carter.

40. Nunda, New York, Oakwood Cemetery: Marker for Lois "Nettie" Carter Foose and her husband, Charles, next to the Carter graves.

41. Buffalo, New York, Forest Lawn Cemetery: Graves for George B. Foose and his wife, Agnes. George Foose was the grandson of Daniel Carter.

42. Ventura, California, Ivy Lawn Memorial Park: Grave for Harry Foose, grandson of Daniel Carter.

43. Vestal, New York, Vestal Cemetery: Graves of Alta Carter Palmer and her husband, James. 44. James Palmer, husband of Alta Carter Palmer.

44. James Palmer, husband of Alta Carter Palmer.

45. L. to R.: Alta Carter Palmer with her sister Lois Carter Foose, maybe at Letchworth State Park, New York.

46. Palmer Family: Standing, L. to R.: Arlene Palmer, Douglas Palmer, Lloyd Murphy, Irene Murphy, Frank Stevens, Arthur

Appendix III: Photographs

Palmer, Florence Palmer. Seated, L. to R.: Alta Carter Palmer, Thomas Murphy, Sally Palmer, Marion Mason, Lillian Stevens.

47. Louise Fuller, daughter of Albert Fuller and Edith Carter. Only known photograph.

48. Johnson City, New York, Calvary Cemetery: Grave of Charles Hungerford, husband of Louise Fuller.

49. Johnson City, New York, Floral Park Cemetery: Grave of Lemuel Stalker, second husband of Edith Carter Fuller.

50. Nunda, New York, Oak Hill Cemetery: Property Map showing lots purchased by Nicholas Adams and Jesse Adams.

51. Nunda, New York, Oak Hill Cemetery: No markers on the cemetery lots of the Nicholas and Jesse Adams families.

52. Nunda New York Town Clerk verifying that Nicholas Adams' father was Jesse Adams.

53. Obituary for Will Adams, grandson of Nicholas Adams, found in a poetry book belonging to Belle Fuller Root.

54. Ceres, Pennsylvania, Evergreen Kings Cemetery: Grave of George Jesse Adams, "half-brother" of Nicholas Adams.

55. Framed photograph of Belle Fuller Root, about 1900.

56. Johnson City, New York, Floral Park Cemetery: Grave of Belle Fuller Root.

57. Belle Fuller Root, about 1904.

58. Ernest Root, husband of Belle Fuller Root, about 1900.

59. L. to R.: Jenny Cox, milliner, and Belle Fuller Root, seamstress, worked together and operated a shop in Binghamton, New York.

60. Johnson City, New York, Floral Park Cemetery: Grave of Leo C. Root, son of Belle Fuller Root.

61. Leo C. Root, son of Belle Fuller Root, about 1908.

62. Leo C. Root and his sister, Nordica Root (Wylie), about 1908.

63. Johnson City, New York, Floral Park Cemetery: Grave of Ethel Bernard Root, wife of Leo C. Root.

64. Jesse Nicholas Fuller and his wife Emma (Graf) at the time of their marriage in 1906.

65. Emma Graf Fuller prior to her marriage with Jesse Fuller.

66. Johnson City, New York, Floral Park Cemetery: Graves of Jesse Nicholas Fuller and his wife Emma (Graf).

67. Donald Robert Fuller (1905-1976) with his grandchildren, Patricia and Albert.

68. Albert Donald Fuller, Sr. when a young boy.

69. Albert Donald Fuller, Sr.

70. Alexi Marie Fuller, daughter of Albert Donald Fuller, Sr.

71. Albert Donald Fuller, Jr.

72. Taylor Steele Fuller, great-grandson of Donald Robert Fuller.

Appendix III: Photographs

APPENDIX III:
The Photographs

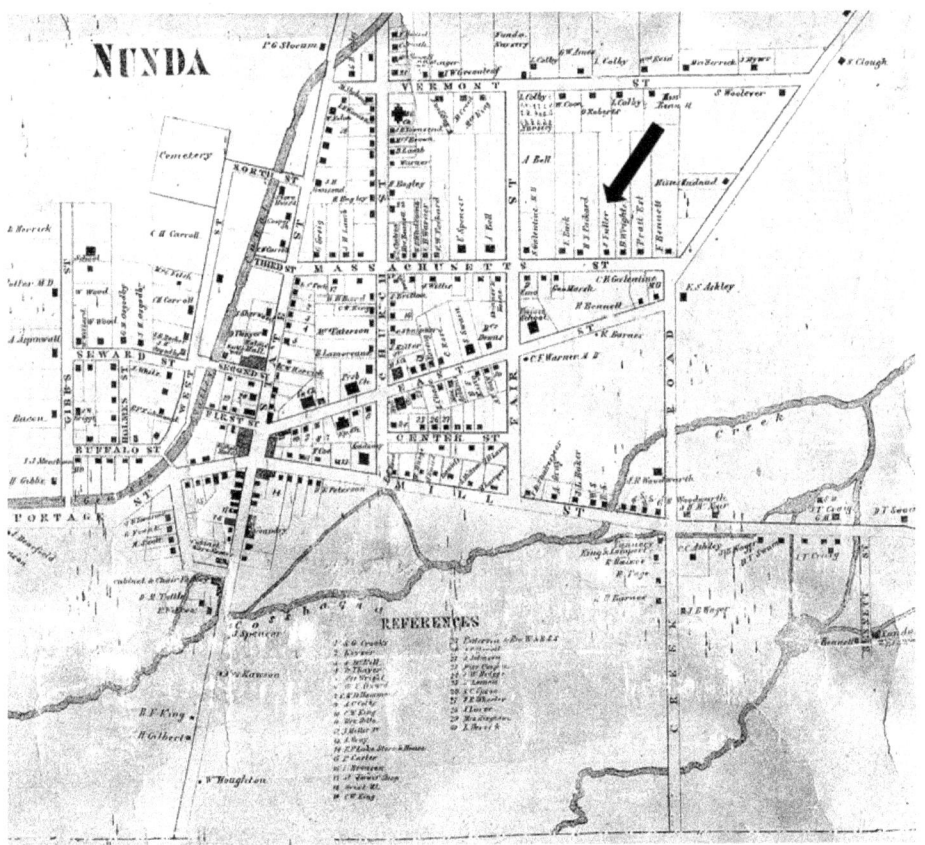

1. Nunda, New York: 1870 Nunda Village map showing the residence of Joshua Fuller on Massachusetts Street.

2. Nunda, New York: 1900, State Street commercial district.

3. Nunda, New York Universalist Church founded by Joshua Fuller.

Appendix III: Photographs

4. Nunda, New York intersection of Fuller Road with Paine Road where the Fuller farms were once located.

5. Nunda, New York Oakwood Cemetery where Fuller graves are located on the extreme front left side of the cemetery.

Appendix III: Photographs

6. Nunda, New York Oakwood Cemetery: Graves for Joshua and Marcy Fuller and John B. Payne (Paine), their son-in-law.

7. Humphrey, New York Chappellsburg Burying Ground: Grave of Pliny Brewer Fuller, son of Joshua Fuller and his first wife, Polly Brewer.

8. Nunda, New York Oakwood Cemetery: Graves for William C. and Louisa Guy Fuller.

Appendix III: Photographs

9. William C. Fuller 1870 signed check.

10. 1861 image of William H. Guy (1830-1895), brother of Louisa Guy Fuller.

11. Nunda, New York Oakwood Cemetery: Graves of Henry and Esther Barker Fuller, son and daughter-in-law of William C. Fuller.

12. Nunda, New York Oakwood Cemetery: Grave of Arthur Fuller, son of William C. Fuller.

Appendix III: Photographs

13. Nunda, New York Oakwood Cemetery: Grave of Charles Fuller, son of William C. Fuller.

14. Kalamazoo, Michigan Riverside Cemetery: Grave of Martha Fuller Drury Cragin Underwood, daughter of William C. Fuller.

15. Kalamazoo, Michigan Riverside Cemetery: Grave of George C. Fuller, son of William C. Fuller.

16. Kalamazoo, Michigan Riverside Cemetery: Graves of Albert Fuller, son of William C. Fuller, with Albert's third wife.

Appendix III: Photographs

17. Sandy Creek, New York Woodlawn Cemetery: Grave of Mary Fuller Paine Slater Rolison, daughter of William C. Fuller.

18. Nunda, New York Oakwood Cemetery: Grave of Alfred Goldthwait, son-in-law of Joshua Fuller, married to Clarissa Caroline Fuller. No marker for Clarissa.

19. Nunda, New York, Oakwood Cemetery: Grave for Norton Goldthwait, Civil War veteran, grandson of Joshua Fuller and his wife, Jane.

20. Madison, Wisconsin, Forest Hill Cemetery: Graves of Sophie Fuller Chittenden, daughter of Joshua Fuller, and her husband, Dr. Nelson Chittenden and their children.

Appendix III: Photographs

21. Dr. Charles Curtis Chittenden (1842-1905), son of Sophie Fuller Chittenden.

22. Vicksburg, Michigan, Clement Cemetery: Graves of James Fuller and his wife Sarah. James was the son of Joshua Fuller.

23. Brochure for the Northern Queen Manufacturing Company founded by George Pliny Fuller, grandson of Joshua Fuller.

24. Washboard invented by George Pliny Fuller with helpful instructions.

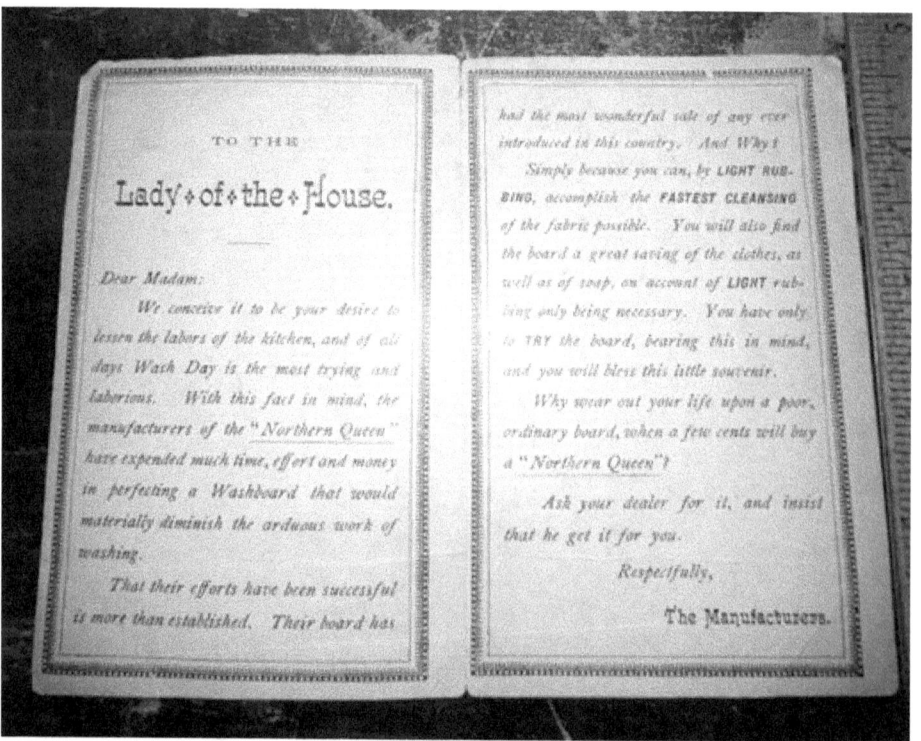

25. Advertising for Northern Queen Washboard manufactured in Kalamazoo, Michigan.

Appendix III: Photographs

26. Burnham Hoyt (1887-1960), internationally known architect and husband of Mildred Fuller (1892-1978), great-granddaughter of Pliny B. Fuller.

27. Hoyt designed 4th Church of Christ Scientist, Denver Colorado.

28. Hoyt designed Red Rocks Amphitheater, Denver, Colorado.

Appendix III: Photographs

29. Hoyt designed Riverside Church, Manhattan, New York City.

30. Bradford Carter (1837-1909), brother of Daniel Carter.

Appendix III: Photographs

31. Ithaca, Michigan, Ithaca Cemetery: Grave of Bradford Carter.

CARTER'S 'BUS LINE!

The only one now between
NUNDA AND DALTON
⸺FARE 25c EACH WAY⸺

Including Oridinary Baggage. Leave calls at hotels or with 'Phone 678.   FRANK CARTER & SON, Nunda, N. Y.

32. Nunda, New York advertisement for the Frank and Alan Carter Bus Line.

Daniel Carter d. Oct 29 1884

Mary E Carter d. Apr. 30 1904

D & M   m. April 16 1863

E.   Sept 13 1865

J.F.   Nov 27 1866

alta   Nov 18 1867

Lois   Dec 18 1868

33. Carter genealogical information written down and found in a New Testament belonging to Edith Carter Fuller Stalker.

Appendix III: Photographs

34. Nunda, New York, Oakwood Cemetery: Marker for Carter graves in the back of the cemetery.

35. Nunda, New York, Oakwood Cemetery: probable burial location for Daniel Carter and his wife, Mary Elizabeth Adams Carter.

36. Nunda, New York, Oakwood Cemetery: Grave for Frank J. Carter.

Appendix III: Photographs

37. Nunda, New York, Frank Carter farm: Jesse Fuller standing with his aunt, Nettie Carter Foose and seated, his aunt, Carrie Angier Carter (Mrs. Frank Carter).

38. Nunda, New York, Oakwood Cemetery: Grave of Carrie Angier Carter.

39. Nunda, New York, Oakwood Cemetery: Grave of Allen J. Carter.

40. Nunda, New York, Oakwood Cemetery: Marker for Lois "Nettie" Carter Foose and her husband, Charles, next to the Carter graves.

Appendix III: Photographs

41. Buffalo, New York, Forest Lawn Cemetery: Graves for George B. Foose and his wife, Agnes. George Foose was the grandson of Daniel Carter.

42. Ventura, California, Ivy Lawn Memorial Park: Grave for Harry Foose, grandson of Daniel Carter.

43. Vestal, New York, Vestal Cemetery: Graves of Alta Carter Palmer and her husband, James.

44. James Palmer, husband of Alta Carter Palmer.

Appendix III: Photographs

45. L. to R.: Alta Carter Palmer with her sister Lois Carter Foose, maybe at Letchworth State Park, New York.

46. Palmer Family: Standing, L. to R.: Arlene Palmer, Douglas Palmer, Lloyd Murphy, Irene Murphy, Frank Stevens, Arthur Palmer, Florence Palmer. Seated, L. to R.: Alta Carter Palmer, Thomas Murphy, Sally Palmer, Marion Mason, Lillian Stevens.

47. Louise Fuller, daughter of Albert Fuller and Edith Carter. Only known photograph.

Appendix III: Photographs

48. Johnson City, New York, Calvary Cemetery: Grave of Charles Hungerford, husband of Louise Fuller.

49. Johnson City, New York, Floral Park Cemetery: Grave of Lemuel Stalker, second husband of Edith Carter Fuller.

Oak Hill Cemetery - Lot Owners

| 94-Jesse Adams | 85-Nicholas Adams | 76-Peter VanDeusen |

50. Nunda, New York, Oak Hill Cemetery: Property Map showing lots purchased by Nicholas Adams and Jesse Adams.

51. Nunda, New York, Oak Hill Cemetery: No markers on the cemetery lots of the Nicholas and Jesse Adams families.

Appendix III: Photographs

Town of Nunda
"A Nice Place To Live"
9261 Water Cure Road
P.O. Box 699
Nunda, N.Y. 14517-0699
www.town-nunda.ny.us

Philip S. Brooks, Supervisor
Cindy Essler, Town Clerk
John Bennett, Highway Superintendent
Robert E. Lloyd, Code and Zoning Officer
Telephone (585) 468-5277

Marcia Ayers, Councilperson
Kirk Brickwedel, Councilperson
David Thompson, Councilperson
John Thompson, Councilperson
Fax (585) 468-5528

March 19, 2006

Dr. William Paquette
13565 Filly Court
Gainesville, VA 20155

Dear Dr. Paquette:

Thank you for sending the CD of the Sanborn Insurance Maps for Nunda, NY. Many people have mentioned using them as part of their research, but I have never taken the time to avail myself to their importance and usefulness in my research. I will inform our local historical society of their presence in Nunda so that they may use them when researching local history as well.

I personally reviewed the death record at our town clerks office for the mother of Nicholas Adams. This record book is the size of the average newspaper and is bound. Unfortunately, the 'Mother's Name and Birthplace' column is on the right hand page and right next to the binding. This coupled with the fact that the towns photocopier is quite limited in its capabilities and accommodates standard letter size paper only, makes it impossible to photocopy the 'Mother's Name and Birthplace' information as I had hoped and as I lead you to believe. In lieu of a photocopy, I laid a piece of paper over the entry and traced it off, twice. Those copies are enclosed. This one bit of information is the most difficult to read on the entire page. I offer two suggestions as to its meaning, either 1) Noto Gioew or 2) not given. The rest of the information is easily readable and is as follows:

June 10th, 1890 – Nicholas Adams, age 78y, 7m, 12d, married, white, farmer
Born - Saritoga [sic] County, father - Jesse Adams, mother - as above
place of death – Nunda, cause of death – suicide,
time from attack til death: 19 hours
medical attendant or other attestant: Wm B. Alley
place of burial: Nunda

I hope this information is helpful to you. As soon as the snow melts, I will travel to the Oak Hill Cemetery and continue to research your request.

I look forward to receiving a copy of your article on the Universalist Church in Nunda.

Sincerely,

Valerie Griffing
Valerie J.V. Griffing
Town and Village Historian

Incorporated March 11, 1808

52. Nunda New York Town Clerk verifying that Nicholas Adams' father was Jesse Adams.

\ARY 18, 1904.

way. He was within a mile of the Grumley Oil Company's well when the blowup took place. The previous evening a cutter went over the bank at the same place and the pathmaster had several times been notified to make the road safe. Two hours work would have made it all right.

"Will" Adams as everyone who knew him called him, had been shooting for Van Curen Bros, nearly four years. He was a quiet young man, very careful in his work and had many friends among the producers. He had met with several accidents before but all of them were what are termed "lucky."

He was born at Nunda and came to Bolivar when a child. His father and mother are both dead. An aunt Louis Sargent, resides in Bolivar and with her he had made his home for several years. He carried a policy of $500 in the New York Safety Reserve Company of Painted Post.

As soon as news of the accident reached Bolivar C. M. Van Curen accompanied by Henry McDowell, left for Barney's Mills. They visited the scene of the accident and ordered the horses buried. The team and sleigh were owned by E. W. McDowell of Bolivar, being hired for the trip. The remains of the shooter were brought to Bolivar and taken Loop's undertaking rooms and placed in a casket. The casket will be sent to Nunda tomorrow where the burial will take place. The funeral expense will be borne by Van Curen Bros. Just who will pay for the damages the house and barn has not yet been decided. Van Curen Bros. may bring an action against the township where the accident occurred claiming that the accident was due to the negligence of the highway commissioner. In any event the loss to Van Curen Bros. in team, sleighs and nitro-glycerine will foot up several hundred dollars.

It has been seven years since a Bolivar shooter has been blown up. The last victim was Henry Young who lost his life at a magazine on the Fassett farm near Wellsville by slipping and falling with a can of nitro-glycerine in each hand while going

Will Adams obituary

53. Obituary for Will Adams, grandson of Nicholas Adams, found in a poetry book belonging to Belle Fuller Root.

Appendix III: Photographs

54. Ceres, Pennsylvania, Evergreen Kings Cemetery: Grave of George Jesse Adams, "half-brother" of Nicholas Adams.

55. Framed photograph of Belle Fuller Root, about 1900.

56. Johnson City, New York, Floral Park Cemetery: Grave of Belle Fuller Root.

57. Belle Fuller Root, about 1904.

Appendix III: Photographs

58. Ernest Root, husband of Belle Fuller Root, about 1900.

59.   L. to R.: Jenny Cox, milliner, and Belle Fuller Root, seamstress, worked together and operated a shop in Binghamton, New York.

Appendix III: Photographs

60. Johnson City, New York, Floral Park Cemetery: Grave of Leo C. Root, son of Belle Fuller Root.

61. Leo C. Root, son of Belle Fuller Root, about 1908.

62. Leo C. Root and his sister, Nordica Root (Wylie), about 1908.

63. Johnson City, New York, Floral Park Cemetery: Grave of Ethel Bernard Root, wife of Leo C. Root.

64. Jesse Nicholas Fuller and his wife Emma (Graf) at the time of their marriage in 1906.

Appendix III: Photographs

65 Emma Graf Fuller prior to her marriage with Jesse Fuller.

66. Johnson City, New York, Floral Park Cemetery: Graves of Jesse Nicholas Fuller and his wife Emma (Graf).

67. Donald Robert Fuller (1905-1976) with his grandchildren, Patricia and Albert.

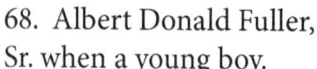

68. Albert Donald Fuller, Sr. when a young boy.

Appendix III: Photographs

69. Albert Donald Fuller, Sr.

70. Alexi Marie Fuller, daughter of Albert Donald Fuller, Sr.

Appendix III: Photographs

71. Albert Donald Fuller, Jr.

72. Taylor Steele Fuller, great-grandson of Donald Robert Fuller.

AUTHOR BIOGRAPHY
Dr. William A. Paquette

William A. Paquette, Ph. D. (United States) was a Professor of History at Tidewater Community College in Portsmouth, Virginia, where he taught Latin American History, World Civilization, U. S. History, and Western Civilization. Professor Paquette received a Master's Degree from Duquesne University (Pittsburgh) and a Ph. D. from Emory University (Atlanta). During his academic career, Dr. Paquette was awarded 14 National Endowment for the Humanities Grants for professional study and Institutional grants that enabled him to study and conduct research in China and Japan. He traveled to southern Mexico over a ten-year period, examining the archaeology at the Maya and Aztec sites, and studied the Maya language at Duke University (Durham, NC). Professor Paquette presented research at international conferences at the University of Louvain (Belgium), the Sorbonne (Paris), the University of Acala de Henares (Spain), the University of Copenhagen (Denmark), Lorand Eotvos University (Budapest), and San Pablo University (Madrid). He has published almost 200 articles and sixteen books and served as a consultant to the U.S. Department of Education, the United States Institute of Peace, the National Endowment for the Humanities, and all major history textbook publishers. For a decade, he was the History Editor for the international MERLOT (Multimedia Education Resources for Learning and Online Teaching) Project, instructing college and university faculty on how to teach online courses. In 2016, Dr. Paquette went to Eastern Europe to study firsthand the legacy of World War II and Communism on the people and nations of Bulgaria, Romania, Serbia, Hungary, Slovakia, Austria, and the Czech Republic. During his professional career, Dr. Paquette met the late King Michael I and the late Queen Anne of Romania, King Simeon II of Bulgaria, the late Pope John Paul II, the Dalai Lama, members of the British Royal Family, and numerous Heads of Government from the European States. Dr. Paquette joined the Mayflower Society of Virginia in 1990 and served that Society as Assistant Historian, Historian, Deputy Governor, and Governor. In 2010, Dr. Paquette was awarded an NEH Grant of $155,000 to bring 50 college faculty to Plymouth to study the most recent research on the Pilgrims and the Wampanoag Indians. He also served the General Society as Chairman of the Education Committee for three years from 2009 to 2012. In retirement, Dr. Paquette joined the District of Columbia Mayflower Society.

www.ingramcontent.com/pod-product-compliance
Lightning Source LLC
Chambersburg PA
CBHW072149070526
44585CB00015B/1060